FOCUSED DETERMINATION

HOW TO ENGINEER YOUR LIFE TO MAXIMISE YOUR HAPPINESS

By
Skills Converged

"If you don't know where you are going,
how can you expect to get there?"

A CIP catalogue record for this book is available from the British Library.

Library of Congress Control Number: 2015908475

Published by CreateSpace Independent Publishing Platform, North Charleston, South Carolina

ISBN-13: 978-1511730099

ISBN-10: 1511730099

Cover Design: E. Honary

Book's Website: www.SkillsConverged.com

Revised V1.2

Contents

Exercises

Foreword

"It is not the strongest of the species that survives, nor the most intelligent, but the one most responsive to change."

Charles Darwin

The world is changing faster than ever before. If you are competing with billions of other people on this planet with its ever-growing population, the way in which you respond to this change can make all the difference to your happiness, success and well-being.

Adapting to change comes with understanding this change and acting quickly on it. It requires self-awareness, periodic review and an informed mind. As you go through your daily activities, process your task list or respond to what the world throws at you, it is easy to lose sight of where you are heading. Pick any five people you know, and the chances are high that each and every one of them is pondering what to do in life and which direction to take. Walk into a coffee shop and listen to any conversation; you will see that the pattern is the same. Everyone is looking for something; a new job, a new skill, a new city, a new adventure, a new project, a new baby or a new friend.

Why is it that we never seem to be satisfied? Why is it that as soon as we get something we desire, we are already looking for something else? Can we channel these interests into tangible results and be happy? What can we do to make sure we avoid wasting time in areas that are fruitless, unnecessary or ultimately doomed? How can we make sure we have a balanced life so that we spend enough time on the things that matters to us?

This book provides a structured approach to help you succeed at whatever you want. It is a practical guide with lots of exercises that will help you to define clear goals and actions, and it uses proven step-by-step methods that you can easily employ and come back to time and time again as you or your life changes.

The book's aim is not to spell out precisely what you need to do. People are different, lifestyles are different and people go through various stages in their lives. No one can provide a generic formula for all to use, and this is simply because none exist. Instead, this book provides a number of tools that can help you find your own way. You will learn what to focus on and spend your energy on. You will learn how to adapt your mindset and how to avoid wasting time. It helps you to ask the right kinds of questions to gain insight into yourself. You will find your ideal work-life balance. How much effort you put into doing the exercises will define how much you get out of this book and, subsequently, how much success and happiness you gain.

This book is the result of the many years of research that have gone into the design, development and delivery of training courses at Skills Converged. As soft skills course designers, we work constantly with the international training community to understand the best ways to teach people how to improve their personal and interpersonal skills. We have, therefore, gained years of experience teaching soft skills and how these can help people become successful. Face-to-face training courses are great for certain interpersonal skills or technical subjects. However, when it comes to personal goals, success and happiness, a self-study course is more suitable. This need led us to write this book. We used our experience in designing training courses to make this book useful, educational, insightful and entertaining.

We hope that you will find it an indispensable resource and a trusted companion that helps you to navigate the rocky landscape of life.

Dr. E. Honary
Director
Skills Converged Ltd.

1 The Principles

"As to methods there may be a million and then some, but principles are few. The man who grasps principles can successfully select his own methods. The man who tries methods, ignoring principle, is sure to have trouble."

Ralph Waldo Emerson

In the 10th century, the Middle East was going through the Islamic Golden Age. As with any empire, golden ages usually occur when there is political stability and the ruling power is well established and unrivalled. With political stability, the arts and sciences flourish as people feel safe and secure enough to pursue such costly adventures. During this period, Avicenna, also known as Ibn-Sina, was born in the Samanid Empire in Persia. At the time of Avicenna's birth, his father was a governor, and he made sure that his son received a quality education in Bukhara, the capital of the Samanid Empire. From an early age, Avicenna displayed extraordinary intelligence and memory. By the age of ten, he had memorised the entire Quran. However, this was not enough for Avicenna. He wanted to learn more about the world to enable him to make sense of it. Avicenna was already showing great interest in the sciences and philosophy. He was so good at learning that by the time he was fourteen years old, he knew more than his teachers. By sixteen, he turned to medicine. He learned medical theory and then started his own experimentation, discovering new methods of treatment. Soon, sick people started to flock to his house for treatment. His fame spread as he often treated them for free, and he could deliver "miracle" cures that other physicians could not. To cure people, Avicenna was, of course, relying solely on science, physics and chemistry rather than on anything supernatural. By eighteen, he had achieved full status as a qualified physician and, in fact, found medicine easier to progress in than mathematics or metaphysics, which he called "thorny sciences."

When Avicenna was twenty-two, he lost his father. Just at that time, the Samanid dynasty came to an end too. Thus came political unrest, and from this point onwards, Avicenna had to move from city to city looking for jobs that could match his talents. Sometimes, he would befriend a ruler or work for a sultan, even becoming a vizier. At court, he still practised as a medical physician while carrying out court duties. In his spare time, he grappled with philosophy and wrote books. According to his autobiography, he enjoyed wine and had a voracious appetite for sex. When a sultan died, he had to find a safe house to escape capture, and then he would eventually move to another area. He even spent four months in prison when he was out of political favour. Nevertheless, during various upheavals, political turbulence, intrigue and rivalry between districts aiming to gain power, Avicenna persevered with his quest for knowledge, even writing books while in prison. Avicenna wrote about 450 books in total, half of which still exist today. He wrote on philosophy, mathematics, logic, physics, Islamic theology, alchemy, geography, astronomy and even poetry. He was a polymath with a life that had all the components of a great thriller.

Avicenna's work was way ahead of his time. He is known as the "Father of Early Modern Medicine." His most famous works, *The Book of Healing* and *The Cannon of Medicine* became standard medical texts in many medieval universities in Europe and were taught to students as late as 1650. He had a significant influence on Islamic philosophy and is credited for his interesting thought experiments on the "floating man" and his investigation on "existence." Avicenna suggested the division between mind and soul 500 years before Descartes, who proposed a similar idea of mind-body dualism with his famous quote, "I think, therefore I am."

Avicenna's writings were in Arabic, the scientific language of the time, though he also wrote several texts in his native New Persian language, pioneering the writing of scientific texts in this language. Ferdowsi, a revered Persian poet who wrote the epic *Book of Kings* or *Shahnameh,* also lived at the time of Avicenna. Ferdowsi's works, along with those of Avicenna, contributed significantly to the preservation of the Persian language, which has changed little to this day. With minimal help, present-day Persian speakers can read and understand the text which was written a thousand years ago; this is quite unusual for most of the languages used in the world today. It is a widely held view that had it not been for the works of thinkers such as Avicenna and Ferdowsi, the Persian language (or Farsi, as it is known to natives) would certainly have been lost and replaced by Arabic, which has been the case with nearly all other Islamic countries in the world today.

What was the secret behind such a significant contribution to sciences, society, Persian and world history? Was it that Avicenna was innately talented and possessed superhuman intelligence? Was it that he didn't have to work much to learn something and so he could progress much faster than others?

To answer this, let's delve into his mind and see what he thought of his own achievements. In his autobiography, Avicenna writes about an experience he had as a teenager. He read *Metaphysics*, one of the principal works of Aristotle. It explores what can be asserted about anything that exists just because of its existence and not because of anything else. It covers the nature of matter, cause, form, the existence of mathematical objects and God.

By this time, Avicenna had mastered logic, the natural sciences and mathematics, and he wanted to learn about metaphysics. He found the topic immensely difficult. Avicenna could not understand it. Despite his superior success in other areas, he was puzzled as to why he couldn't get it. So he decided to read Aristotle's book one more time. What is existence? Why should something exist? How can something continue to exist despite the change it goes through? Why should something not exist? In every change, there is something that persists through the change. There is also something else which did not exist before but which now comes into existence as a result of that change. The world around us is in a flux, but there is only one truth or reality . . .

After reading the book for the second time, Avicenna again had trouble understanding it. He was not going to give up, though. He read it for the third time but still could not understand what Aristotle meant.

Ordinary people, especially teenagers, would stop after a few tries, if that. They would not continue reading a book (and, for that matter, one on philosophy) over and over again to understand it. Most people would think that it is either beyond them or, more likely, just dismiss the work, thinking that it isn't interesting, useful or well-written. They would just come up with some excuse. Avicenna, however, was not ordinary. He was *determined*.

What does it mean to be determined? It means that he went on to read Aristotle's book on philosophy a total of forty times!

By then, Avicenna had memorised every word, and he knew each page by heart. He desperately wanted to understand the work, and he was not willing to give up.

One day, while wandering in town, Avicenna decided to visit the book bazaar. A travelling bookseller approached him to sell some books. Just like modern-day shoppers who try to get rid of a clingy salesman, Avicenna said he didn't need any of his books. The bookseller was persistent, though, and chased

Avicenna while he explored the bazaar. Eventually, Avicenna decided to have a look at the bookseller's small collection. There he found a book by Farabi titled *A Commentary of Metaphysics by Aristotle*. Amazed, he bought the book on the spot for three dirhams. When he got home, he started reading it straight away. As he had already memorised *Metaphysics*, he didn't even need to look at Aristotle's book. He read the commentary and understood what Aristotle meant. He was so happy that he could not believe his good fortune, and he consequently decided to donate a lot of money to charity the next day. He was only seventeen at the time.

Avicenna's understanding of the subject subsequently had a significant effect on the development of his philosophy. He thought there must be an explanation for the existence or non-existence of things. He distinguished between essence and existence. He reasoned that existence must be because of an agent cause that necessitates and adds existence to an essence. If something exists because of something else, then this cycle can go on forever. Where does it stop? He then went on to suggest proof for the existence of God. This was independent thinking that differed from the prevailing Islamic beliefs of the era or the works of other Islamic scholars on philosophy. It became highly influential. We now consider this the "Cosmological Argument," though, of course, after several hundred years of progress, there are many counter-arguments to it. Nevertheless, by the 12th century, Avicennism became the leading school of Islamic philosophy, and Avicenna was considered the central authority on philosophy in most of the Middle East. Avicenna divided medieval philosophy into two parts—one before Avicenna and one after him—simply because after Avicenna, any scholar who wanted to write about philosophy and be taken seriously had to respond to him.

His life is greatly inspiring when it comes to understanding success. There is a method to success; it does not happen by chance. Success is not given to you on a silver platter. It has to be earned, relentlessly, enthusiastically and with *focused deliberate determination*. Avicenna's story gives us a vivid example of one way of finding and applying the methods. His example makes it easier to see how he devised his own methods based on the *principles of success*. This book aims to show you these principles so that you can devise your own methods. Using them, you can find your way to success and life satisfaction however you choose to define these. As you go through the book, you will see time and again that the most successful people— Avicenna and others—took advantage of the fundamental principles that are explored in this book, and they are incredibly disciplined in following the rules of success.

These principles or methods are nothing new; in fact, much has been written about their power throughout the last hundred years. Perhaps people don't follow them or are still unaware of the immense power of some seemingly simple principles. Perhaps they need a step-by-step, systematic approach that helps them define what they want so that they can then go about achieving it. This book aims to provide this systematic approach along with examples and inspirational stories that support or illustrate the power of these approaches.

1.1 What Is This Book About?

As you go through this book, you will learn about inspiring stories that illustrate how various methods were used by successful people. Many motivational books include such stories, but they leave it at that without providing any clear structure regarding what to do next.

If you read such books, you may feel strongly motivated while reading them and even a few weeks afterwards. Soon, however, you are likely to drift back to your old habits and forget the stories and the books. After several books, it can lead to despair, as you may wonder why nothing seems to help with your life even though you read these books. You may even conclude wrongly that you are not good enough, are not lucky enough or that, somehow, the universe is set against your success while favouring others'.

This book is different.

You may have seen statements in some motivational books that you agree with but then wonder how they apply to you. Such statements may lead a typical reader to have the following reactions:

Statement in some book: "You must see how you feel inside and go with that."

A typical reader: "Well, what does that mean exactly?"

Statement in some book: "You must silence the voice within in order to concentrate better."

A typical reader: "OK, I agree. But how do I actually stop the negative self-talk that simply increases my anxiety at random points during my day?"

Statement in some book: "You must pick the ideal career."

A typical reader: "Yeah, you bet. But what is an ideal career? What is ideal for *me*?"

Statement in some book:	"People who have goals tend to be more successful."
A typical reader:	"This makes a lot of sense, and I have heard it countless times. My problem is not that I don't set goals. My problem is that I don't follow them. If you can help me on that, then I am listening."
Statement in some book:	"Happy people achieve a lot."
A typical reader:	"I agree. But I am not happy, and I am wondering what would make me happy."

This book avoids such lousy statements. In contrast, the focus is firmly on actions without which nothing would change. Step-by-step guides and methodical exercises will help you formulate specific actions to achieve results.

By the end of the book, you will understand why Avicenna or other high achievers have become so successful and what it takes specifically to imitate their success. You will know how to analyse your attitude and take specific steps to make yourself as happy as you can be.

Success is hard. It takes effort, determination and persistence. There is no easy way to achieve success, but there is a systematic way. If you want to stand out, you will have to do something beyond what everybody else is doing. This is much like engaging in sports or going to a gym to build your muscles. If you follow a number of fundamental principles, you are guaranteed to get results, just as you would when you consciously aim to improve your health and fitness. It is all in your head (read *attitude*) and your approach (read *daily activities*); these define your success. Luck is just a catalyst that will come to you if you persist.

1.2 How Is This Book Structured?

The book has a top-down structure which guides you through areas that are more important first and then focuses on tips and tricks that can help you define your way to success.

This book is structured as a self-study course. It is not the kind of book that you read cover to cover in one or two sessions. You read, think and then take action. Then you think again. You should not be in a hurry to finish the book; only be in a hurry to take action.

In each chapter, you will read through inspiring stories that illustrate key points. You will then go through a number of how-to guides that further show you what you need to consider to improve your skills.

At the end of each chapter, you can go through the exercises. You will need to examine your own attitude towards key concepts and then answer a number of questions to reflect on it.

The book is based on extensive research carried out by experts on productivity, motivation, goal setting, attention, expertise, time management and happiness. It presents such research in the form of easy-to-follow, step-by-step guidelines. The intention is to help you ask a lot of questions of yourself. You know yourself best. The book is here to help you become a high achiever. As you go through the chapters, each set of questions will help you to better understand your needs. Your answers will then prepare you for the next chapter and more questions, and this sequence continues to the end of the book.

1.3 How to Get the Most from This Book

While reading each chapter, you need to pause and go through the exercises. Use the forms in the book and an extra notebook that can give you more space to record your thoughts and answers.

Be honest with yourself. You don't have to show your answers to anyone else, so you can be as honest as possible. This will help you to avoid self-censoring, as you don't have to worry about being judged by others.

Remember, you need to write down your answers. Do not just read the questions and answer them in your head. Writing down your answers has several benefits:

- It focuses your mind.
- You will spend more time answering a question than quickly moving on to the next question. This will, in turn, help you think deeply about the subject.
- You are more likely to provide a longer answer, leading to an in-depth self-analysis.
- You will have a record of what you thought about the concepts raised at the time you were reading the chapter. You can then refer to and reflect on this later.
- You can go back and forth between the chapters and the exercises. It is possible that you might inadvertently omit an answer in an earlier

exercise. As you go to the next chapters, you may discover that a specific area in your life is more significant than you originally thought. You can then go back and update your new answers. You can review other exercises that rely on these answers and reflect on them accordingly.

Due to the limitation of the English language when referring to a third person, we always use "he" in the text. However, this is not a bias; we are not only referring to men and ignoring ladies. It's just that we are following what is customary to avoid bad grammar by using "they" or making the text unreadable by constantly using "he/she" and "him/her".

As you go through the book, you will read about many examples and inspiring stories. They will help to illustrate various points using real-world examples that are easy to remember. In several places, examples are based on artists or the world of art. Most people can easily relate to the field and might even have had some experience in producing artwork. This is why we chose art examples—because readers from all backgrounds can easily understand them and then apply the lessons to their own specific fields.

1.4 Focusing on the Ultimate

Throughout this book, we assume that, philosophically, a man's highest aim in life is to maximise his happiness. It is not necessarily about getting the most from life, becoming rich, having many friends or going to heaven; ultimately, you can only judge your life based on your own subjective happiness. This book is a tool to help you find what makes you happy and keeps you happy for as long as you live, so that towards the end, when you look back at your life, you will feel satisfied with what you have achieved.

People's interests vary greatly over a lifetime. In today's complex world, there are many interests and desires that can make you happy. However, they don't necessarily make you happy to the same degree. You may achieve more in some areas than others, and these higher achievements can make you happier and more satisfied in life.

To find out what makes you happy, you will start by thinking about a set of actions and desires systematically. As you go through the book, you will review this set and filter through it. This will allow you to zoom in on those areas that would make you happiest not just now but also way into the future. Step by step, you will put aside wishes and desires that might be superficial or, in comparison with your other interests, not that appealing. This systematic self-discovery and pruning of your wishes will help you stay focused on what you aspire to most and will ultimately help you become happier faster and for longer.

2 Know Your Ultimate Goal

"Desire is the starting point of all achievement, not a hope, not a wish, but a keen pulsating desire which transcends everything."

Napoleon Hill

"If an ant seeks the ranks of Solomon, don't smile contemptuously upon its quest. Everything you possess of skills and wealth and handicraft, wasn't it first merely a thought and a quest."

Rumi

Let's have a quick look at an interesting episode in Arnold Schwarzenegger's life whose story you will be introduced to in more detail later on. In the late 1970s, Arnold was going through an important phase in his life—the switch from bodybuilding to acting. He was always interested in becoming an actor and was planning to find the right roles and movie projects.

While searching for roles and movies, his agent got him an appointment with Dino De Laurentiis, a legend in the movie business and the man behind the production of many classic movies, such as *La Strada*, *Serpico* and *Barbarella*. De Laurentiis was particularly interested in adapting comic books into movies. Arnold went to meet De Laurentiis, but his encounter with him did not go well. De Laurentiis had an ornate antique desk which was bigger than a standard desk. Arnold looked at De Laurentiis, who was very short, and thought to say something funny, perhaps to lighten up the mood. He said, "Why does a little guy like you need such a big desk?" De Laurentiis looked at Arnold and said, "You have an accent, I cannot use you!"

Arnold was out of De Laurentiis's office in about one minute and forty seconds, having potentially offended the important producer without intending to. From then on, De Laurentiis did not seem to like Arnold at all.

Having alienated an important producer, Arnold continued with his search for a good movie to act in. Eventually, after some experience of acting in TV series and his movie documentary *Pumping Iron*, he came across a project to make a movie version of a comic. This project eventually led to the creation of *Conan the Barbarian*. Having met the producer and directors, Arnold was considered an ideal cast for this movie given his well-built body, his young age, his attitude, his Austrian origin and his reputation of having won the Mr. Universe bodybuilding championships several times. They thought he already had a fan base in the bodybuilding community who would come to watch any movie he acted in. It would be a good head start in terms of promoting the movie. After considering the role, Arnold and his agent negotiated that he should get 5% of the profits once the movie was made. After all, he had the title role, and the success of the movie depended heavily on his delivery and performance.

The project proved to be complex and required a lot of upfront investment in building sets and preparing costumes, as well as training actors for sword fighting and horseriding in order to create a convincing world that the comic fans would accept. As a result, the project had some funding issues and was delayed several times.

Through a series of negotiations, the producers came to an agreement with De Laurentiis. The result was that De Laurentiis effectively bought the project from them. De Laurentiis was rich and influential. With him in charge, and with the movie rights sorted, the project suddenly got a strong kick-start.

The next move by De Laurentiis was perhaps predictable. He approached the director, John Milius, and asked him to get rid of Arnold. De Laurentiis never liked him anyway. Milius argued that Arnold should stay. Not content, De Laurentiis then decided to send his company lawyer to negotiate with Arnold.

What happened next is quite extraordinary, as it shows what it means to have your eyes set firmly on your goal.

Arnold met with De Laurentiis's lawyer. The lawyer said that De Laurentiis didn't want to give 5% of the profits to Arnold as per their contract. He in fact didn't want to give anything to Arnold . . . 0%.

Now let's pause at this point. Five percent can lead to hundreds of thousands of dollars when a film becomes successful. To give up a percentage is indeed a lot. Arnold was at the beginning of his career, so he had not made much money yet, and as a young immigrant, the money certainly looked attractive.

Most people in such a situation would probably negotiate, aiming to retain at least a percentage, thinking that it is only fair to negotiate to get as much as they can get away with. Arnold, however, had his eyes firmly set on his target. He knew *exactly* what he wanted in the long term. Here is what happened next.

Arnold said, "I am in no position to negotiate." The lawyer was shocked. He was expecting a fight, so he replied, "All five points?" Arnold said, "All the points. Take it, take it all."

Arnold's reasoning was very clear. He was thinking that De Laurentiis had all the money, and he needed a career. A lot of money was going to be invested in him to make the movie a success. There was simply no point in arguing. As he put it later, when recalling the event, it was simply supply and demand. He also thought that there would come a time when De Laurentiis had to pay, but this was not that time.

This story is a powerful example of what it means to know your goals. Arnold did not view the movie as a money-making opportunity but rather as a great way to promote himself and his acting career. De Laurentiis and his men were going to spend millions of dollars to promote Arnold's name, movie and brand. He wasn't too bothered about how much he was going to be paid at this point. In addition, he had already prepared himself for this moment. He had made a fantastic move by getting into the real estate business to create an independent source of income. This would free him from becoming dependent on what producers were going to pay him. He could treat acting as a hobby, with his long-term goal of becoming an international star. Setting a long-term goal helped Arnold not to become confused by money and to remain totally committed to his ultimate goal. He knew that once he made it big, he could negotiate from a position of strength. But he could not do that now because his acting career had not really taken off. The cancellation of a movie project such as *Conan the Barbarian* or the recasting of his role could have been much more damaging than losing the 5% profit.

In short, Arnold had a firm idea of what he wanted and was prepared to be a tremendously patient man to get it.

2.1 Why Goals Matter

Alice came to a fork in the road.

Alice:	"Which road do I take?"
Cheshire cat:	"Where do you want to go?"
Alice:	"I don't know."
Cheshire cat:	"Then, it doesn't matter."

As nicely presented by Lewis Carroll in *Alice in Wonderland*, if you don't know your goals, it doesn't matter what you choose. The most important starting point is to have goals which can then come to define your life.

In 1953, the final-year students at Yale University were asked to complete a questionnaire. One question asked, "Do you set clear specific goals?" To this, one out of ten replied "Yes." A second question asked, "If you set goals, do you write them down?" To this, four out of ten people who set goals replied "Yes."

Hence, the questionnaire showed that only 4% of students set goals for themselves and wrote them down.

Fast-forward twenty years.

In 1973, the university contacted the students of 1953 to see where they were and how much they had achieved in their lives.

The survey showed that the 4% who had said that they set goals for themselves and wrote them down were ahead of the other 96% of the class in a range of indicators, including health and relationships.

However, the comparison for the financial indicator was perhaps the most amazing. All of the 4% declared that they were financially independent. In addition, the 4% had a total financial wealth greater than the other 96% combined.

Goal setting and goal monitoring are perhaps the most important skills required for success.

> ### You can get it if you want it.
> ### If you don't know what you want, you are not going to get it.

2.2 How to Generate Goals

You are convinced that having goals is essential. In fact, no one is likely to dispute this. The problem is how to come up with them in the first place. Most productivity gurus at this point suggest that you go into an empty room, lock the door and keep thinking until you sort it all out. They may even give you a number of ground rules, but after that, you are on your own. If you have ever tried this method or something similar, you have probably noticed that your mind goes blank and you end up thinking about your immediate issues more than anything else. The experience may prove so boring or unfruitful that you may put it aside, thinking that there is something wrong with you and that you just don't know what you want in life. Fortunately, this is far from the truth.

The more you have experienced life, the more likely it is that you have an understanding of your own capabilities, talents and skills, as well as the areas and activities that you are enthusiastic about. What you might be lacking is a valid and systematic approach to structuring your thoughts and your goals so that they can empower you to achieve more in life.

Some well-known researchers have suggested motivational systems that are truly effective and inspiring. In parallel, other researchers have been looking into developing tools or methods that can enhance creativity and allow the mind to explore concepts and ideas freely. In the following sections, you will be introduced to a combined system that captures the essence of these methods and provides a comprehensive step-by-step technique that can be used to define goals, missions and, ultimately, the meaning of life. The system inherits and extends the work of giants in the field, including Napoleon Hill's six-step approach to the riches, Tony Buzan's research on creativity and memory, Stephen Covey's mission statements, Daniel Goleman's five components of emotional intelligence with an emphasis on self-awareness and Anthony Robbins and his work. It also includes the use of Neuro-Linguistic Programming (NLP) methodology in some exercises.

This session is a starting point in preparing you to define your mission statement later. You will need a number of tools and to follow a procedure before starting to define your mission. First, you will be introduced to a very powerful creativity tool, and then you will be shown how to approach and incrementally update your mission statement. Let's start with the basic tools.

2.3 Using Lists

The usual method to document thoughts and record ideas is to make lists. Let's go through a simple exercise.

Exercise 2-1
Make a List
Think of a concept and try to make a list of related terms. For example, think of man-made vehicles and make a list. The list can then include car, bicycle, helicopter and so on. Keep going and see how many things you can come up with whilst writing non-stop. Do this in the space provided below. Continue reading the book only after you have done this exercise so that you don't spoil what follows.

How many items did you manage to have in your list? Here is a guess; you listed about seventeen items. You may wonder how we know this. It turns out that this is what people tend to do when making lists. When we think linearly about associations, we end up with about this many before running out of ideas. It is as if we hit a block and we feel we cannot think of any more ideas.

In reality, you are aware of more associations, but the list-making method stops you from finding them. List making has serious drawbacks, as it can be very limiting. Here are some of the problems you may encounter when making lists:

- Keywords are obscured.
- Lists are visually boring.
- Items in a list are difficult to remember.
- A written list is difficult to search. There is no categorisation.
- Re-reading is time-consuming.
- Lists prevent the brain from making associations.
- It is easy to lose concentration when making lists.

Fortunately, there is a much better way to make associations and unleash the power of your brain.

2.4 Mind Mapping

Mind mapping is a particularly powerful technique based on a method which is similar to how our brains structure data. This visual technique is designed to collect and organise information. The modern mind map was invented by British psychology author Tony Buzan in the 70s. A mind map is a diagram that represents ideas, words, concepts, images and other items which are arranged around a central concept. Concepts are related to each other through branching (Buzan 2006).

A mind map effectively translates concepts into an image. Since our brain is quite powerful when it comes to processing images, it can pick up relations much more easily from an image than from an alternative capturing mechanism, such as a list. A mind map evolves over time as you add more concepts. Mind mapping encourages you to classify new concepts based on the current categories and branches you have put on the map, and as a result, you get to collect and organise your thoughts simultaneously. In turn, the addition of new major branches and categories leads to even more *associations*. Hence, mind mapping is also an effective brainstorming tool.

Research shows that the use of mind mapping can increase your productivity. The increase in efficiency is most profound for visual people, although most people pick up mind mapping very quickly and find it helpful.

2.5 How to Create a Mind Map

Start at the centre of a space (be it paper or a software solution) and keep adding branches. As more concepts are introduced, categorise them appropriately based on what you have on the map. After a while, you may realise that the concepts you have added belong to a different set of categories. Rearrange the map appropriately as more concepts are added. The following is an example of animals divided into a number of basic categories.

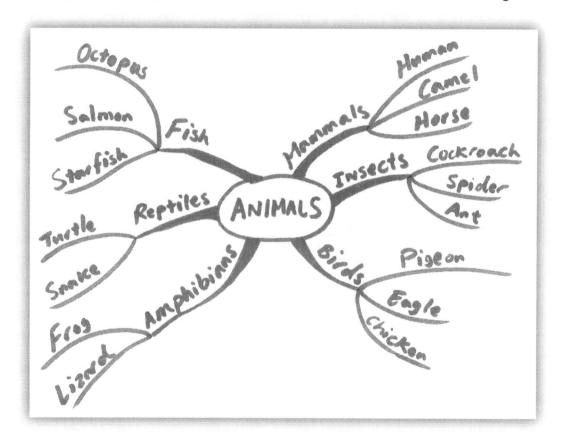

Notice that the more colourful the mind map, the more memorable it becomes[1]. The main branches are drawn thicker to enhance their importance. The first-level branches are called *Basic Ordering Ideas (BOI)*. Other branches then follow all the way to the end leaves.

2.6 Step 1: Create Your Happiness Mind Map

Let's start by going through an exercise on mind mapping for happiness. The idea is to quickly capture what you think would make you happy. However, rather than making a list and inevitably coming to a quick halt, you will use an approach that is suited to how your brain makes associations.

The following is an example of a first attempt at creating a mind map of what makes you happy.

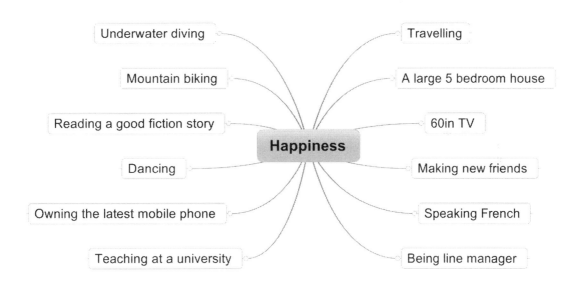

So far, the process is not too different from making a normal list. The next step makes mind mapping immensely more powerful. At this point, you may decide to create a number of categories to group various branches. You may then end up with the following:

---

[1] The mind map printed here is in black and white due to the format used for publication of this book. Ideally, to get the most from mind maps, you should make them in colour.

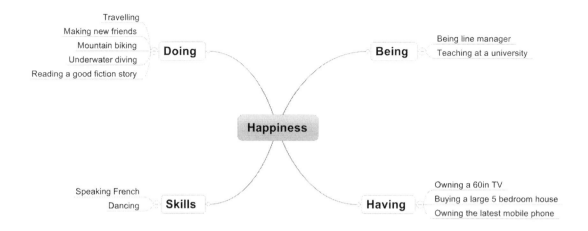

You still have the same branches as before, but each one is now part of a BOI. It is already much more useful than just a list. The new categorisation, along with the branches, will immediately inspire you to add more items to the map. You may then end up with the following:

Now you can categorise within each BOI to further define the map:

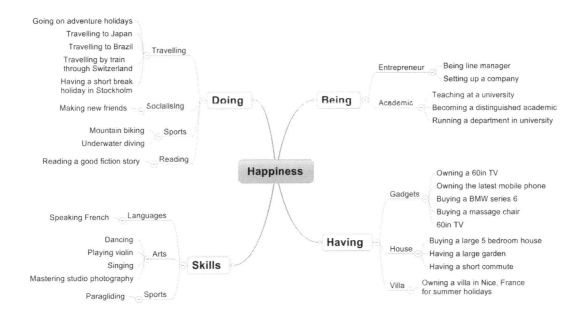

It is starting to look more and more like a mind map. You can carry on extending and rearranging the map. You are allowed to change your mind as often as you want. In fact, you are encouraged to do so until you have something that best represents your thoughts.

Now it is time to create your own happiness mind map.

Mind-Mapping Benefits and Applications

You can use mind maps for a wide variety of applications, such as the following:

- Enhancing memory
- Note taking
- Creativity/Brainstorming
- Tasking/Exploring
- Taking notes in meetings
- Designing, preparing and rehearsing presentations
- Solving interpersonal issues
- Storytelling and fiction writing
- Writing project reports and conducting research
- Teaching
- Helping those with learning disabilities
- Serving as a knowledge repository
- Blogging
- Planning and scheduling

Exercise 2-2

STEP 1: Create Your Happiness Mind Map

1. Identify the first ten associations that come to your mind when you think about *happiness*. As they come to your mind, write them down without pausing, and include them in the map. You can use a large blank paper or mind map software, such as Mind Manager by Mindjet.
2. Rearrange the mind map to introduce a number of first-level associations or BOIs. These categories will help you organise your mind map.
3. Extend your map with more branches related to the concepts and categories you have already identified. As you come up with new associations for one concept, you may become inspired and think of other associations, which you can then add to the appropriate BOIs as you expand the map.
4. Continue doing what you have done with the examples above to rearrange your map, and add more ideas about what makes you happy.

Note:

You don't have to start on one piece of paper and finish everything there. It can become messy as you keep adding and updating. Consider using a fresh sheet and transferring what you already have before updating some more. It is highly recommended that you use a software solution for creativity exercises in this book, as the real power of mind mapping is in the rearrangement of the branches, and software can facilitate this greatly. There are many free software solutions available which a simple online search will bring up.

2.7 Step 2: Identify Your Desires

Now that you have become familiar with the mind-mapping tool, it is time to use it for your quest to find your mission statement. Remember, we don't want you to stare into blankness and hope to find out what you want to do in life. Hence, the next step encourages you to think about your desires. Think about the things you want to have. Do not limit yourself in any way. Think about all your small or significant desires. Here, even the sky is not the limit! You will not be judged. Be as honest as you can be with yourself. Do you fancy becoming an astronaut so that you can walk on Mars? Do you want to have the most famous kebab restaurant in the city? Do you want to have sex with a particular person? Write them down.

Exercise 2-3

STEP 2: Identify Your Desires

Use a mind map similar to the following, and expand on your desires based on the main branches given. Do not limit yourself. Use a similar approach to mind mapping as you did in the previous exercise. Allocate as much time as necessary to get everything you have in mind down on paper.

Categorise your desires based on the following:

1. *What I want and have.* These are things that you have achieved simply because you wanted them enough.
2. *What I want and don't have.* These are things that you haven't achieved or accumulated yet but desire strongly.

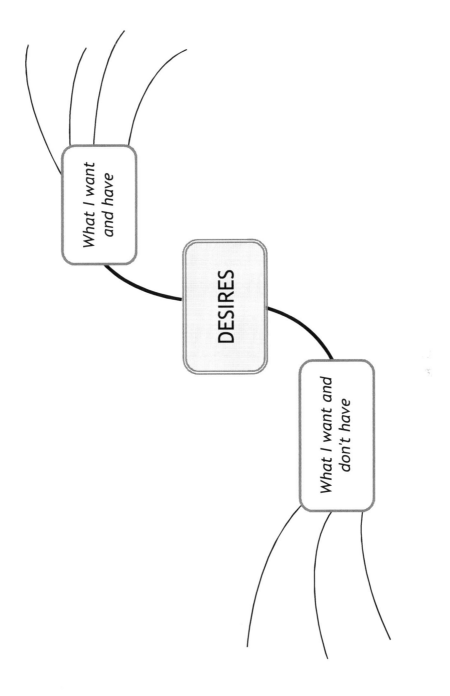

How did this exercise make you feel? We tend to easily forget what we have already achieved and instead focus more on what we don't have. Worse, we tend to forget that there was a time we dreamed of having something we didn't have, and when we got it, we simply took it for granted.

Anything you have now is the result of the realisation of some desire you had in the past. This exercise helps you record your future desires, though these might be similar to what you have already identified in your happiness mind map. This is fine, as the aim here is to make sure you don't leave anything out. If you are not aware of a desire, it is unlikely that you have achieved it. If you feel the need to go back to the mind map and review it, now is your chance to do so before moving on to the next chapter.

One more reminder; do not carry on if you have skipped the exercises in this chapter. Remember, this is not a book for you to read cover to cover. Treat it as a training course. Stop and think carefully about the topics explored and reflect. Spend as much time as you need, and when you are ready, continue to the next chapter. You will need the answers to the exercises here in future exercises.

3 Find Your Ideal Career

"We cannot change the cards we are dealt, just how we play the hand."

Randy Pausch

Excitement was in the air. It was 1984, and the Olympics was taking place in Los Angeles. Mark had trained for this day for the past six years. Olympic swimming is very competitive and requires miles of swimming up and down a pool for hours on end. Getting accepted into an Olympic competition is a major accomplishment that many fail to achieve. Yet, Mark had made it, and he was starting to feel that he actually had a chance to get a medal.

Mark was born in Nottingham, United Kingdom. When he was twelve, he won a series of school swimming competitions. His PE instructor was impressed and encouraged him to pursue swimming more seriously. Mark followed suit, and with practice, he became better and better, winning at the city level, the county level and, finally, at the national level. As he won more competitions, he became more passionate about swimming, which, in turn, made him train harder and win more international competitions. Soon, his eyes were set on winning an Olympic medal.

Mark was determined to win. He had decided to make swimming an absolute priority. Nothing else mattered as much. Friends, social interactions or any other entertainment commonly favoured by people his age became secondary to his main goal of obtaining an Olympic medal. He was totally focused.

In 1984, Mark was twenty-five years old and was ready to win an Olympic medal. He had narrowly missed participating in the 1980 Olympics, so this was his first attendance. At the next Olympics, he would be twenty-nine, so he was very determined to win this time around.

As is common in swimming, Mark was participating in several swimming competitions, though he was best in the 200m and 400m freestyle.

The day before, Mark had come fifth in the 400m, but he had a firm belief that he could get a medal in the 200m. Swimming was dominated by Americans at the time, so Mark was dreaming of becoming a national hero for his country, Britain. That day, Mark was competing in the final round of the 200m—his very last competition in this Olympics. He had done his training and was ready. He just had to win . . . win something . . . anything.

One minute and fifty seconds later, it was all over. He knew. He didn't even have to wait for the scoreboard to update. He had tried hard and, at his best, was ranked number four. Two Germans and an American snapped up the medals. He fell short of a bronze medal by 0.49 of a second.

And that was the end of Mark's swimming career.

He was devastated. He had nothing left. The career and fame he had trained for and aspired to for the past six years were gone because of a mere 0.49 of a second.

After returning home, Mark sank into depression. He had no motivation. Nothing excited him. Now what? He had spent most of his adult life so far focusing on swimming, and yet he didn't even have a single medal to show for it. He looked around to see what careers he could pursue. It was then that he realised that there weren't many good career options for winning swimmers, let alone for those who lost. Swimming was different from lucrative sports, such as tennis. There was no huge demand for international coaches, reporters, consultants or strategists. Swimming did not have as many fans as other popular sports. Swimming was just something you did in addition to everything else you knew. Mark was only good at swimming. He didn't have any other strong skills.

Eventually, Mark pulled himself together. He got a job at a restaurant and carried on with his life. Nevertheless, the experience made a permanent mark on him. He concluded that putting a lot of effort into something may not necessarily get you anywhere. The taste of trying so hard and getting so little was bitter and had a profound effect on his attitude. He was lost in the sea of life, not knowing which way to swim.

Fast-forward thirty years. Mark is fifty-five years old and runs a bar. To make ends meet, he also holds occasional parties at the bar for clients. He drinks a lot, occasionally takes drugs and doesn't look after his health. Although a charming man and a fantastic entertainer, there is something sad about what he has gone through. He no longer has any strong reasons to push forward and succeed; what is the point of trying hard? He has been there, done that and gotten nowhere. Why bother now?

What does Mark's story tell us? What can we do to avoid a similar depressing end?[2]

3.1 Avoid Dead-End Careers

Most of us make our career choices when we are about eighteen. At eighteen, you have limited experience, very limited skills and most of what you know comes from your parents, your environment and the structured school system you have gone through. You are usually slightly better at some skills because you have spent a bit more time on them. Maybe someone in your environment was good at something and passionate enough to get you interested in spending more time in that area. It is also possible that you might have a specific physical feature—such as being tall—that might make you better at certain activities, such as playing basketball. In any case, most people make a decision regarding their career and direction in life based on their limited experiences and biases in their childhood and teenage years. This decision will come to dominate their life for many years to come. No wonder so many get it wrong! It is easier to get it wrong than to get it right, because statistically, there are more wrong ways than right ways.

However, there is a crucial point to consider. Some choices allow you to gracefully change from one career or topic to another while benefiting from what you have already achieved. Unfortunately, some other choices lead to dead ends—directions that don't help you with anything else in life if you ever decide to leave that domain. Avoid these dead ends, even if you think the money is good or that you will somehow turn it around. The last thing you want is to be stuck in your career because there is nowhere to go.

To illustrate this, here is an example. Suppose you are a software developer in the late 90s. Focusing on a career in COBOL[3] computer language just because you like it or someone hires you and pays you to learn it may not be wise. The language was invented in the 1950s and was pretty much obsolete

---

[2] Mark is a fictional character, and his story is presented to illustrate a point.

[3] The name stands for Common Business-Oriented Language.

way before the 90s. A COBOL programmer was either needed to maintain code that was already written or to customise it based on some clients' rare requests. Why go in a direction that is already doomed from the outset? It takes effort to learn a new language, so it will distract you from other more useful areas, including other trendier languages that can benefit your career much more than COBOL.

This is not to say that pursuing a career just for joy or money is wrong. By all means, if you are an academic and find the exercise useful, then go for it. You just have to appreciate the risk every time you decide to spend a significant amount of your time in a given area. There is a possibility that you might not be able to convert that time into a tangible accumulated result that can be used in your future career.

Some jobs are bad in the sense that they do not allow you to realise your full potential. They do not challenge you and help you to learn a lot, grow, enjoy your newly learned skills, make a lot of money or move to another job once you are bored with this one. They are just dead-end jobs. Here are some examples:

- Lifeguards
- Parking wardens
- Customs officers
- Train ticket conductors
- Lumberjacks

There are many respected individuals who have these jobs, and we are indeed grateful for what they do. However, if you choose such jobs, you can't expect much in return.

3.2 *What Leads to Success?*

As Mark's story suggests, success is closely linked to the area you choose to pursue as a career. These areas are not all equal. Some are more forgiving when you decide to switch to something else—others, not so much. Some careers actually help you to progress and to move to a new career while allowing you to utilise whatever skills or achievements you have acquired.

Bruce Lee is a legend. In his relatively short life, he elevated himself to become an acclaimed international star who was known the world over. Let's have a quick look at the important phases of his life.

Lee was born in 1940 in San Francisco, though he and his parents returned to Hong Kong, their home country, when he was three months old. Lee's father was a leading Cantonese opera and film actor. His mother was from one of the wealthiest clans in Hong Kong. Thus, he was born into a privileged environment; yet, as is often the case, not everything was in Lee's favour.

Just a few months after his parents returned home, Japan invaded Hong Kong and occupied it for the next three years. This led to a politically destabilised environment, as a large number of refugees from communist China flocked to Hong Kong. Gradually, Lee's neighbourhood became overcrowded and dangerous. Rival gangs started to fight each other, creating a rough environment. In this setting, Lee inevitably became involved in a number of street fights. The situation got so bad that Lee's parents decided that he should be trained in martial arts. Lee learned the basics from his father. At age sixteen, he began learning Wing Chun under Yip Man, the master of the martial arts technique.

The path was not easy, though. Within a year of training, other students had learned that Lee had a mixed ancestry as his mother was half Caucasian. They did not want to train with Lee. At this time, Chinese were strongly against teaching martial arts techniques to non-Asians. Rather than seeing this as a setback, Lee was determined to learn martial arts. He started to practise in private with his master. He specifically worked on his precision and speed and soon started to amaze his observers.

At the age of nineteen, Lee got into several more street fights, and on these occasions, the police were called. At one point, he ended up beating the son of a rival gang leader. The police believed that there could be a contract out on Lee's life! His father was also concerned.

Because of the risk to their son's life, Lee's parents decided to send him to San Francisco. Lee had a mere $100 in his pocket when he arrived, but he did have his intense passion for the martial arts. Initially, he stayed with his sister and got some odd jobs. He enrolled in university and studied philosophy and psychology. Before long, his focus turned back to his main passion—martial arts.

Lee started teaching martial arts to a number of his friends. While at university, he also met Linda Emery, whom he later married. With Linda's help, Lee opened his first martial arts school.

Lee appeared in an international karate championship held in Long Beach, California. With his novel and somewhat magical techniques, such as the "one-inch punch," he truly impressed the crowd and made a name for himself.

This, however, was not seen positively everywhere. His demonstration of such techniques, along with his teachings, started to alarm a number of Chinese people. According to Lee, the Chinese community was unhappy about him teaching martial arts to non-Chinese. They issued an ultimatum to him, which he rejected. Next, they challenged him to a combat match; if he lost, he had to quit. The controversial private fight was eventually settled. Lee won decisively; consequently, he continued to teach and popularise his methods.

Lee's passion for the field intensified, and he developed his own system. He evaluated his controversial risky fight. He was not really happy with his own performance, even though he won the fight. He thought the fight had lasted too long and that he had been too formulaic. He was following the tradition too rigidly. He had to modernise the technique. Lee decided to develop a system that could cater for the dynamic environment of a street fight. He focused on speed, practicality, flexibility and efficiency. His style was, "the style of no style." In fact, this is how he put it:

> "I said, empty your mind. Be formless, shapeless, like water. Now you put water into a cup, it becomes the cup. You put water into a bottle, it becomes the bottle. You put it in a teapot, it becomes the teapot. Now, water can flow or it can crash . . . be water, my friend."

He was determined to push the field ahead and take it to the next level. He experimented with different training methods and devised his own. He used weight training for strength. He then combined this with stretching for flexibility and running for endurance. With intense and focused training, he achieved a level of physical fitness that was legendary. He believed that martial artists did not spend enough time on physical training and that fitness was essential for a successful performance.

His appearance in international competitions earned Lee a great deal of attention. Before long, he was offered several supporting roles in a number of TV series. Because his father was an actor, Lee had already been exposed to acting since his childhood and soon saw the potential in taking this direction. He was, however, firmly focused on martial arts. This new direction was only a tool to facilitate his self-expression. Lee believed that knowledge ultimately led to self-knowledge and that one could then take steps to express this knowledge. For him, it meant that he could express himself through martial arts.

Lee's incredible screen presence earned him the nickname "The Kato Kid," which is the character he was playing.

As his teaching continued, a couple of his students turned out to be Hollywood script writers. In 1969, the three of them started to work on a script for a film. They went to India to search for a location to shoot the film, but the project never took off. Lee did not see this as a failure; it only fuelled his interest. He continued to play a number of supporting roles in more television series. He was planning for the next opportunity.

Next, Lee pitched his own TV series, with himself as the main lead, to a number of Hollywood studios. This proved to be difficult. Studios such as Warner Brothers had their own ideas about how such TV series ought to be developed. In particular, they thought that casting Lee as the main role was too risky due to his ethnicity and thick accent. So they went ahead and developed a TV series with the same theme, but they cast someone else instead.

Did Lee take this as a setback? Certainly not. He was on a mission. He wanted to express his passion for martial arts, and his specific expression of it, to the whole world. Nothing was going to get in his way. It was only a matter of finding out how he could get there. Lee was *focused* and *determined*.

Lee returned to Hong Kong with the intention of producing his movies there instead of doing so in Hollywood. He could then pitch the finished movies to executives in Hollywood and win their backing. In short, he wanted to reduce the risk and simply show what he was capable of.

When he arrived in Hong Kong, Lee was in for a surprise. He realised that he was already a hit! His role in *The Green Hornet* TV series had made him famous there. Many recognised him in the street as the "The Kato Kid."

Lee soon set out to work with a number of local studios. His first leading role was in *The Big Boss* (1971), which made him an international star across Asia. This was then followed by *Fist of Fury* (1972). Studio bosses could now see Lee's potential, and for his next movie, *Way of the Dragon* (1972), he was given total control over the film's production. He was the director, writer, choreographer and the lead star. He could now express his ideas as freely as he'd always wanted. Lee's perseverance was paying off.

By now, Lee had gained the attention of Hollywood studios, namely Warner Brothers. While before they had considered Lee's appearance too risky for a lead role, they now saw it as an opportunity to make a successful movie. This served Lee well. He held no grudges. All he cared about was the chance to express himself to a wider audience through his martial arts.

Lee set out to work on his next movie, *Enter the Dragon* (1973). This time, the local Hong Kong studio and Warner Brothers worked together to produce the movie. This was now the first martial arts movie with Lee as the lead actor that involved a big Hollywood studio. Unfortunately, as fate would have it, this also turned out to be his last. A few months after completing the movie, and only six days before the release of *Enter the Dragon* in 1973, Lee died due to a cerebral oedema. The cause of his death has been rather controversial, but it is now generally believed that it was due to a reaction to a headache medication.

Enter the Dragon went on to become one of the highest-grossing films of the year, making Lee a martial arts legend.

Bruce Lee's and Arnold Schwarzenegger's stories suggest that choosing an ideal career early can make it easier for you to progress or switch to other careers later in life. Of course, you should choose something that you are passionate about, but you *always* have more than one choice. You should aim to choose a career that has an easier path to success as you jump from one area to another in the span of sixty years or so of a healthy adult life.

This is a prime example of how *focused determination* along with *accumulated results* can lead to tremendous success.

3.3 Pursue the Right Hobbies

As with your career, it is also a great idea to choose your hobbies early on. Just as with a career, there is a choice to make when you want to engage in a new hobby. First, let's look at some examples:

Case 1	Chloe works as a customer service representative at a bank. Outside work, Chloe's greatest interest is food. She is a food enthusiast. She likes going to restaurants and tries every single one of their meals. She likes to eat exotic foods and is proud that she eats anything and everything. Being European and having travelled to Asia and Japan, she is fascinated by the range of new foods she can try. She loves telling people about all the weird things she's eaten on her travels. Chloe is interested in the wining and dining part of food—not its production. She doesn't cook and is not really that keen to pursue it. Chloe is obese, which is a direct result of her excessive interest in eating out, eating a lot and eating anything with no regard for her health.

Case 2	Olivia is a receptionist at a dental surgery office. She deals with patients' appointments, responds to their queries on services provided and does a lot of customer service on the phone. Outside of work, Olivia's greatest interest is in photography. She likes both studio and nature photography. She has several high-end SLR cameras with various lenses and accessories. On weekends, Olivia always allocates some time to her specific photography expeditions. She likes to experiment with her shots and to shoot just at the ideal time when the light is exactly as she wants it. She usually takes many shots of the same scene as she experiments with exposure settings and various effects. Back at home, she enhances her photos further using Photoshop. She has a blog as well as a popular Flickr account and posts her photos online. She recently bought a soft box studio lighting kit to experiment with photography in a controlled environment, and she's very excited about it.

What do you think of Chloe's and Olivia's lives? What do you think of their hobbies? Whose hobby do you think will help the person to become more skilled? Who will find it easier to switch to a different career should there be a need for change? All things being equal, who is healthier?

In every case, Olivia seems to have a better deal. The contrast between the two lifestyles illustrates a fundamental principle—that not all hobbies are equal; some are naturally more constructive than others.

All things being equal, Chloe is more likely to have a premature heart attack than Olivia. Olivia would find it easy to start pursuing a new career in photography, but for Chloe, it may not be that easy to pursue something in the food industry. She doesn't like cooking, so she doesn't have that skill, and eating itself is not really a skill. The nature of the fields is different too. Olivia can easily put a portfolio of her work together. She already does something similar by posting her work online. She has accumulated results; she has tons of photos to illustrate her passion and skills. This is not the case for Chloe. All she has is her stories of eating, which are a personal and subjective matter.

These contrasting lifestyles serve to demonstrate an important point—that you should think twice before you embark on a new interest or hobby. People acquire hobbies primarily to do something that makes them feel good— something other than a potentially boring day job. Hobbies can also provide people with opportunities to socialise more and to find friends. It is important to understand and appreciate the consequences of pursuing a given hobby.

Those that can make you happy while also helping you develop skills or accumulate results are always better than those that don't add any value to your life. Avoid hobbies that do not lead to any new skills or achievements or that cannot be carried over to a new career, another hobby or a desired lifestyle. These days, there is no shortage of choice when it comes to hobbies. With humanity's ever-expanding knowledge and experience, there seems to be a whole host of new niche areas. You simply need to be careful about what you get yourself into.

3.4 Beware of Career Risks

- *Don't pursue a career just because you like it now*. Think clearly about how you see a potential career now, and compare it with how you might view it in five, ten or twenty years if you stay in the same field. Don't let your excitement make you think that of course you will love it. Consider its future carefully—where the industry is now and where it is heading. Consider your age, the environment and the country you are living in and the changes that they are going through now and will undergo then. Predicting the future is very hard, but not seeing the obvious is unforgivable. For example, once digital photography was invented, it was only going to be a matter of time before it became the dominant technology. Deciding to go into the film-processing industry at that point would obviously lead to a dead-end career.
- *Don't pursue a career just because it's fun*. It might be fun now, but will it help you convert your time into something tangible and long-lasting? Will it lead to something that suits you when you are older? Can you sustain the fun you are experiencing over a long period?
- *Make sure you understand the risks of staying in a given career*. Does this career follow the winner-takes-all format, such as the swimming example you saw earlier? Is there a risk that you might end up with nothing? Alternatively, does your career help you accumulate results or skills, much like an artist's or a musician's?
- *Consider what results you can take with you if you need to switch careers*. It is all too common that, in the course of life, people change focus, lose interest in what they have been doing or become excited about something else. Being able to carry what you have achieved in your previous career into your new career can give you a great head start. By the time you want to switch, it is too late to think about what you can take with you. The time to think about this is when you choose your original career or hobby.

- *Being stuck in a dead-end job is your own fault.* In the majority of cases, no one can force you to stay in a job. You can quit at any time and find something else, and there are plenty options if you look for them and spend some time researching them. When you choose a job, it is, therefore, your responsibility if it turns out to be a dead end or if you fail to leave before it gets worse. If a given technology in which you are an expert becomes obsolete and you are still hanging on, expect the worst. By holding yourself responsible, rather than blaming your luck, the economy or the government, you become proactive in looking for signs of a dead-end career so that you can avoid it or get out of it as soon as you recognise the signs.

3.5 Beware of the Mediocre Trap

Have you noticed that people who stay with the same company for years tend to be mediocre and unambitious? Have they always been like this, or is it that staying with a given company has this effect on them?

Successful companies are always on the lookout for talent. They want to keep talented and ambitious people and place them in strategically important positions which enable them to benefit the company the most. Yet, if you look carefully, you will notice that the higher the employees are in an organisation, the dimmer they get. These people would rather stick to tradition than try something new; they would rather use the old, proven methods than change; they would rather machine-gun a new idea than let it flourish; and they would rather silence an aspiring graduate who could be aiming for their job than let novel ideals take hold.

A number of factors contribute to this trend. Examining these reasons can help you see how to avoid the *mediocre trap*:

- *Clever graduates now use employment as a training ground.* They get paid, are mentored, learn the ropes and then use all this as a springboard to a bigger ship.
- *It is not that the mediocre stay; it is that those who stay become mediocre.* The lack of brightness comes as a result of sticking to a job, holding on to old ideas for too long and engaging in a lot of office politics to keep the job. These people aim to receive a high salary while doing the least rather than solving a useful problem.
- *Years of corporate labour contribute to reducing brightness.* Tight deadlines for poorly managed projects and the stress of dealing with stubborn management take their toll on anyone who could have been bright and energetic at the start. The need to conform in order to avoid

being isolated from the crowd or being labelled as a naysayer can also lead to reduced brightness.

- ***Soft skills become more critical than hard skills.*** It is well known that people in a corporate environment gain a lot more by working on their soft skills than their hard skills. Learning how to communicate with people, making quick decisions, being a leader and knowing how to manage others in a friendly way are much more effective ways of climbing the ladder than working on hard, technical skills. In itself, this is not a problem, as having good people skills has tremendous benefits in the long term. Conversely, this suggests why those who tend to climb the corporate ladder are likely to be more of a salesman type than a technically knowledgeable problem solver. This, in turn, explains why, over time, these employees tend to become mediocre workers who are not as bright as the more technically skilled workers at the bottom of the ladder.

To become and remain successful, be wary of falling into the mediocre trap. Stay hungry, change your environment, go into a different field and never forget that knowledge and good technical skills are ultimately the backbone of success and that they command respect. You must be willing to take chances to achieve superiority in your craft, and this, along with good social skills, will make you unstoppable.

It's time to do some reflection by going through a number of exercises.

Exercise 3-1

Self-Analysis

Answer the following questions. Include when and why in your answers.

The last time I felt successful was . . .	
The last time I felt truly happy was . . .	
The last time I learned a new skill was . . .	
The last time I was totally satisfied with my work was . . .	
The last time I did something that I really, really didn't want to do, but did it anyway, was . . .	
The last time I felt totally focused was . . .	
The last time I felt really proud of myself was . . .	

Exercise 3-2

Have You Chosen Your Interests Wisely?

Does your choice of career or potential interests help you succeed in the future?

To answer this question, consider a hobby or career that you are interested in. Answer the following questions to see if your career choices or interests are wise and whether they can help you become successful and happy. No one can accurately predict the future, and that is certainly not the aim here. All you aim to do by answering the following questions is to plan ahead based on what you *already know*. Ask yourself the right questions to get the right answers and an insight into your direction. Armed with this insight, you can take actions *now* to adjust your direction.

Consider going through this form for every major interest you have. This can be done for your main career or for a number of important hobbies. These are the areas that take up most of your time. Use a copy of the form for each interest and answer the questions.

Aim to write at least one paragraph for each question.

Questions

What is the interest under consideration?	
1	Does this interest lead to products or results that you can easily showcase to others? What results do you expect? If not, what are the implications?

2	Does this interest help you to interact with others, socialise and become part of a community?
3	Does this interest lead to a skill that you can easily demonstrate to others?
4	Does this interest produce a useful portfolio of work that can precede you? Describe an ideal portfolio that you would like to aim for.

5	Does this interest lead to something that is understood and recognised by people you know, or is it highly technical and niche? As a test, pick five random people from among your friends and family. For each, write down what they would think of what you have produced and if they can understand it. Would they appreciate the effort that goes into your accomplishments?
6	Similar to the above question, does this interest lead to something that is understood and recognised by people across society, or is it highly technical and niche? As a test, consider it from the point of view of the following characters: • A supermarket cashier • A medical doctor • A mechanic • A software engineer • A bus driver

7	Does this interest lead you to produce timeless products that retain their value or even gain value as you become more well known and as the world changes? For example, if you are an artist or a filmmaker, your earlier work can always remain interesting or become even more treasured as you become more famous. On the other hand, a software tool might be obsolete or completely unusable a decade later.
8	In contrast to the above, does this interest lead you to work that will eventually become obsolete? Will anything remain other than the fact that you worked on a particular project or domain at some point? For example, is this interest similar to doing tax calculations for a client?
9	Describe the industry and the direction it will follow based on what you know now. Predicting the future is tough, but if you can already see it

coming, then this is your chance to record it and consider it in your decision-making. If you have *no idea* about what can happen in the future, record that too. At least you can't blame yourself for ignoring the signs.

5 years	
10 years	
15 years	
30 years	

	Describe your role in this industry. This can be your ideal role or roles that you are most likely to have. What will you be doing in:	
10	5 years	
	10 years	

	15 years	
	30 years	
11	Given your desired personal and professional circumstances, describe a typical day of your life in:	
	5 years	
	10 years	
	15 years	
	30 years	

Exercise 3-3

Mind Map Your Interests

In this exercise, based on what you have analysed so far, you get to shortlist your most important desires and interests that lead to an ideal career—one that would help you grow while remaining satisfied.

To do this, consider the two mind maps you created in *Exercise 2-2* and *Exercise 2-3*: the *Happiness Mind Map* and the *Desires Mind Map*.

Create a new mind map based on the two maps while leaving out any areas that do not lead to an ideal career, as you have identified above. Your aim is to focus on areas that will help you the most, so you may need to compromise. Get rid of areas that are not fruitful or that can lead to a dead-end career.

4 Recognise What Makes You Happy

"A musician must make music, an artist must paint, a poet must write, if he is to be ultimately at peace with himself. What a man can be, he must be."

Abraham Maslow

Andrea worked at a call centre. She worked closely with her team and got along well with them. It was a high-pressure job, and time went very quickly when she was absorbed in her work. She liked this because her mind couldn't wander off too much. The job made Andrea very tired, and by the end of the day, she could not do much at home other than just lie on the sofa and watch TV passively. After a year at this job, the work was becoming routine, which suited her fine; it meant that she didn't have to think much or stress herself out. Her social group pretty much comprised her colleagues. She went out with them almost every week and generally had a good time—when there was no drama, that is. She was single and was actively looking for a partner.

Andrea didn't feel that her parents thought very highly of her. She had dropped out of university after only a year. Since then, she thought her parents had given up on her ever having a successful career. She wanted to prove them wrong, but she was not succeeding. She liked the job because of the people she worked with, but she knew this was not the kind of job she could do for the rest of her life. It was a convenient job for now, but the only way up in the company was to become a manager. That position, however, was always given to someone with a degree, which she did not have.

Andrea was not happy with her basic wage either. She wished she could make more money. Going out in a capital city every weekend costs a lot. Andrea always dreamed of an ideal future in which she would own and run a coffee shop. She would get some antique furniture, have shelves full of old books and serve a large variety of coffees. She was fond of going to coffee-drinking festivals with friends.

During the past year, the economy had been deteriorating. The global financial crisis had repercussions, and the problems were spreading everywhere. Two months ago, the company Andrea was working for announced that that it needed to lay off 10% of its staff. A few days later, Andrea was told that she would be made redundant as part of the restructuring. Her last day at work had been a week ago. She was now desperately looking for a job. She had just enough money for a month of rent, and she needed to find another job quickly or risk being homeless.

Today was certainly not one of the best days of her life. Her landlord was standing in front of her, but he was not talking about the rent, because that wasn't due for another two weeks. He was saying that he had decided to sell the house, and he was giving her a month's notice to move out.

Andrea couldn't believe how everything was happening at once. She now had to find a job *and* a new place to rent and all this without much cash in her account. Andrea didn't want to ask her parents for money. That would just confirm their fear they they wasn't going anywhere professionally, and Andrea was determined to prove them wrong. Renting another place wasn't going to be easy, as many buy-to-rent landlords were selling their houses. Even if she managed to find a place quickly, she could be given notice again, as the next landlord might decide to sell too.

Andrea's main priorities at this point were to find a job and a place to live and to regain control of her life. Her dreams of running a coffee shop and even finding a boyfriend were relegated to the back of her mind. Andrea had to cut down on her socialising too, but she didn't want to lose her friends. She had lost her job and was afraid she was going to lose her friends too. If she didn't go out with them, they would think that she had forgotten them already, but she couldn't go out with them because she had no money. She had to sort out her house, get a new job and save some money before she could even think about anything else.

What a mess . . .

Let's analyse what is happing to Andrea. There seems to be a significant shift in her behaviours and her interests as a result of her life experiences so far, as well as the change in her environment. The threat to her finances and security seems to have completely derailed her from thinking about her dreams of starting a business and finding a partner. In other words, Andrea's motivations have changed dramatically.

A fairly established and popular theory of motivation can explain what is happening to Andrea and, in fact, predict the way in which Andrea's concerns will shift. Let's explore this theory, apply it to Andrea and see what she is going through.

4.1 A Theory of Motivation

By the 1940s, psychology had become a major field. Sigmund Freud, Carl Jung and their peers opened up the field significantly through their respective approaches to *psychoanalysis* and *psychological types*. Most of their work was achieved through examining psychiatric patients who had issues of some kind or another. Through careful examination, analysis, conversations and therapy, they discovered a great deal about human psychology. This trend continued, and by the 1940s, it had become normal for any ambitious psychologist in search of more insight to examine psychopaths, schizophrenics and the mentally ill. The aim was to see what it is that leads to such dramatic failure in people and to use these discoveries to deduce how a normal person functioned. This research was in parallel with research on animals, particularly rats and mice. Various theories on motivation were popping up all the time.

However, the problem with such approaches was spotted by the brilliant Abraham Maslow. He thought that in order to understand how functioning healthy humans made decisions, we could not rely solely on examining those who malfunctioned or study only animals. Instead, we should focus on those who performed exceptionally well to get an insight into how a healthy life ought to be. In fact, he went on to famously say, "The study of crippled, stunted, immature and unhealthy specimens can yield only a cripple psychology and a cripple philosophy."

In his approach, Maslow studied the healthiest 1% of the college student population. He then studied people such as Albert Einstein, Mother Teresa, Gandhi, Eleanor Roosevelt, Beethoven, Lincoln and Jane Addams, all of whom he considered "exemplary" or "self-actualisers." His approach led to what is now famously known as Maslow's theory of human needs, leading to *A Theory of Human Motivation*, which was published in 1943. Maslow later represented this in detail in his book *Motivation and Personality* (1954).

Maslow's theory was ground-breaking. It was intensely debated. From this, various derivative models emerged and followed the same core ideas. His ideas and theory are still taught today in training courses, in business or when you need to use a simple and elegant model to analyse human behaviour. With more than sixty years of research on human psychology, his model has since been superseded by more sophisticated theories, especially in clinical psychology. However, such theories are more complex and are more useful when examining a mentally ill or mentally abused person. Maslow's theory of motivation is powerful in its simplicity and ease of use, which is why it is still very popular after all these years.

4.2 Maslow's Hierarchy of Needs

Needs can be shown as a pyramid, indicating that basic needs must be satisfied first and that higher needs only become important when lower needs are addressed. According to Maslow, lower needs come to dominate an individual's behaviour, and until they are satisfied, the individual will not be motivated by higher needs. For example, a hungry person will think about food. A person who is extremely hungry will not be thinking about his career or education. His utopia is a place full of food. This individual will only start considering other needs once his hunger is satisfied. As Maslow put it:

> "Man is a wanting animal and rarely reaches a state of complete satisfaction except for a short time. As one desire is satisfied, another pops up to take its place. When this is satisfied, still another comes into the foreground, etc. It is a characteristic of the human being throughout his whole life that he is practically always desiring something."

Various needs can influence a person's behaviour in combination with each other, although, in general, a person wants to satisfy lower-level needs first. Maslow was very careful to use the word *domination* to indicate that needs are not independent of each other. The fundamental point of Maslow's theory of motivation is that humans do not act based only on the *deprivation* of some needs but also based on the *gratification* of certain needs.

The hierarchy of needs is depicted as a pyramid because higher needs only become important once lower needs are satisfied. A great analogy is to consider that each need is like a box that contains other boxes. For example, physiological needs include the need for food. In turn, the need for food includes the need for proteins. Proteins are necessary to build amino acids and so on. All needs can, therefore, be categorised into five fundamental types. The hierarchy shows that when two given needs are not satisfied, an individual will be motivated to satisfy the more basic need first.

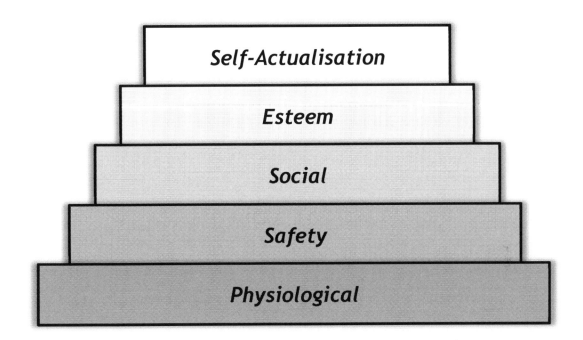

Maslow's Hierarchy of Needs

4.2.1 Physiological Needs

Needs:

These are physical requirements for the survival of a person in the environment. Since many of these needs are biological, they are fairly independent of each other. You will need to satisfy your thirst independent of your hunger for food or your desire for sex.

Examples:

- Air
- Water
- Food
- Sex
- Sleep

If These Needs Are Not Satisfied:

These physiological needs are so fundamental that if they are not satisfied, they can immediately bring all other activities to a halt. Failure to address these needs will ultimately lead to the failure of the body in the environment.

4.2.2 Safety Needs

Needs:

Once physiological needs are gratified, an individual considers the need for safety. These are needs related to security and staying out of harm's way. They include disruptions caused by war, family feuds, crimes and childhood abuse. Safety is not limited only to physical safety. It also includes economic, psychological and job security.

Examples:

- Home
- Shelter
- Physical safety
- Freedom from fear, anxiety and chaos
- Financial security
- Personal security
- Job stability
- Threats to law and order or authority in society

If These Needs Are Not Satisfied:

Without safety, people cannot concentrate on any task for long and will need to attend to the safety issue as soon as they can. For example, if someone is in a rented property and has received notice from the landlord to evacuate the building, then he has to drop almost all other tasks and immediately make arrangements to move to a new place.

If these needs are not satisfied, this can lead to post-traumatic and stress disorders.

4.2.3   *Social Needs*

Needs:

Once both physiological and safety needs are adequately gratified, an individual will consider the need for love and affection. While hungry, an individual might have sneered at love, viewing it as unimportant. He now focuses sharply on it. He will want to belong to a community. He will feel the absence of friends and will constantly think of ways to have an intimate relationship. Otherwise, he will feel lonely and rejected.

We as humans have evolved to become social creatures. Social needs are incredibly important to us. These needs involve the feeling of *belongingness*. Many studies show that the healthiest and happiest people tend to be those who are involved in their communities.

Studies show that people who tend to have one or more close relationships are happier. It seems that what matters is not the quantity but the quality of relationships. Relationships that lead to greater happiness are those in which we can share our personal feelings, engage in shared activities and provide support to others (Jackson *et al.* 2000).

Social needs are particularly critical in today's world due to the widespread feelings of loneliness and isolation that exist. This is mainly as a result of mobilisation, the breakdown of traditional family interactions and our hectic lifestyles. The demanding nature of our competitive and digitalised society means that we have little time for face-to-face interaction with others and for forming meaningful relationships.

Examples:

- Loving and being loved
- Sharing thoughts and feelings with others
- Belonging to a community
- Being part of a team
- Intimacy
- Family
- Being cared for

If These Needs Are Not Satisfied:

Humans need to be loved both sexually and non-sexually. The lack of such needs leads to social anxiety, loneliness, social isolation and clinical depression.

To remedy this, focus on making close friends so that you can share your personal feelings and receive support, which will help you to form stronger ties. Shallow relationships can be troubling for this need, as they prevent you from connecting deeply enough to feel that you are cared for.

4.2.4   Esteem Needs

Needs:

This is about a person's concern about his status within a group, team or community. Esteem represents people's desire to be accepted and valued by others. People usually engage in activities and professions that lead to a sense of contribution.

Maslow identified two versions of esteem needs—a *lower* and a *higher* version:

- **Lower version.** This refers to the need for *respect from others*, including the need for fame, prestige, reputation and attention.
- **Higher version.** This refers to *self-respect*, including the need for competence, mastery, freedom, independence and confidence.

Examples:

- Respect from others
- Confidence in carrying out a task
- Being recognised as an expert in a given field
- Having a high-status role, such as manager

If These Needs Are Not Satisfied:

A lack of self-esteem can lead to weakness and an inferiority complex. It makes people think very little of themselves, leading to unmotivated and unproductive behaviour. It is also dangerous to base self-esteem on the opinions of others rather than on real competence and capacity. A healthy self-esteem is, therefore, based on *deserved* respect.

Fame will not necessarily help to increase people's self-esteem until they have come to accept who they are internally. Fame and praise from others suggest respect from others, which is the *lower version*. To fully satisfy the need for self-esteem, a person must come to believe in his own competence and achievement. This is the *higher version,* which cannot be faked by praise and recognition from society alone.

4.2.5   Self-Actualisation Needs

Needs:

Even if all the previous needs are gratified, an individual may still feel restless and discontent. This need is about how a person can *actualise* himself in the world. It is about the need to express one's full potential and achieve the most of what one likes to be. It refers to the actualisation of full potential capability. An artist needs to paint, and a musician needs to make music. What a man *can* be, he *must* be. Self-actualisation captures an individual's desire for *self-fulfilment.* It is about becoming everything that one is capable of becoming. As you can imagine, self-actualisation is expressed differently between people, and each person pursues his own desires.

Examples:

- Realisation of a lifetime achievement
- Producing a work of art that comes to define capability and what a person can accomplish

If These Needs Are Not Satisfied:

If these needs are not satisfied, a person will feel unfulfilled. Life will feel incomplete and unsatisfying.

Self-Actualisation

**Lifetime Achievement - Full Potential
Capability - Legacy - Peak Experiences
Plateau Experiences**

Esteem

**Respect from Others - Self-Respect
Achievements - Voice and Opinion - Expertise**

Social

**Loving Others - Being Loved - Friendship - Intimacy
Belonging to Community**

Safety

**Home and Shelter - Personal Security - Financial Security
Job Stability - Insurance against Accidents**

Physiological

Food - Sleep - Exercise - Health - Sex

4.3 How Needs Relate to Each Other

From what you have seen so far, you may think that once a need is satisfied, another one emerges. This would then suggest that a need should be 100% satisfied before the next need arises. However, in reality, most people in society have their needs only partially satisfied. In reality, needs are satisfied from the basic needs to the higher needs. For example, for the average person, the following could be the case:

- 80% of physiological needs satisfied
- 75% of safety needs satisfied
- 55% of social needs satisfied
- 40% of esteem needs satisfied
- 10% of self-actualisation needs satisfied

In addition, new needs don't emerge abruptly. You may not be consciously aware of a higher need before the lower needs are satisfied. As a given need is satisfied, a previously non-existent higher need gradually emerges. For example, if you have a pressing financial need, you may not be thinking much about making new friends. As you get back in control of your financial needs, you may start thinking of finding new people to socialise with.

This also works backwards in regard to frustration, and here is another insight into what motivates people. If you are going to be worried about something, you are better off worrying about a higher need than a lower one. This applies to the society as a whole too. You would be better off wondering how to gain the respect of your community through demonstrating your skills than to worry about food and shelter. The society would be better off in this case too. It would be much better for you and the society if you worry about your lifetime achievements rather than wasting time figuring out how to pay complicated taxes, which is something for politicians and policymakers to think about.

4.4 Exceptions and Variations

In presenting his theory, Maslow also identified when and how the hierarchy might need to be adjusted to fit the data in rare and unusual cases. There are a number of variations to the model:

- *Suspending the needs of lower levels consciously.* Some people might satisfy their lower-level needs progressively until they reach a higher-level need, such as the need for self-actualisation. They may feel passionate about a cause and want to pursue it at all costs to the extent that they may sacrifice other needs for it. Such individuals may then pursue a higher need at the expense of a lower one. For example, a person may go on a hunger strike to prove a political point that he feels passionate about. Maslow states that such cases usually occur when lower needs have been satisfied previously and the individual has now decided to suspend the need momentarily for a specific goal.
- *Reversal of esteem and love needs.* This reversal in the hierarchy is one of the most common reversals, whereby an individual may consider self-esteem to be more important than love. A person may feel that in order for him to be loved, he must be strong, powerful, confident and respected. He may want to put up a front which is aggressive, dominant

and self-confident in order to gain love and affection. He may assert himself strongly not for self-esteem but, paradoxically, to gain love. A person with such a reversal may be task-oriented, preferring to stay on his own to get better at a given skill rather than to go out and socialise. Sometimes, this is not even about being seen as powerful by others. As with the higher version of esteem, this can be about self-respect. With a reversal, a person may not feel the need to socialise until he thinks he is worthy enough and respects himself for what he is.

- *Ignoring a lower need over time.* Another reversal in the hierarchy is that some people may be dominated by a higher need and treat lower needs as unimportant. For example, while absorbed in self-actualisation and creativity, some people may come to consider food as unimportant. After a long deprivation, they will then evaluate both needs and take actions to satisfy the basic need too.

- *There can be a difference between behaviour and desire.* Looking at behaviour itself may give you the wrong impression of what someone wants. The hierarchy shows that a given person will *want* to have the more basic version of two given needs when deprived of both of them. This doesn't mean that he will *necessarily* act on this desire, though—just that he wants it.

- *It takes more than being with people to satisfy social needs.* One aspect of satisfying social needs is spending time with others. However, just turning up and talking to friends in a pub or meeting close family members for a meal over the weekend may not be enough. Despite such interactions, a person may still feel lonely and isolated. Satisfying social needs also includes intimacy. This can include love and intimacy with a partner. This is different from sex, which is a physiological need. Beyond interaction with a partner, satisfying social needs also includes sharing internal feelings with a close and trustworthy friend. This intimate sharing of one's personal life and the empathic communication that follows prevent a person from feeling lonely. A partner is, of course, an ideal choice for this but may not be enough. If a person's partner is often away or is focused on a demanding career or if the relationship is not strong, the person may still feel lonely. Higher needs will then be forgotten. There won't be any desire to pursue a lifelong ambition, and the focus comes back to satisfying social needs in order to address the loneliness.

4.5 What Is the Highest Need All About?

Maslow called the highest need—the one at the top of the hierarchy—self-actualisation, which is indeed different from the previous needs. Maslow called the other four needs *deficiency needs*. When you don't have enough food, you are motivated to go and eat. When you don't get enough love and affection, you tend to seek people. In contrast, self-actualisation is about growth. It is about finding out how we can become more of what we want to be. When deficiency needs are not satisfied, this affects people's psychological health. When deficiency needs, which are *necessities,* are satisfied, people can act based on their desire to *grow* rather than being motivated by deficiency needs.

Other needs suggest that humans are biological machines with certain needs. Self-actualisation refers to our need to have a sense of *purpose*—to have a meaningful life. It allows us to pursue our universal human tendency for growth, individual identity, autonomy and excellence.

Self-actualising people in general enjoy life in all its aspects. In contrast, other people enjoy only stray moments of triumph. As Maslow puts it, "Growth takes place when the next step forward is subjectively more delightful, more joyous, more intrinsically satisfying than the previous gratification with which we have become familiar and even bored."

In fact, as later expanded on by Maslow, humans can have what he called *peak experiences*. These are significant experiences that may change a person's view of life and can make a person feel more alive, happy and complete. Such peak experiences usually come suddenly and can be experienced by having intense exposure to a great piece of art, listening to great music, falling in love, appreciating the beauty of nature or having profound insight while solving a problem. Their most important contribution is that they promote growth and help a person to change in a significant way.

Maslow observed that peak experiences tend to release creative energies, give the person a sense of purpose, provide a meaningful existence and indeed make a permanent mark on the individual. It leads to a strong sense of self-determination with limitless horizons opening up. Self-actualising people have a sense of awe, wonder and gratitude about life. They are independent thinkers and are not overly influenced by the general culture.

Peak experiences are, however, temporary. Not all self-actualising people experience them, but those who do are reportedly more satisfied than those who do not.

According to Maslow, only 2% of people reach the stage of self-actualisation. Such people are unusually creative, spontaneous and interesting, and they can have a strange, philosophical, and life-affirming sense of humour!

At the highest level, you get what Maslow termed *plateau experiences*. These are lengthy, wilfully induced peak experiences which lead to a state of *cognitive blissfulness*. To get there, you will need to go through a lifetime of effortful practice and self-actualisation.

Maslow's model continues to be popular. The following diagram applies the model to the 21st century—the era we live in!

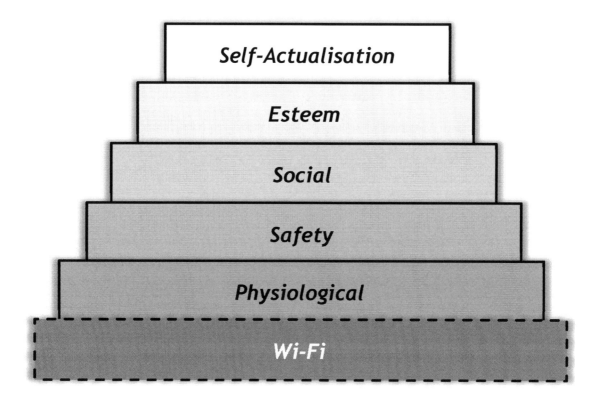

4.6 What Happened to Andrea?

Let's go back to Andrea, whom you were introduced to at the beginning of this chapter. Andrea has five basic needs. Let's see how gratified she was for each set of needs *before* her world turned upside down.

Andrea's Needs Before the Change

Physiological Needs	
Analysis	**Estimated Satisfaction**
She seems to have most of these needs satisfied, as she is focusing on other areas.	Andrea is about 90% satisfied.

Safety Needs	
Analysis	**Estimated Satisfaction**
She is happy with her personal security. She likes the place she is renting. She wishes that she could make more money, but in general, she earns what she needs to spend. She has been at her job for a year, and her performance has been positive. She doesn't want to stay there forever, but she feels secure in her job.	Andrea is about 80% satisfied. This is partly because she feels safe in her job and is not aware of the financial vulnerability of the company.

Social Needs	
Analysis	*Estimated Satisfaction*
Andrea has friends and meets them regularly. Although they are her work colleagues, she gets along well enough with them to prevent her from feeling isolated or lonely. They support her, and she shares many aspects of her life with them. Meanwhile, she is looking for an intimate relationship—a partner whom she can care for deeply and from whom she can expect love in return. She meets with her family often, but because she still feels she needs to prove herself to them, deep inside, she doesn't feel particularly close to them. It is as if they don't understand her or her world. She certainly feels that there is a generation gap, and she wishes she could be closer to them, just like her friends are close to their parents.	Some of Andrea's needs are satisfied, but she has a few that remain relatively unsatisfied. She is about 50% satisfied.

Esteem Needs		
	Analysis	*Estimated Satisfaction*
Lower Version: Respect from Others *This includes the need for fame, prestige, reputation and attention.*	Andrea is respected and liked by her colleagues. She also thinks her managers are happy with her performance. However, she does not have the kind of reputation she would like to have. It is an ordinary job, and beyond that, she is not known at all in the industry.	Andrea's overall sense of self-esteem is poor—about 30%.

| *Higher Version: Self-Respect* *This includes the need for competence, mastery, freedom, independence and confidence.* | Andrea knows her job, but she doesn't think that this is a particularly important skill. She doesn't have a degree, which dampens her self-esteem and confidence. She thinks that without one, she will never be considered for a managerial position. | |

Self-Actualisation Needs	
Analysis	*Estimated Satisfaction*
Andrea doesn't have much self-actualisation. She doesn't think she has achieved her full potential. She has yet to set up her coffee shop to realise her dream of independence and express her full creativity and passion. She still wants to prove herself to her parents, whose opinions matter to her. She knows that her current job has no long-term prospects. She knows that she needs to move on so that she can pursue her dream job.	Andrea is about 10% satisfied.

By looking at the satisfaction levels of Andrea's needs, it is easy to see that she is most motivated by her social and esteem needs at the moment. Until these needs are satisfied, there is little chance for her to consider improving her self-actualisation and possibly achieving her dream of setting up a coffee shop. Of course, once she feels confident enough to make the jump, setting up a coffee shop will no longer remain such a high goal and will be replaced by others, such as leaving a legacy or producing a work of art.

Now let's see how Andrea's needs changed when she lost her job and home.

Andrea's Needs After the Change

Physiological Needs	
Analysis	*Estimated Satisfaction*
Andrea now has an immediate need for shelter. She will soon be homeless and needs to find a place to rent as soon as possible. Shelter is a basic need that overshadows all else. Finding a place to rent might be difficult since many buy-to-rent houses are being sold, thereby increasing the competition to find a place.	Andrea is about 60% satisfied.

Safety Needs	
Analysis	*Estimated Satisfaction*
Andrea is now jobless, and her financial security is, therefore, in danger. Considering the economic downturn, finding a new job will prove to be difficult.	Andrea is about 40% satisfied.

Social Needs	
Analysis	**Estimated Satisfaction**
By losing her job, Andrea is also risking losing touch with her colleagues, who have become her friends and comprise her social circle. If she wants to remain friends with them, she needs to keep socialising with them, but this, in turn, means spending money she doesn't have. On top of this, she is yet to find a partner to share her life with. She also doesn't think her current situation will strengthen her connection with her parents.	Andrea is about 20% satisfied.

Esteem Needs		
	Analysis	**Estimated Satisfaction**
Lower Version: Respect from Others *This includes the need for fame, prestige, reputation and attention.*	By becoming redundant, Andrea has just realised that the management did not think highly of her after all; otherwise, they would have kept her employed much like her colleagues. Maybe her parents are right after all that she is not doing very well in her professional life.	Andrea is about 10% satisfied.
Higher Version: Self-Respect *This includes the need for competence, mastery, freedom, independence and confidence.*	This has lessened her confidence in herself. Is she not good enough?	

Self-Actualisation Needs	
Analysis	*Estimated Satisfaction*
If there was any satisfaction for such high needs before, with her current circumstances, Andrea is not going to be concerned about them at all.	Andrea is about 0% satisfied.

Andrea is now going to be most concerned about her basic physiological needs, such as shelter and safety, as she gets her job and finances in order. Before these needs are addressed, she will not be too concerned about her higher needs.

Maslow's hierarchy of needs provides an elegant structure to analyse motivation, including self-motivation. The hierarchy helps us to see which needs are not being fulfilled and need to be addressed. This, in turn, helps us recognise the underlying problems affecting our overall quality of life.

Exercise 4-1

Reflect on Your Needs

The following exercise will help you to reflect on the hierarchy of needs. The aim is to provide you with a quick insight to enable you to see which ones are satisfied and which ones are being ignored. The exercise is designed to be systematic so that you can use it regularly. You should consider going through this exercise on a quarterly basis. Having evaluated your needs, you will draw up a number of actions for the next quarter that will help you satisfy your most important needs. The periodic review is critical because, as your circumstances and environment change, your needs change too. The review will help you stay in control.

PART 1

For each need, consider five domains. Go through the following table and examine each domain one by one using the following instructions:

- Rate each domain from 0 to 10. For each rating, consider the quantity and quality in respect of that domain. For example, for the *social* need, you should consider rating *friendships* based on the number and quality of the friends you have. Similarly, rate yourself from 0 to 10 for *financial security, respect for expertise* and so on.
- Identify what makes you give a domain a rating of less than 10. Record the first few words that come to your mind when you think of each of these domains.
- Calculate an average rating for each need by averaging the ratings of its five domains, and record this in the area provided.

Physiological Needs		
Domain	**Rating (0 to 10)**	**If the rating is less than 10, what are the main causes?**
Food		
Sleep		
Exercise		
Health		
Sex		
Average Rating		

Safety Needs		
Domain	Rating (0 to 10)	If the rating is less than 10, what are the main causes?
Home and shelter		
Personal security		
Financial security		
Political stability		
Environmental stability		
Average Rating		

Social Needs		
Domain	**Rating (0 to 10)**	**If the rating is less than 10, what are the main causes?**
Loving others		
Being loved		
Making friends		
Having intimacy		
Belonging to a community or a team		
Average Rating		

Esteem Needs		
Domain	**Rating (0 to 10)**	**If the rating is less than 10, what are the main causes?**
Respect from others indicated by fame, prestige, attention and being valued by them		
Self-respect indicated by competence, mastery, freedom, independence and confidence		
Respect for achievements		
Respect for your voice and opinion		
Respect for expertise		
Average Rating		

Self-Actualisation Needs		
Domain	**Rating (0 to 10)**	**If the rating is less than 10, what are the main causes?**
Realisation of a lifetime achievement		
Actualisation of full potential		
The leaving of a legacy		
Peak experiences		
Plateau experiences which are wilfully induced peak experiences, thereby leading to a state of cognitive blissfulness		
Average Rating		

PART 2
Visualise your rating in the diagram below by placing a bar and shading it based on the average ratings you identified above. Use the example diagram below as a guide. Record your average ratings as a percentage.

Example Bar Chart	
Physiological Needs	92%
Safety Needs	73%
Social Needs	61%
Esteem Needs	43%
Self-Actualisation Needs	9%

Your Ratings	
Physiological Needs	
Safety Needs	
Social Needs	
Esteem Needs	
Self-Actualisation Needs	

Analysis
What do you think of your chart? Are your basic needs, on average, satisfied more than your higher needs? If not, what does this suggest? For example, you may rate your social needs lower than your esteem needs. This may suggest that your social needs and esteem needs are reversed (See *Section 4.4*). The data are just guides to help you analyse yourself further.

PART 3

Use the table below to evaluate each of your needs subjectively. For example, you may identify that within your social needs, your lowest ratings are for *friendship* and *belonging to a community*. Highlight this below, and then draw up actions to address it.

Remember, your basic needs require more immediate attention, so this exercise will help you focus on them.

Physiological Needs	
For this need, which domain has the lowest rating?	
What can you do to maximise your rating for this domain?	
What can you do to improve your average rating for this need to get it closer to the maximum of 10? Consider all domains within this need, and formulate a number of actions for the next period.	

Safety Needs	
For this need, which domain has the lowest rating?	
What can you do to maximise your rating for this domain?	
What can you do to improve your average rating for this need to get it closer to the maximum of 10? Consider all domains within this need, and formulate a number of actions for the next period.	

Social Needs	
For this need, which domain has the lowest rating?	
What can you do to maximise your rating for this domain?	
What can you do to improve your average rating for this need to get it closer to the maximum of 10? Consider all domains within this need, and formulate a number of actions for the next period.	

Esteem Needs	
For this need, which domain has the lowest rating?	
What can you do to maximise your rating for this domain?	
What can you do to improve your average rating for this need to get it closer to the maximum of 10? Consider all domains within this need, and formulate a number of actions for the next period.	

Self-Actualisation Needs	
For this need, which domain has the lowest rating?	
What can you do to maximise your rating for this domain?	
What can you do to improve your average rating for this need to get it closer to the maximum of 10? Consider all domains within this need, and formulate a number of actions for the next period.	

PART 4

After your analysis is completed for this quarter (and if this is not the first time you are doing this exercise), you should refer to your analysis of your previous quarter to see if you have improved your ratings for your needs. Compare and analyse your forms to see if your previously identified actions helped you to satisfy your needs. Write your reflection and conclusions below.

5 Don't Work for Money

*"Money will not purchase happiness for the man
who has no concept of what he wants."*

Ayn Rand

*"I worked out what I liked doing and then
found someone to pay me to do it."*

An entrepreneur

On doctor's orders, an American investor went on holiday to a coastal Mexican village. After a difficult night without much sleep, the American went to the pier early the next morning.

A small boat with one fisherman had just docked, and you could see several large yellowfin tuna inside it. The American was impressed by the quality of the fish.

"How long did it take you to catch them?" the American asked.

The fisherman replied, "Only a little while."

"Why didn't you stay out longer to catch more fish?" the American asked.

While unloading the fish, the fisherman replied, "Well, I caught enough to support my family and a few for friends too."

"But what do you do with the rest of your time?"

The fisherman paused, looked up and smiled. "I sleep late; fish a little; play with my children; take siestas with my wife, Judith; and, each evening, I stroll into the village, where I sip wine and play guitar with my amigos. I have a full and busy life."

The American laughed. "Sir, I have an MBA from Harvard, and I've got a great idea. You should spend more time fishing and, with the proceeds, buy a bigger boat. With the proceeds from the bigger boat, soon you could buy several boats. Imagine, you could have a fleet of fishing boats!"

The American was now getting more excited and continued, "Instead of selling your catch to a middleman, you could sell it directly to customers. You could then open up your own cannery. You would control the product, processing and distribution."

The American was visibly excited, and as if suddenly remembering something, he said, "Of course, you can leave this small place and move to Mexico City, then Los Angeles and eventually to New York City. You can then run your ever-expanding enterprise from there with easy access to qualified management professionals."

The fisherman asked, "But, how long will all this take?"

The American replied, "Fifteen to twenty years. Maximum twenty-five years."

"But what then?" asked the fisherman.

The American laughed and, as if waiting for this moment, said, "That's the best part. When the time is right, you would announce an IPO, sell your company stock to the public and become very rich. You could make millions!"

"Millions, señor? Then what?"

The American said proudly, "Then you could retire and move to a small coastal fishing village, where you could sleep late, fish a little, play with your kids, take siestas with your wife and stroll to the village in the evenings, where you could sip wine and play guitar with your amigos . . ."

5.1 Create a Cascading Success

Greg is a mechanical engineer who works in a German factory. The factory produces wheels that are used for a whole host of products, such as trolleys, toy cars, office chairs, conveyor belts and rollerblades. Greg studied mechanical engineering at a well-known local university. He had to work hard in school to be able to pass the university's entrance exam. The comprehensive course took four years to complete, and unlike some other universities, where students seem to be more concerned with dating and clubbing, Greg had to study hard to meet the high standards of his engineering course. Despite being a bright student, Greg's studies took up so much of his time that he had little time left for socialising or attending to his hobbies. The last couple of years of the course were intense, as Greg had to pass complex modules, complete a demanding project and look into finding a job for after graduation.

Being a mechanical engineer meant that Greg was not going to be part of a particular association of qualified specialists, such as medical doctors, dentists or lawyers. In such professions, the supply of specialists is controlled across the market, and the path to finding a job is clearer. In such professions, people need to be certified to be able to work. A national association controls and monitors qualified specialists to make sure they are fit for the job and are up to date. The immigrants in these professions cannot start competing with such specialists straight away. As a result, graduates often start making good money right out of university.

This was not the case for Greg, the mechanical engineer. After his gruelling studies, he had to compete with cheap labour flocking into Germany from Eastern Europe or the Far East. His best chance was to get a job as a test engineer or a technician and to be utilised as cheap but smart labour for the team. After several years of intense work—which was mainly on stuff no other engineer wanted to work on—and low pay, he might be lucky to find his way up and at least start to work on a project that he actually liked. As with the average trends for a young person's life, having had a job, Greg focused his attention on finding a partner. He succeeded, and they subsequently settled down as a couple. His next focus was to work for a few years to pile up enough of a deposit to get a mortgage and buy a house. House prices kept going up, and the sooner he got the house, the better. If he was lucky, he might even have time to spend a few hours every week on a hobby. That, however, was difficult, as he had to spend long hours at work. With the current pace of technology, it was as if he had to study as much as he had for his degree every year just to remain competitive in his field. Everyone everywhere was outsourcing work to cheaper countries while cheap labour entered the country from newly joined European countries. Greg's job was constantly under threat, and he felt that he had no choice but to work harder and gain more qualifications, learning CAD, 3D printing, on-demand manufacturing and so on.

Greg wondered if becoming a line manager would improve the quality of his life and make his professional situation more fulfilling and less hectic. Looking at his current line manager, David, did not fill him with much confidence. David was a fossil when it came to technical knowledge; he was also unhealthy, out of shape, stressed out and overworked. Greg wondered if that was his future. He'd had to work hard for every single thing in his life so far, and his life seemed like a succession of challenges.

Now, let's compare this with another life. Recall Bruce Lee's life story that you went through earlier. His life is a classic example of a *cascading success*, as he went from martial arts to setting up a teaching school to acting and, finally, to writing and directing movies.

For Lee, his choices helped him to succeed, and each success prepared him for the next phase and, in turn, more success. It was a *cascade*, whereby each choice he made helped him directly and prepared him indirectly for the next success in his life. The cascade ultimately allowed Lee to express his knowledge and passion as freely as he wanted.

In contrast, some people have to work sequentially for everything. They have to work hard to get educated, to find a job, to find a partner and to make money. This leaves little time for their hobbies and interests. Before they know it, they are old and life is over. On the other hand, others seem to cruise along as if the world changes just to suit them. In reality, it is because the *domain* they have started with, along with their *environment* and their *decisions,* has helped them succeed in one area and has simultaneously prepared them for the next. Even if they find themselves in a negative environment, they turn this negativity into an advantage. Before focusing on the next item, these people are already halfway there. Such cascades can lead to an incredibly successful life that sometimes outsiders may put down to good luck, but in reality, it is nothing more than the results of making the right choices at the right time. Bruce Lee is indeed a legend—but only because he made himself into one.

5.2 Types of Motivators

When it comes to jobs, many people consider the wage as a critical factor in making their decision. A range of thoughts, such as the following, may pass through their minds:

- Does this job pay well?
- Is there a lot of money in this?
- I need to find another job that pays me at least £3,000 more. I will threaten to leave unless they give me a pay rise.
- With this job, they give good bonuses, private health insurance at reduced cost, a laptop I can take anywhere and free lunch at the canteen.

All of these can be classified as *extrinsic motivators* which come to influence a person's behaviour. Motivators can be divided into two types: *intrinsic* motivators and *extrinsic* motivators.

- *Intrinsic motivators.* These are motivators that are driven by interest in the task itself. The individual feels internally motivated as opposed to being influenced by external factors, such as rewards or pressure.
- *Extrinsic motivators.* These are motivators that come from the outside of the individual. Examples are rewards, money, perks, threat of punishment and competition.

5.3 Is Money a Good Motivator?

When it comes to choosing a career, money and perks are considered extrinsic motivators. This is in contrast with your deep internal interests in a subject or career. The question is, are external motivators any good, and what are their long-term effects on your behaviour and success?

There have been numerous studies on the differences between intrinsic and extrinsic motivators. Let's explore some of them here.

5.3.1 Extrinsic Motivators Can Reduce Intrinsic Motivators

In a study on preschool children, researchers investigated the use of motivators (Lepper *et al.* 1973). They divided the children into three groups:

- *Group 1.* Researchers told Group 1 that each person would get a reward for his drawings.
- *Group 2.* For this group, researchers did not mention any rewards before the children engaged in a drawing task. However, after the drawing task was completed, the children were given an unexpected reward.
- *Group 3.* This was the control group. They were not told that they would get a reward, nor were they given any rewards after the drawing task.

A couple of weeks later, the same groups of children were put in a room for a free-play session and were provided with pens and papers for drawing. The result was that the children in Group 1 drew less than those in the other two groups.

Concluding Principle:

> This and similar studies in this area suggest that when external rewards are provided for a given task, people pay more attention to these rewards than to their own interest in the activity. When rewards are

given for a previously unrewarded activity, people come to depend on these rewards when it comes to doing the task. If the rewards are withdrawn, interest in the activity is lost. The previous internal interest does not return, and the reward must be continuously provided to sustain interest.

In social psychology, this is known as the *overjustification effect,* and it has profound consequences. Consider the following: If you get a job primarily because of what an employer pays you, any change in the level of payment can immediately make you feel disinterested in the job. For example, if due to some financial difficulties, the company freezes wages, making you lose money as inflation eats your wages, you are likely to lose interest in the job. You may turn up to work later than normal, work more slowly and appear demotivated even though the daily tasks remain exactly as they were before.

If the company gives you a bonus every year, you start to expect it and feel entitled to it. If one year the bonus is not given, the overjustification effect suggests that your previous interest in the job may not return.

You may decide to set up a new company to provide products and services to make money. In the beginning, you might be excited about the products you are developing and the methods you use to expand your company to take a foothold in the market. Gradually, your sales start to go up, and you feel really good about making money. You may then become more and more focused on making more money, turning it into your main goal. You may start to think that cash is all that matters to the health of your company and that this is all you need to care about. As they say, cash is king. Sooner than later, there comes a year or a period in which the company takes a dive and generates less revenue and profit than before. The lost profit can then lead to the overjustification effect. You may no longer remain as interested in the company or its products and services; this is because the extrinsic reward—namely money—is gone. Once monetary incentive is withdrawn, your previous interest in producing top-quality products may not necessarily return, and this leads to disinterest, demotivation and, eventually, a failing company.

5.3.2 *Extrinsic Motivators Reduce Creativity*

Studies on artists show that when they create artwork primarily to make money, they are less creative or take a narrower perspective than when they create art for themselves and have total control over the outcome.

This is, in fact, something that some artists take advantage of. As an example, a really capable artist living in the UK produces outstanding figurative oil paintings that are good enough to be exhibited in places such as the National Portrait Gallery in London. In fact, the artist's students exhibit their work there. Nevertheless, the artist refuses to do any paintings for sale, enter competitions or attend exhibitions to showcase his work. He makes his living separately from a business in interior design. His oil paintings, according to him, are all for him and him alone; he paints purely for the pleasure of going through the experience of transferring what he finds interesting in a person onto a canvas.

Naturally, at some point in the past, he had discovered that the best work he produced was one that he did only for himself—not one to get money, recognition or fame.

Concluding Principle:

> Extrinsic motivators can make an activity rigid and limited based on the perceived value of the extrinsic rewards. In contrast, intrinsic motivators are freeing, leading to unlimited creativity and joy.

5.3.3 *Extrinsic Motivators Lead to Short-Term Thinking*

Studies show that corporations that are obsessed with producing strong quarterly earning guidelines end up having significantly lower long-term growth than companies that are not.

Concluding Principle:

> Extrinsic motivators lead to short-term interest in a given task. Once the external motivators are withdrawn, interest is reduced, and hence, in the long term, external motivators can do more harm than good as focus becomes limited and priorities shift towards the short term.

5.3.4 *Extrinsic Motivators Lead to Long-Term Negative Effects*

Going back to the studies by Lepper *et al.* (1973) on giving rewards to children for their drawings, it was found that when the children were rewarded once, their interest in the drawing task was diminished for two weeks.

In another study on creating headlines for a newspaper, the subjects were divided into two groups. One group was paid to design the headlines for a few issues. The other group was simply given a chance to design them without being paid. Those in the group that was rewarded became less motivated to design the headlines after the pay stopped, and it was five months before their interest was restored to the original level.

Concluding Principle:

External rewards can reduce internal motivation in the long term.

5.4 Money as an End in Itself

From what you have seen so far, it is clear that working directly for money is not as productive as aiming for something that comes from within and motivates you internally. This doesn't necessarily mean there is something wrong with wanting money or that there is something inherently bad about the desire to get rich. Getting rich is sometimes seen as an exploitation of the poor or is looked down on as mere materialism that is beneath a high-level mind (whatever that might be).

The problem is not money itself; it is the way in which people see it that makes all the difference. Consider the following guidelines that help clarify this difference. You will also see why working for someone else can be destructive:

- *You will never make enough or have enough money.* As you saw with the hierarchy of needs, once a need is satisfied, people swiftly move on to address the next need. A certain level of money addresses certain needs, only leading you to want to satisfy other needs. You will never get to a stage where all needs are covered. That's just human nature. You cannot satisfy your higher-level needs just by having cash, so aiming for cash will not get you there. Hence, thinking, *one day when I am rich, all my problems will be solved and all my needs satisfied,* is wrong. Use money as a tool, not as an end.

- *Working for someone else in a fixed job with a fixed salary is extremely limiting.* If you work for someone else on a fixed salary (with a potential small raise every year or some random bonus), understand that you are taking a safe approach and won't get very far. You will never get seriously rich by working for someone else, and that is not the biggest problem. The worst part is that by working for someone else, if you are smart, sooner or later, you learn how to become productive in your job. In other words, you learn how to do something in half the time. For the rest of the time, you have to either pretend you are busy when you are not or make what you do look twice as big as it actually is. You may also get credit for things other people do or delegate all the donkey work to others while you are busy enjoying the perks. Remember, you get to this stage if you are good; if not, you won't even get this far! This leads to *stagnation*. In a fixed-salary job, the only way to succeed is to do the least and get the most. That's a logical way to approach a fixed resource. As you may guess, the problem is with the "doing the least" part. Over time, this only leads to *fossilisation* of an individual in a fixed-salary environment. This is why in just about every organisation, you will find senior employees—usually in their fifties—who are rigid against new ideas, slow to work, fond of regulations and policies, defensive about their abilities and very much engaged in office politics in order to protect their jobs at all costs. You don't want to become like them, so quit while you are ahead and work for *yourself*. Create an environment in which more productivity leads to more success and hard cash, which in turn, allows you to do the next big thing all the way until you achieve ultimate satisfaction and self-actualisation.

- ***You end up borrowing from your future at a great cost.*** Everybody wants to have a better job, bigger house, better car, more gadgets and simply more luxury. There's nothing wrong with that, except that people on fixed salaries tend to feel safe in their jobs and tend to borrow from their future for the luxury they want to experience now. This only leads to a debt spiral. You get a job, and then you get a mortgage on the back of your salary and buy a house. Next, you use your credit cards to fill up the house with the latest furniture, gadgets and niceties. To repay the debt, you feel even more attached to your job, become more protective of it and so take fewer risks. You may get a small salary raise and then decide to get a bigger mortgage to get a bigger house. Now you need to buy more furniture; otherwise, the giant house will look empty! Your mission in life now turns into paying off your mortgage and various debts. You will always feel vulnerable. What happens if you lose your job? What happens if the company goes down? What if your partner leaves you? You will be chasing this debt for the rest of your life, unable to be creative and ambitious. It is, as Robert Kiyosaki (2000) calls it, a *poor dad's mentality*.

- ***When you don't make enough, you are likely to blame others.*** When working for someone else, you become attached to your salary. Most people in paid jobs just make ends meet. Any disruption to their salary will have immediate consequences for their lives. This creates fear and anger. You start to feel that it is other people's fault that you are not earning enough. You blame your manager for not giving you a raise. You blame your colleagues for out-competing you on a bonus. You blame company management for falling behind a competitor. You blame the wealthy bankers for the poor state of the economy. You blame the president for everything else. All this would really be an indirect projection of your anger towards yourself. The only way out is to learn to control and use money as a tool rather than letting it control you.

- ***When you work for others, you pay more tax.*** In today's world, taxation is an important factor that influences quality of life greatly.

You want to live in a prosperous nation while avoiding paying too much tax. In most of the developed countries, you get to pay less tax if you take more risks. It is how the system is designed—to encourage entrepreneurship for developing new products and services. You are encouraged to take risks to solve a problem in society and receive the rewards once you succeed. Being employed means taking the least amount of risk, which, in turn, means you will have to pay a lot more tax than those who take risks.

- ***It doesn't mean you should quit your job and go into real estate.*** There are plenty of books and articles by success gurus that seem to recommend that working for money is bad, and then they immediately follow this by saying that having a real-estate asset is a great way to generate cash! In recent years, it has become fashionable to invest in a property, hoping that once the market goes up, you can sell at an advantage and get more than what you invested in its purchase, as well as on maintenance, taxes and insurance. This is a very limiting view. It is a buy-and-pray mentality. It is more of a gambler's attitude than that of a person who wants to succeed by adding *value*. If everybody was just buying houses and aiming to sell higher, nothing new would be invented or produced. We would be fooling ourselves. Civilisations would simply not flourish and progress. We would just have a market of get-rich-quick people whose only concern in life is to second-guess each other. The essence of making money in a successful way is to *create* something that generates the money for you as a result of your thoughts, creativity and originality. Building a factory can lead to manufacturing thousands of products that can satisfy many customers' needs. Writing software can help millions of users to access information more effectively. Setting up a distribution network can save people a lot of travel time. Such endeavours lead to tangible positive results for you and for society. Guessing how the property market or shares move up and down is not as rewarding to the society as solving a real problem. It is only when you solve a real problem to help people that you *deserve* the reward, and you *will* be rewarded more than you dreamed of. Aim to solve a tangible problem in your society. Don't invent a problem to solve, and don't look for ways to exploit the system like a gambler with a short-term mentality.

5.5 It is Called "Making" Money for a Reason

In English, we tend to say things like "I want to *make* money." It turns out that this is perhaps the best way to think of money—not to hope to find it somewhere, steal it or beg it but to *make* it. It might be difficult to find anything more elegant to capture this than the following script by Ayn Rand on what making money really means. This statement was made by one of the characters in Rand's *Atlas Shrugged* (1957), explaining the nature of money:

> "Money is the tool of men who have reached a high level of productivity and a long-range control over their lives. Money is not merely a tool of exchange: much more importantly, it is a tool of saving, which permits delayed consumption and buys time for future production. To fulfil this requirement, money has to be some material commodity which is imperishable, rare, homogeneous, easily stored, not subject to wide fluctuations of value, and always in demand among those you trade with. This leads you to the decision to use gold as money. Gold money is a tangible value in itself and a token of wealth actually produced. When you accept a gold coin in payment for your goods, you actually deliver the goods to the buyer; the transaction is as safe as simple barter. When you store your savings in the form of gold coins, they represent the goods which you have actually produced and which have gone to buy time for other producers, who will keep the productive process going, so that you'll be able to trade your coins for goods any time you wish.
>
> So you think that money is the root of all evil? . . . Have you ever asked what is the root of money? Money is a tool of exchange, which can't exist unless there are goods produced and men able to produce them. Money is the material shape of the principle that men who wish to deal with one another must deal by trade and give value for value. Money is not the tool of the moochers, who claim your product by tears, or of the looters, who take it from you by force. Money is made possible only by the men who produce. Is this what you consider evil?
>
> When you accept money in payment for your effort, you do so only on the conviction that you will exchange it for the product of the effort of others. It is not the moochers or the looters who give value to money. Not an ocean of tears nor all the guns in the world can transform those pieces of paper in your wallet into the bread you will need to survive tomorrow. Those pieces of paper, which should have been gold, are a token of honor—your claim upon the energy of the men who produce. Your wallet is your statement of hope that somewhere in the world around you there are men who will not default on that moral principle which is the root of money. Is this what you consider evil?
>
> Have you ever looked for the root of production? Take a look at an electric generator and dare tell yourself that it was created by the muscular effort of unthinking brutes. Try to grow a seed of wheat

without the knowledge left to you by men who had to discover it for the first time. Try to obtain your food by means of nothing but physical motions—and you'll learn that man's mind is the root of all the goods produced and of all the wealth that has ever existed on Earth.

But you say that money is made by the strong at the expense of the weak? What strength do you mean? It is not the strength of guns or muscles. Wealth is the product of man's capacity to think. Then is money made by the man who invents a motor at the expense of those who did not invent it? Is money made by the intelligent at the expense of the fools? By the able at the expense of the incompetent? By the ambitious at the expense of the lazy? Money is *made*—before it can be looted or mooched—made by the effort of every honest man, each to the extent of his ability. An honest man is one who knows that he can't consume more than he has produced."

5.6 *Making Money or Saving Money?*

Consider Jane. She is totally focused on saving. She is proud of what she can achieve while bargain hunting. She can easily spend hours going from store to store to get what she wants at the lowest price. She is a voucher junkie. She actually carries a dedicated purse just for keeping all the store vouchers and discount coupons. She is also very involved in online shopping, wanting to get the cheapest prices everywhere. She buys a lot of stuff from eBay and knows all the best car boot sales. She always boasts to her friends about how good she is at finding a bargain. Within minutes of any conversation, she is talking about the costs of something, how expensive or cheap it is and how she cannot afford X or Y. Jane lives with her husband and five-year-old son in a mortgaged house. They regularly go on holidays to France and Spain, and they eat out often.

Now consider Calum. When working on a product, the first thing Calum asks himself is who it is for and what they are willing to pay for it. He is always on the lookout for new investments to increase the value of his current assets. Any news always makes him think of new potential markets that could be served by new products. In a way, Calum is focused on making more money and using it as a tool to make even more. It is not just the money that he is after; his main interest is in the challenge of creating wealth by his own creativity, hard work, risk taking and clever thinking.

What do these two stories tell you? Who do you think becomes richer? Who do you think becomes more successful? Which focus leads to more achievements and probably more happiness?

There tend to be two general attitudes towards money; some like to save it and some like to make it. Which one of these would you rather focus on?

At the end of the day, there is only so much you can save; you can only save as much as you already have. In contrast, imagine if you are determined to increase wealth as a concept, very much like Warren Buffet—not just to get rich to have money and spend it but to focus on increasing the value of your assets and on turning each dollar into two and treating it as a challenge. It is well known that Buffet, despite being one of the richest men on Earth, still lives in the same house he bought in 1958. He is known for his simple tastes. His success is certainly related to his attitude towards investment as an interesting and challenging activity as opposed to wanting to make quick money so he can spend it.

Exercise 5-1

Define Your Future Questionnaire

It is not the money that matters; it is what you can do with it—perhaps to create the next big thing or use it as a tool. This exercise helps you recognise what it is that you want when you get access to that money. Consider the following questions, and answer them honestly.

PART 1: What If You Won £1 Million?

You have just won a big prize with certain conditions. The conditions are as follows. You are not allowed to invest this money, buy shares, put it into a bank or carry out similar investment activities. You cannot give away the money to friends, family or charity. It has to be spent on products or services that you truly desire the most.

What would you buy with this money? Treat this exercise as a thought experiment. It is designed to force you to think about what you would do irrespective of what society thinks. You don't have to be heroic here by giving it to family or charity. The exercise is a tool to help you realise what you truly want.

Make a list of anything you can buy with this money, and for each item, explain your reasoning and what you expect to achieve.

Thing/service to buy	Why are you buying this?	What do you expect to achieve by buying this?

Thing/service to buy	Why are you buying this?	What do you expect to achieve by buying this?

PART 2: What If You Got the Top Job?

Overnight, there has been a significant shift in attitudes and mentality in your company. The company has decided to place you as the top managing director or CEO. You are now in charge of the company. How would you lead the company? What strategy would you follow? What products or services do you want your company to offer? Where do you see your company in five or ten years with you in charge?

If you are self-employed, still go through the exercise by focusing on what you would do for the future of your trade.

PART 3: What If You Had Financial Freedom?

You have made it. You are now earning £1 million a year. Your investment or the company you set up will pay you enough that you don't ever have to work again. You are also lucky to have people who can take care of your wealth so you don't have to worry about anything.

Considering this, what would you do? Where would you go? How would you spend your day? What would you desire the most? How do you visualise such a life?

While visualising, aim to use all your senses. See yourself in the environment; how does it feel? What do you hear? What does it smell like?

5.7 Define Your Heaven

Contrary to certain religious beliefs, you don't have to wait until you die to go to an imaginary heaven. In fact, humanity would be much better off if people collectively believed that heaven could be created on Earth. They would then be more likely to do something about it and would be more likely to succeed. As a bonus, there would be far less murder, as the need to become a martyr in order to get to heaven would be negated!

Anyway, there is no reason why you shouldn't be able to create your own personal heaven on Earth. The first step is to know what you'd like this personal heaven to look like. The following systematic exercise will help to reveal this.

Exercise 5-2

Define Your Ideal Heaven

The purpose of this exercise is to help you think of a desirable day that is perfectly achievable. The exercise also helps you to see that what you desire is not just a wish or a nice-to-have. You want to see that you want something so much that you are willing to sacrifice for it. Once you have this world in mind, you can start thinking about how to create it. You will see how to approach this systematically in the coming chapters. Go through the following main steps to imagine your believable heaven. You can use additional blank sheets, and be as imaginative as possible.

STEP 1: Imagine Your Personal Heaven

To create your own heaven on Earth, you will first need to imagine it as precisely as you can. This is just a mental exercise. Don't limit yourself. You can have anything you want. The aim is to express your desires. In this initial step, write down your ideas as quickly as you can. Don't worry about consistency at this point; just make sure you capture everything.

What does your day look like? What are you doing? What possessions do you have? Who do you interact with? Where do you live? How is the weather? What is the view like from your house? Where do you go? What resources— whether tangible or intangible—do you have access to? How do you feel?

Be honest. Write what you desire the most without censoring yourself. If you like it, get it out; this is your chance to express it. You can judge yourself later.

Consider using a mind map if you think it will help you to come up with more ideas.

STEP 2: Make It Rational

Once you have captured your ideas, go through the list to check for rationality. Unlike a religious heaven, you cannot have an irrational world. For example, you cannot be in two places at once or be tall and petite at the same time. Go through the list and update it until you have a rational and realistic heaven on Earth.

At this point, don't worry about society's limitations or reactions to your desires. Only check for rational consistency.

STEP 3: *Think of Real-World Consistencies*

To create your heaven on Earth, apart from making it rational, you must also make it consistent with Earthly rules. For example, you cannot have a lot of money without making sure it is secure. You cannot be the richest person on Earth without anybody knowing about you. You cannot be with the most beautiful woman in the world without half the world desiring her too. Think about the consequences of the features of the world you have imagined, and rethink them to make sure you actually want to have what you have written down.

Exercise 5-3

Put It All Together

Go through the updated mind map of your interests that you created in *Exercise 3-3*. Update this mind map based on your analysis of Maslow's hierarchy of needs and the exercises you completed in this chapter on your ideal heaven.

Focus on areas with intrinsic motivators as opposed to extrinsic motivators that can distort your judgment when considering your desires. Reorganise and redraw your map below or on a separate sheet, and prepare this for use in future exercises.

6 Beware of Attention Economy

"In an information-rich world, the wealth of information means a dearth of something else: a scarcity of whatever it is that information consumes. What information consumes is rather obvious: it consumes the attention of its recipients. Hence a wealth of information creates a poverty of attention and a need to allocate that attention efficiently among the overabundance of information sources that might consume it."

Herbert A. Simon

A group of young students are out for a hiking trip in a remote location. They get off the bus and approach the entrance of a national park. A beautiful, calm lake and gorgeous hills in the background make the place look magical. While standing by the lake, a guide approaches the students and explains which directions they can take to explore the area. He also adds, "There is no mobile phone signal out here, so I'm afraid you just have to look at the lake!"

The comical nature of this scene says something profound about the era we live in—that there is a lot of competition for our attention wherever we go, and that even traditional "competitors" for our attention, such as enjoying natural tranquillity, are under threat from the real-time, always-available, complex digital world that seems to be engulfing us like air.

What exactly is in the air? Let's have a look. You will agree that it is immense! Here is just a fraction of what's out there.

What Is in the Air or on the Ground?	
YouTube[4]	<ul><li>100 hours of video is uploaded to YouTube every minute.</li><li>Four billion YouTube videos are viewed per day.</li><li>Six billion hours of video are watched every month.</li></ul>
Movies[5]	<ul><li>According to IMDB, there have been about 315,000 feature films made so far. According to the Academy of Picture Arts and Sciences and the British Film Institute, a feature is a film that has a running time of forty minutes or longer. The total number of movies ever made around the world is much higher than that—all potential content to consume.</li><li>IMDB has a record of about 1.9 million TV episodes.</li><li>According to the Motion Picture Association of America, about 600 movies were released in 2013. This is in contrast to 1,300 movies released in India, 400 in China and 240 in France.</li></ul>
Games[5]	<ul><li>IMDB has a record of 14,000 video games.</li></ul>
Internet[6]	<ul><li>There are 276 million registered domains.</li><li>The total domains grew by 19.3 million in 2013.</li></ul>
Books[7]	<ul><li>According to Google's infamous research on the total number of books ever published in all of modern history, 129,864,880 books have been written. A book is defined as a "tome; an idealised bound volume that can have millions of copies or just one or two such as a thesis filed in a university library."</li></ul>

---

[4] Statistics as of 2015

[5] Statistics as of 2015 from www.imdb.com/stats

[6] Statistics as of July 2014, according to Verisign:
www.verisigninc.com/assets/domain-name-brief-july2014.pdf

[7] See Google Books: booksearch.blogspot.co.uk/2010/08/books-of-world-stand-up-and-be-counted.html

Products[8]	• Amazon.com has about 296 million products listed. • Thirty-six million products alone were added to amazon.com during the second half of 2014. • Amazon.co.uk has about 166 million products listed. • Amazon.de has about 156 million products listed. • Amazon.fr has about 130 million products listed.
Travel	• There are 190 independent countries in the world. If you travel three times a year, just visiting each country's capital once in a lifetime, it will take about sixty-three years. This excludes all other cities, areas, parks, mountains, islands and beaches.
Mobile Apps[9]	• The Apple Store has 1.4 million apps that are on available for iOS devices, such as the iPhone, and 725,000 of them have been made for iPads. • There are 1.5 million Google Play apps available for Android.

6.1 What is Attention Economy?

Right. That seems to be a lot of content. And that's not counting a whole lot of other types of content you can find across the entire Internet. There is simply an unimaginable amount of information to consume in about 100 years or so of a lifetime if you live really well. Then, there is a whole lot of stuff to do too, from learning to play an instrument, to travelling, to kitesurfing, to writing a book, to appreciating art and much more. You have no chance to even scratch the surface of all that is there to experience!

This doesn't suggest that we need to worry. What *attention economy* suggests is that we need to accept that there is only so much we can pay attention to.

---

[8] Statistics as of 2015. You can easily see the total number of products in each Amazon domain at any time by searching for gibberish, such as "-hbgnkkl" and checking the total results.

[9] Statistics for Apple Store as of Jan. 2015: www.apple.com/pr/library/2015/01/08App-Store-Rings-in-2015-with-New-Records.html. Google Play statistics as of Feb. 2015: www.appbrain.com/stats/number-of-android-apps

We each have a finite amount of attention that we can spend on things. Attention works both ways. Spending the right kind of attention can lead to improved quality of life, while receiving a generous amount of attention can lead to success. When people pay attention to you or your products, you are more likely to sell your ideas or products to them, thereby leading to more benefits to you. This is why understanding attention economy is crucial to success and happiness. Let's explore both sides of attention in more detail.

6.2 How to Pay Attention

You are a hard worker. You feel that you need to give 100% to your work in order to progress professionally. You believe that being successful at work will help you to better provide for your family. You are happy to spend long hours at work. You work long hours, and by the time you get home from work, your five-year-old daughter is already asleep, so all you get to do is give her a kiss while she sleeps. You have dinner with your partner, who is telling you a story about her day, but you are far away, thinking about a million other things related to your work. You just nod to keep her talking. Next, you are too tired to do anything and want to go straight to bed. You have three meetings tomorrow, and you know it's going to be a long day.

You continue like this for weeks and then months. Due to not spending much time with your family, you are almost out of touch with them. You only exercise when you get a chance, and that is rare. Beyond work, you are not engaged in any exciting activity or hobby; you simply don't have enough time, as you believe your job takes precedence.

Six months later, your hard work pays off, and you are promoted to departmental manager. As part of the promotion, your wage is increased by £5,000. You feel very pleased. You must be doing really well.

However, you have a feeling that not everything is going well. Your partner feels distant. She has already warned you that you are not there for them. You don't really get to interact with your daughter and be a father to her when she needs you.

This trend continues until your partner tells you that your relationship is not working. She is unhappy with the way you work, which seems to be getting in the way of your personal life. She doesn't think you care enough about your family. On top of your job, you now have to deal with the emotional roller coaster of a divorce.

The divorce gets more and more complicated as you go through it. This takes its toll on you as you have to utilise every minute of your free time to get the case through the court. Sometimes, you even have to take time off work. Your mind is not on the job. A few months later, your boss calls you in and gives you a strongly worded warning. You are not delivering as much as they expected when they promoted you. You are told to get yourself sorted or you may have to look for another job.

You are sinking deeper and deeper. Your partner is gone. Your relationship with your only child is in jeopardy because she doesn't know you very well. And now you are losing your job too. You have no hobby, and you will lose your social circle, which consists of your colleagues, when you lose your job.

What do you think is happening here? You have been enthusiastic about your job and have wanted a successful career. In fact, you have been determined to succeed. There is nothing wrong with this, except that your approach has been to sacrifice everything else for it. The problem is that by neglecting other areas of your life, you have created issues elsewhere.

As more problems emerged, they started to affect the very job you were aiming to succeed in. In short, your strategy backfired because you did not pay the right kind of attention to all the areas that matter in your life.

While it is crucial to be able to pay attention to several important areas, you cannot pay attention to everything. *You must choose.* Choosing is best done using a systematic approach so that you don't get carried away by an emotional impulse or simply react to whatever fights for your attention.

A great systematic method was advocated by Stephen Covey in his influential book, *The 7 Habits of Highly Effective People* (1989). Here, you will go through an extended version of this approach, which will help you prioritise your life and control your *attention expenditure*, which is much like spending money.

6.3 Define Your Roles

In earlier chapters, you identified your desires in life and created a mind map to capture what you wanted most. You also analysed your needs based on Maslow's hierarchy of needs, which should have given you further insight into what you need to focus your attention on. This, along with the guidelines on attention economy, aiming for intrinsic motivators and choosing interests that don't lead to dead-end careers should have prepared you for the next step in the process.

In this step, you identify your *roles*. For example, you might be a company manager, author, researcher, charity worker, tennis player, singer, sister or mother. In the context of your life, you need to pay attention to every single one of these roles. Failure to spend time in a given role may result in all sorts of inconveniences later on. For example, if you spend too much time on your professional role, you may end up upsetting your family a few years later with serious life-changing consequences.

The identification of your roles helps you understand the scale of your engagement with tasks and people and the amount of time and energy you wish to spend on each area.

There are two sets of roles:

- *Automatic*. These are roles that you are automatically assigned to in life. For example, you might be a son and a brother, and you might later become an uncle. You simply have to deal with the duties of these roles in line with your mission statement.
- *Non-automatic*. These are roles that you choose yourself and roles that ultimately define you. As you can imagine, these are critical roles that you need to think continuously about and balance based on your available time. These roles *must* match your mission statement. Otherwise, you will be pursuing roles that will not provide any meaning to your life and are probably a waste of time.

You will define your mission statement in later chapters. Defining the roles at this point will prepare you for that. Some examples of roles are shown below.

Examples of Automatic Roles	
Brother	Sister
Son	Daughter
Uncle	Aunt
Father-in-law	Mother-in-law
Nephew	Niece
Stepfather	Stepmother

Examples of Non-Automatic Roles	
Author	Salesman
Artist	Receptionist
Coach	Nurse
Doctor	Entrepreneur
Lawyer	Associate
Student	Mentor
Leader	Badminton player
Teacher	Traveller
Father	Mother

You probably cannot be the world's best mother, sister, wife, author, visionary and surgeon while being insanely rich, fit and charming and spending most of your time being pampered. In order to be great at some of the roles, you may have to compromise others. The following exercise helps you identify your roles. Later, you will go through the set to explore the importance of each one.

Exercise 6-1

Identify Your Roles

In this exercise, you should think of your roles and use a mind-mapping approach to document them. Identify these roles based on your interests and desires. Use the updated mind map created as part of *Exercise 5-3* as a reference.

Tips:

- To get the most from this exercise, focus more on your non-automatic roles as opposed to your automatic roles since the former are more difficult to identify. You will, however, need to capture all your roles.
- Think of your important long-term roles. This helps you focus on the future and not on the short-term roles, such as the project management role you were just assigned by your boss.
- Use the power of mind mapping to create branches and sub-branches, and reorganise the map as you add more roles. This categorisation and reorganisation will help you discover all the roles that interest you. For example, you may create an *Adventures* category and list a few roles there, such as *sailor* and *off-road driver*, and then suddenly realise that you also need to include *snowboarder*.
- Aim to add every role you can think of. You will have a chance later on to prune the list, but at this point, your aim is to not miss any.
- A list of roles is not a wish list of things you like to do; it is a list of blocks of time you need to allocate to various interests and commitments.
- Be as specific as possible when defining each role. For example, don't name a role "artist." Instead, define it specifically such as, "painter", "photographer", "guitarist", or "writer."

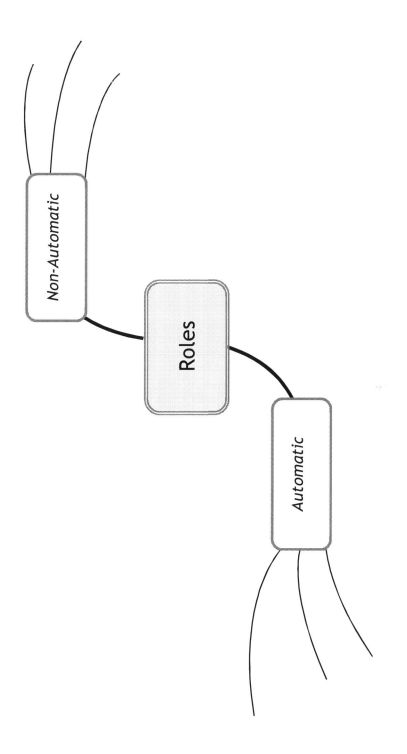

6.4 How to Gain Attention

It can be argued that perhaps the only critical commodity is attention. Attention leads directly to success, wealth, influence and, ultimately, control.

There is only so much attention in the world, as defined by its inhabiting population. To succeed, you must carve out a slice of attention for yourself. The more you can get, the more successful you will be.

With the current explosion of content, its abundance and immediate availability, everyone is fighting for attention. Lack of attention is, therefore, the major limiting factor in relation to the growth of just about anything. Abundance of content is leading to *information overload* in many areas, which means that in order to stand out, you need to go beyond shouting more loudly. It means you need to use branding and attention-grabbing activities with a specific goal and strategy in mind so that your attention resources are not wasted. You need to carve out a very specific type of attention—*niche attention*—to have a chance at grabbing any at all.

Think of attention as a currency. A great way to increase wealth is to invest what you already have; in other words, use money to make more money. The same applies to attention. Initially, you aim to gain any attention you can get. Next, you must consider using whatever attention you are getting to receive more attention. This investment will give you a quick head start and put you on a positive cycle.

Let's look at an example to illustrate this.

Your colleague, Jonathan, was planning to give a presentation at a conference on a project that the team, including you, has been working on. He is the project's technical lead and a senior member. Hence, he is well suited for the presentation.

You have recently joined the team, and although you are extremely enthusiastic about the subject and your involvement in the project, you have never had a chance to showcase your work publicly.

Each week, members of the team are supposed to present what they have accomplished. This week, you come to share your achievements in the weekly meeting. It is an exceptionally interesting area, and because of your enthusiasm, you deliver it passionately. Your presentation makes people feel excited about the whole project too. This is noticed by Jonathan and other senior managers.

So far, you have gained a bit of attention because of your dedication, enthusiasm and passionate presentation.

As if by chance, a few days later, a week before the main conference presentation, Jonathan is assigned by top management to visit a potential new multinational collaborator abroad. As this is a priority, Jonathon cannot give the presentation at the conference; someone else must cover for him. Jonathan approaches you and asks if you are happy to do this.

Now, your original attention grab has led to gaining more attention, this time from Jonathan, who is a senior member of your team. You have a choice to reject the offer because you don't have time, or you might be afraid of public presentations. If you reject it, you have lost a great opportunity to grab yet more attention for yourself. However, if you accept it, you can go to the conference and, through another solid performance, receive much more attention from the industry.

In short, use a bit of attention you have received to grab more of it. Just be on the lookout for opportunities to turn any attention you receive into more. There simply isn't much of it, and as with current trends, there will be less of it in the future.

6.5 Aim to Create Value

Think of people whom you would consider successful. They can be founders of successful corporations, famous venture capitalists, scientists and authors. Now look for patterns in their approach. Do you think their success was primarily the result of aiming to get rich and famous, or was it due to their determination to *create value*? Were they more interested in solving a problem, addressing a need, contributing to knowledge with a novel insight, or were they just chasing money? If you examine them closely, you will see that aiming to create *value* comes first with almost every single one of these people.

Do not confuse this with a call to be altruistic or with popular slogans about helping the society. You may choose to do that too if it makes you happy. However, creating value does not have to be altruistic. You may do it for your own selfish interests, just as you may want to get rich for your own selfish needs. It is just that aiming to create value will get you there faster. Think of money and attention as *votes*. There is a finite number of votes in the world. Having wealth is basically about *control*. To succeed and to remain worthy of that wealth and success, aim to get people to vote to you so you gain control. Getting rich is only an indication that society has given you more control because you are on the right track. It means you are doing something that is of value to the people in society, changing their lives or doing something that they simply want to see more of. This is why people will give you control. If you are a successful author, every purchase means readers are voting to read more of what you can write. If you are selling a lot of products, every purchase means that your customers want you to have more control over this specific field so that you can produce better and more elaborate products in this area. With their purchase, they are telling you that they believe you are on the right track and should keep doing what you are doing.

Here is an example to illustrate. Back in 1998, the founders of Google became interested in the market of search engines and considered search a vital function of the future of computing and the Internet. The market leader at the time was Yahoo. The solution provided by Yahoo, however, was inadequate, and the Google founders thought they could do better. Yahoo's website was full of ads, and the company appeared to be more interested in making money than providing value, such as clear and relevant search results. Yahoo seemed more focused on maximising revenue and appeared actively hostile towards their rival, Microsoft. Boosting their share price for their stakeholders also seemed to be Yahoo's most important aim; in other words, Yahoo was aiming for quick money.

Yahoo saw itself fundamentally as a *portal*—a site that people would visit before starting to head elsewhere, such as to check news and email or find businesses in a directory (Yahoo stands for Yet Another Hierarchical Officious Oracle). Once people were on the site, Yahoo could feed them tons of ads and get advertisers to fight each other for that front-page banner.

Google founders took a different approach. While doing their PhDs, they researched academic citations and, from there, came up with a new ranking method that could show significant results. Next, they focused on search algorithms based on the same research, using linking instead of citations to rank web pages for a given search. Despising Yahoo's approach, the Google people came up with a clean and ad-free home page that produced relevant results for a given search term. They insisted that Google was not a portal like Yahoo. Instead, it was about searching and organising data. Even to this day, Google tries hard not to be a portal, while Yahoo still seems to be lost in the same old approach. For years, Google simply focused on improving the search results and leaving direct revenue making for later. Google wanted to create value first and foremost to help people. Their main priority was to produce a scalable solution. They knew that once they got people's attention, their attention votes could be converted into revenue. Eventually, they found that search-specific advertisement was the solution, which not only created revenue for them but also provided value for customers who were searching for products and services. Advertisers could bid against each other for a given search term so that their ads could appear on top of the page for that keyword.

This win-win solution led to Google's massive success. Their system turned out to be one of the most lucrative money-making machines ever invented.

In short, always aim to create value. This way, you can grab people's attention faster and for longer, leading to more success and, ultimately, happiness.

6.6 Position Yourself to Be Lucky

It was the year 2001, and the age of the Internet was upon us. It was now obvious to consumers and corporations alike that the Internet was the most disruptive technology ever. Everyone was trying hard to set up websites, provide content, sell products, develop software and simply make the best of this new technology. All this meant that there was an increasing demand to distribute more and more digital content, such as software, data files, images, music, videos, games and many other types of data. Digital distribution was based primarily on a simple system that had been invented years earlier. The essence of this system was that you set up a computer as a server with the appropriate software (known as an FTP server). You assign an address to it and then share this address with end users. The users can then browse the server using FTP software to access it and download the files they want. As the Internet developed, this system became more elaborate and had easier user interfaces to access and browse the files. The download system, however, stayed the same. Many users had to connect to a single server to download files. A server could handle only a finite number of users. Hence, once a file became too popular, it became difficult and sometimes next to impossible to download it unless more servers were added to the network by the people who hosted the files.

As the Internet boomed, this became a major problem. A software company could make a new version of its software available for download, and soon everyone would be accessing the server simultaneously, all wanting to get the new large files quickly. This also meant that other users who wanted to access other files on the server could not access them while the servers were overloaded. This was also the case for the distribution of videos, which, considering the average download bandwidth of the day, were considered very large. You could place a video on your website, and as soon as it became popular, your server would go down, and no more users could access the video or, for that matter, the rest of the site.

Soon, a new technology dubbed peer-to-peer networking or P2P emerged. Rather than downloading content from servers, people could just share it with each other. Software, such as Napster and later KaZaA, allowed users to connect to another person's computer and download files. While there was always a need to share files legitimately, such technologies were soon used to share movies, music and other copyrighted content. Technically, the system was the same as the server–client model. Downloading was still done from a single computer hosting a file and acting as a server for a KaZaA client, say on a teenager's computer. Again, as soon as a file became popular, many people (peers) started downloading it, which made the server (the other peer) unresponsive. Ultimately, few people could download the files as the server rejected new connections.

This was a problem, and a new approach became necessary. We take it for granted that if a lot of people want something, it should become scarce and difficult to find. It is coded in our brain. If we see free food, we run to get it before others do. We fear that if we are late, the food will finish. Was this really true for the digital age too?

As with many new technologies, necessity is the mother of invention. It was time to turn a very basic idea on its head and think completely differently to find a novel solution.

This is, in fact, what twenty-six-year-old Bram Cohen thought at the time. He was a college dropout software programmer whose main interests were recreational mathematics, origami, juggling and puzzles.

After extensive deliberation and experimentation, Cohen came up with a new protocol and a system to connect users and data. This was to eliminate the inevitable server overloads. He succeeded spectacularly. In the old system, the popularity of the data made access worse. With Cohen's new system, popularity actually improved access!

To realise how profound this breakthrough was, let's go through a simple analogy. Suppose you have a common grazing ground which is easily and freely accessible by everyone. Farmers can bring their sheep to this ground for grazing. What follows is that there is a rush to use the grounds as quickly as possible, for every farmer is competing with all others. Those who get there first and stay there longer will benefit the most. Soon, the ground will be totally utilised and will become useless to everyone. As Garrett Hardin put it, "Freedom in a common brings ruin to all." In fact, he coined this phenomenon as the *tragedy of the commons*. This was a fairly established piece of philosophical thinking—until Cohen, that is.

What Cohen did was to make it exactly the opposite. His new software protocol for exchanging files meant that as more and more people went to download something, it became easier and faster to do so! More downloaders didn't mean more traffic; it meant more opportunities to access what you wanted! The idea sounded too good to be true, but that is exactly what the new protocol achieved. He named it BitTorrent.

The fundamental idea behind BitTorrent was simple, but the implementation was much more complex. Here is a brief explanation of how BitTorrent works. Basically, when a lot of people connect to a network, they bring along with them two things—a *computer* and their *Internet bandwidth*. Cohen thought that when computer and bandwidth resources become abundant, it shouldn't lead to a clogged network; instead, it should actually make it easier for users to access the files. So the idea was that rather than downloading a file from a single *uploader* or *seed* (traditionally a server), it should be possible to download various bits of it from other people who were also trying to download the same file. These other downloaders are known as *peers*. So you could divide a file into a lot of small parts. Rather than everyone connecting to a single server to get all the parts, you could just search other peers' computers nearby to see if they had a copy of a specific part that they had already downloaded and could share with you. You could then download this specific part from them instead of downloading it from the seed, thereby reducing server demand on the seed. Equally, once you got the piece, you could broadcast to other peers that you had a copy of this part and, in turn, share it with them. This way, a file would be downloaded non-sequentially piece by piece. Once you had the whole file, you could turn it into a seed, which meant that all other remaining peers could then connect to you to look for any missing pieces they had failed to get from other peers. As more and more peers joined the network, more of these bits could be downloaded simultaneously, and there was a higher chance of having several complete sequences, which could, in turn, be shared with others. Hence, this led to an acceleration of download speeds as a given file became more and more popular.

Cohen released the first version of this software protocol in 2001, and this was followed by a series of updates until 2008. The breakthrough protocol completely changed the way in which large files were distributed on the Internet. By 2004, 35% of all Internet traffic was exchanged through BitTorrent. By 2009, usage increased to between 43% and 70% of all Internet traffic, depending on region.

In short, Cohen had managed to invent something profoundly useful for millions of people worldwide. Usually, we expect a lot of fame, money and prestige to follow such success, especially when it can be associated with a single person. This, however, did not turn out to be the case. Despite pursuing a passion with determination—spending hours and hours on cutting-edge coding of the kind that the world had never seen before—the rewards were not as tangible as one would expect. Why was this the case? As you will see, this had nothing to do with Cohen himself; it was more to do with what people could do with what he had invented.

The main reason that the BitTorrent system became insanely popular was perhaps the type of content that was shared through it. It turned out that a lot of people simply wanted a faster way to share copyrighted movies, music, software or porn. They wanted a system that was better than KaZaA and other similar peer-to-peer networks which became slow when certain movies became a hit, and no one could access them as the servers became saturated. As the BitTorrent system became more popular, it started to cause problems for content producers. Movie studios were not keen on this new technology and started fighting it. An easy and simple solution was to target the designer himself. Although there was no grounds on which to sue him directly just because the users of his software shared copyrighted content, he was watched and monitored carefully by hostile lawyers. Studios and distributers saw BitTorrent as a threat and wanted to get rid of it. In other words, the industry and the guys with the money wanted to kill it, but the end users who didn't want to spend any money loved it.

The subject matter itself is largely responsible for how lucky a person can get when it comes to cashing the rewards. If the scale of financial success is what you are looking for, then you need to choose wisely to be lucky. While in the example of Google's founders, the breakthrough in search algorithms led to the creation of a giant technology company that is still strong today, a similar level of effort, passion and determination to design BitTorrent did not lead to a marketable product or service that could become as big as Google is today. In the early years, Cohen had a website with a click-to-donate button, hoping that with people's donations, he could continue with his software development. Eventually, he set up his company, BitTorrent Inc., with his brother and other investors for the ongoing development of the BitTorrent protocol. It now licenses its technology and its brand to corporate customers. The company also made specific deals with major studios and distributors to make sure copyrighted materials did not appear on its search website. Despite such progress, BitTorrent is nowhere as big as Google.

There is nothing wrong with pursuing a given route for your own personal satisfaction or self-actualisation. Cohen's story suggests that it pays to pause and think about the eventuality of a given endeavour and choose a route that is more fruitful based on what you ultimately want. In short, position yourself to be lucky while choosing your roles or making decisions about inventing new services, products or artwork.

Sometimes, you won't know and should just hope to get lucky. However, it pays to think about this upfront while you are choosing your direction. Is what you are developing going to help a lot of people in legitimate ways, and can you actually cash it in (think Google)? Is what you are developing going to be big but will not necessarily lead to a lot of cash or corporate power (think Wikipedia)? Is what you are developing going to solve a big problem for some people, while creating a big problem for others (think BitTorrent)? Is what you are developing not going to solve a significant problem and the only reason you are doing it is to chase the cash (think spammy article websites)? Is what you are passionate about potentially lucrative but borderline illegal (think setting up a business to sell illegal posters of famous paintings)?

This then becomes a question of ethics. What are your values, and how can you avoid crossing the line? Would you consider developing software to hack into people's phones? Even if the hacking is done in the name of something good—say, because you are working for GCHQ[10] and your boss asked you to do it—it can be problematic. Your efforts can be easily taken advantage of by someone who doesn't have the same ethics as you. You will need to think carefully about this. You cannot go down a line of work for a few years that eventually leads to something you don't feel ethically comfortable with or that attracts a lot of hostility from industry or society. You might as well quit early to avoid wasting time by heading in a direction that will ultimately be a dead end.

In short, position yourself in such a way that can help you ultimately get the right kind of attention. This will then lead to the right kind of success in a way that you are most comfortable with ethically and morally.

6.7 *Be Prepared to Switch*

Anthony Quinn, the American actor, is familiar to many through his iconic roles in *Lawrence of Arabia*, *The Guns of Navarone* and *La Strada*. He won Academy Awards for best supporting actor for both *Viva Zapata* and *Lust for Life*. At the height of his career, Quinn was known all over the world. He has acted in more than 200 movies. You may assume that he was a second-generation actor born and bred to act; however, he was anything but. Quinn's life was not an ordinary one by any standard.

Anthony Quinn was born in Mexico in 1915. His mother had Aztec ancestry, and his father was born in Mexico to an Irish immigrant and a Mexican mother. His maternal grandmother was Cherokee. When Anthony was a boy, the family moved to California, where they worked as grape pickers. His parents were devoted Catholics. At the age of six, Anthony started to attend a Catholic church regularly, and he turned to religion. He decided that he wanted to

---

[10] Government Communication Headquarters of United Kingdom

become a priest. For a while, he was an apprentice preacher and a renowned evangelist.

Anthony's father died in a car accident when he was only nine. His father's absence forced him to support his mother and to take odd jobs, including shining shoes, digging ditches and driving a taxi. One such random job was boxing. Starting at sixteen, Anthony went on to win sixteen consecutive games, but then he was knocked out completely in his seventeenth game. He'd had enough. Boxing wasn't for him.

Next, Anthony started to learn the saxophone and formed a small orchestra. He joined a band with the Foursquare Gospel Church and did some preaching. This got him more interested in music, literature and art. Anthony taught himself these subjects, and with his increasing knowledge and interests, he started focusing more on art and architecture.

Anthony worked hard to enter an architecture drawing contest, and he won. Following that, he met Frank Lloyd Wright, one of the most famous architects of the 20th century. After a meeting with him, Anthony decided to become an architect, and he studied art and architecture under Wright at his Arizona residence and his Wisconsin studio, Taliesin.

The two men were very different but soon became friends. Later, Wright advised Quinn to get medical help to improve his speech impediment (stammer). After the surgery, Quinn's speech actually deteriorated. He sought help to improve his stammer and started to go to acting classes conducted by a former actress, Katherine Hamil. This gradually got him interested in acting and shifted his focus away from architecture.

Anthony discussed his newfound passion for acting with Wright since he felt close to him and could use his advice. He told Wright that he was offered $800 per week by a film studio and wasn't sure what to do. Wright simply replied, "Take it; you'll never make that much with me." Wright encouraged Anthony to pursue his acting, and thus began a long and successful acting career which lasted for decades.

The path, however, was not straightforward. Initially, Quinn was given wordless roles. Next, he was repeatedly cast as a foreign heavy. By 1947, he had appeared in more than fifty films. He had played the roles of Chinese guerrilla, Indian, Hawaiian chief, mafia don, Filipino freedom fighter and Arab sheik; yet, he was still not considered a major star. The pattern was that he died in most roles. He barely made it to the final reel, often being dispatched by a knife, a gun or a length of twine. He was often the bad guy's bad guy.

This also had an effect on how Quinn saw himself in regard to his sense of identity. His rich multi-ethnic heritage directly influenced the roles he played. He recalled in an interview:

> "Those were rough times, right from the beginning. With a name like Quinn, I wasn't totally accepted by the Mexican community in those days, and as a Mexican, I wasn't accepted as an American. So as a kid, I just decided, well, 'A plague on both your houses. I'll just become a world citizen.' So that's what I did. Acting is my nationality."

After many years of viewing his ethnicity as a disadvantage, Quinn started to see that he could turn it into an advantage. As the decade approached its end, Quinn went through a major transformation. He allowed his age to show and built up his physique. His hair greyed, and his weathered and rugged face showed his age and a tough life.

Next, he acted alongside Marlon Brando as the brother of Zapata. This won him an Academy Award for best supporting actor. Thus began an era in which he acted in increasingly high-profile movies.

At this stage, Quinn was spending much of his time in Italy. He worked with several acclaimed Italian filmmakers, including Dino De Laurentiis—the very same producer you were introduced to earlier: the one with whom Arnold Schwarzenegger had an eventful encounter. The world is perhaps smaller than we think.

Quinn continued to act in more movies, and his career reached its peak in the sixties when he acted in *Lawrence of Arabia* opposite Peter O'Toole and Alec Guinness.

As the years passed and he aged, interests declined. As he recalled, "The parts dried up as I reached my sixtieth birthday, loosely coinciding with my growing disinclination to pursue them. Indeed, I could not see the point in playing old men on screen when I rejected the role for myself."

Thus, once again, it was time to switch to something else. This time, Quinn started focusing on art, going back to the initial interest of his youth. He concentrated on painting, sculpting and designing jewellery. The styles that appealed to him most were cubist and post-impressionist in oils. He got his inspiration from the masters, "Some days, I paint like an Indian. Some days, I paint like a Mexican . . . I steal from everybody—Picasso, Kandinsky . . . I steal, but only from the best."

He got his inspiration from his Mexican ancestry, decades of living in Europe and extensive stays in Africa and the Middle East during film productions in his long career.

By the beginning of the 1980s, gallery owners started to show an interest in Quinn's art. He was exhibited internationally in New York, Paris, Mexico City and Los Angeles. He sold his paintings for thousands of dollars.

His work is now represented in both public and private collections throughout the world. Quinn has achieved this despite having learned everything on his own. Apart from some art classes which he took in 1950s, he never attended an art school. He was, however, keen to use what he had access to—books, museums and art galleries—as he travelled the world during his acting career. He also acquired a sizable collection of artwork which, in turn, helped to inspire him.

What does Anthony Quinn's life story suggest? It illustrates that you may not really know the direction you need to take, but if you persist, you can eventually succeed. It is not obvious what may appeal to you the most, and even when you discover it, your interests can eventually change. Hence, you must always be prepared to borrow from one field and prepare yourself for an eventual switch. Don't assume that you will remain interested in your current endeavours. Be flexible and ready to jump.

What made Quinn's art career successful? Let's look at his advantages:

- For an extended amount of time, Quinn lived in Europe and, in particular, in Italy, where he was exposed to a tremendous amount of art and history.
- His acting career made him rich. He converted his cash into a sizable art collection that could then inspire him later in life.
- Being rich also meant that Quinn had easy access to resources and materials to produce more paintings. Unlike most artists, he didn't have to worry about selling them initially to make a living. This also meant that he could focus on the skill rather than worrying about selling his art, or worse, making art with the intention of selling it, which usually leads to poor results. Instead, he could focus on expressing himself.
- Quinn's long acting career in the entertainment industry meant that he had access to contacts, important galleries and art hubs, such as New York, London and Paris.
- He could do a self-portrait, and the painting would be immediately recognisable because he was already a famous actor with a very familiar face.

In short, Quinn could continuously tap into accumulated results, skills, contacts and know-how to switch to the next area when required. Place yourself in a position of advantage, and be ready to switch when you see the need.

Exercise 6-2

PART 1: Analyse Your Past Contributions

Consider your life up to now. What have you contributed to society so far? Think about what you have contributed to your customers. Focus on the values you have created that you are most proud of. Your customers include not only those whom you have sold a product or service to but also those whom you have mentored, inspired and in any way influenced with your ideas. List your most important contributions below.

PART 2: Analyse Your Future Contributions

What values do you want to create in the future? List the most important values. These can include some of the values you have created in the past. Here are a number of guidelines that can help you compile your list:

- Think of the needs of people you can address.
- Think of solutions to tangible and important problems that can help many people.
- Think of lives you can improve by inspiring them.
- Think of how you can make people happier.
- Think of how you can contribute to humanity's knowledge.

ID	Contribution
1	
2	
3	
4	

PART 3: Identify Who You Would Be Helping

For each value, identify the type of people you would be helping. The aim is to understand the scale. For example, you may decide to spend years researching the effects of underwater volcanic sources on deep sea creatures. You want to analyse who would benefit from this, how they would benefit and how important it is that you should provide this given your skills and background. Consider answering the following questions about each value. You can use extra blank sheets to capture more ideas. Use the ID references in *Part 2* to relate an answer to the corresponding contribution.

For each contribution, consider the following:

- What type of people would you be helping?
- How many people would benefit from your contribution?
- Who would care about it?
- How much impact would this work have on your country?
- How much impact would this work have on the world?
- Would your contribution be significant and unique?
- Would this contribution represent your best based on your background and skills?
- Who would *not* like to see this work?
- Could your work be exploited by someone who wants to engage in suspicious or illegal activity?
- Would you be able to isolate yourself from such activities?

ID	Benefits and Impacts
1	

2	
3	
4	

Exercise 6-3

Choose your Roles Based on Your Contributions

Now that you have identified your values, it is time to identify how you can create them. For this, you need to know how creating these values will fit into your roles. As you have seen, roles can help you organise your time based on your most important interests and keep you focused on what matters the most.

PART 1: Map Your Roles

Consider the list of future contributions you just made in *Exercise 6-2,* as well as the roles you identified earlier in *Exercise 6-1.*

1. List all automatic and non-automatic roles below. In the mind map in *Exercise 6-1,* focus on the leaves of the map. Ignore any categorisation that helped you to come up with the roles. You now want to summarise a list of them in the following table.
2. Analyse each future contribution and see which role it fits into. Aim to assign at least one role to each contribution. If you don't have an appropriate role for it, you will need to add one. If some roles don't map into any contribution, just keep them in the list for the time being.

Automatic Roles	Contribution

Non-Automatic Roles	**Contribution**

PART 2: Rank Your Roles

1. Rank your roles based on importance, listing the most important first. To rank, consider what each role represents and what contribution it leads to, as you identified in *Part 1*. List them below from rank 1 to N (as many roles as you have). Automatic and non-automatic roles can now be mixed up. All that matters is ranking them based on their significance to you.
2. Next, consider getting rid of non-automatic roles that don't lead to any significant contribution. In addition, review roles that are ranked at the bottom of the list. If these roles take valuable time that you can spend on more significant roles, they should be removed. Tick in the *eliminate* column to indicate this.

Rank	Role	Eliminate ✓
1		
2		
3		
4		
5		
6		
7		
8		
9		
10		

Exercise 6-4

Review Your Roles Based on Your Needs

When you applied Maslow's model in *Exercise 4-1,* you identified your needs. In the previous exercise, you identified your ideal roles based on your future contributions. In this exercise, you will review your needs to make sure none have been left unaddressed.

PART 1: Match Your Needs with Your Roles

Consider the five main needs identified in Maslow's model. For each need, list the roles that you think will satisfy that need. For example, what roles feed your need for self-esteem? What roles contribute to your self-respect, as well as to the respect you receive from others? Perhaps this requires learning new skills. Do you have roles that would lead to tangible skills and command respect? If not, you will need to review your roles and include some that satisfy this need.

Needs	What roles contribute to this need? List them here. Include both automatic and non-automatic roles.
Physiological Needs	
Safety Needs	
Social Needs	

Esteem Needs	
Self-Actualisation Needs	

PART 2: Define New Roles If Necessary

If you have needs that are not satisfied by your roles, you will need to reconsider your roles. What do you need to do to make sure these needs are not neglected? Do you need new roles, or can you express certain roles differently to address these needs? Write your thoughts below.

Exercise 6-5

Finalise Your Roles

Create a final list of your automatic and non-automatic roles based on all the exercises you have gone through so far.

Automatic Roles	Non-Automatic Roles

7 Design Your Mission Statement: First Draft

"Riches do not respond to wishes. They respond only to definite plans, backed by definite desires, through constant PERSISTENCE."

Napoleon Hill

A boy and a girl in their twenties who are on a student budget have the following conversation:

Girl: "You know what car I'd like to have. I want to have a big BMW X5. It's so pretty and so large."

Boy: "But I would rather go with something smaller and use the rest of the money on cool gadgets or to travel to new places."

Do you notice anything wrong here? It would seem natural to most people, and this is indeed for a good reason. Throughout our lives, we become conditioned to think of everything as a limited resource. You have only X amount of something. If you want something else, you have to sacrifice from somewhere else. We tend to assume that there is only so much we are going to earn and, therefore, that the question is to choose A *or* B because we simply cannot have both A *and* B at the same time. In fact, we do this kind of decision-making so often that it becomes second nature. It starts to become a problem when we end up applying it to everything, including our dreams. Let's go back to the example. The girl is simply *dreaming* about an ideal future. She thinks a big car would be cool. The boy, however, treats the car as a finite, limited resource. Either you can have the BMW X5 or you can have a small car—say a Renault—buy a large TV and travel to two countries for the same price. But why does a dream have to be limited to a specific price? Why not have a big car *and* the TV *and* travel to two countries? It's just dreaming up a future; why limit it in *any* way?

If you aim higher, you get more. So never think of how you are going to get it when you are dreaming it up. That can come later. All you should care about is to see how enthusiastic you are about it. How far are you willing to go to get it? If you really want it, you will eventually get it, but while dreaming it up, don't ever make a compromise thinking that to have X, you need to give up Y. This is not necessarily the case, and certainly not when you are thinking of an ideal future. Is getting a BMW X5 something that you truly want and cannot wait to have, or is it just a wish because you saw your neighbour driving one the other day and now you fancy having one?

Then there is the question of what to desire. Consider the following statements:

- "I want to make a living out of selling paintings."
- "I want to be a famous painter."
- "I want to be a nationally well-known artist."
- "I want to become the world's most famous contemporary artist."
- "I want to become the greatest artist in the history of mankind."

Which one of these would you rather aim for? Why go for a lower objective when you can aim for a higher one? There is something common between all these statements—that you are always aiming to be an artist. After that, if you had free choice, there would be no reason to aim for anything less than the best. Why shouldn't you aim to be the world's best artist? You are already unique. There has never been a person like you in history, given your genetic make-up and life experiences. There will never be one like you ever again either. There is no reason to believe you are incapable of being history's greatest, so if you don't believe in this, you are cutting yourself short unnecessarily. The critical point is to define exactly what it is that you want to become. In the above statements, it is expressed as "becoming an artist." But what exactly is an "artist"? This is not enough. You cannot aim to become history's greatest *everything*, but you can certainly aim to become history's greatest *something* as long as you clearly understand what that something is.

In short, don't limit yourself from the outset when you are dreaming. Bear this in mind as you go through this chapter and craft your mission statement.

The aim here is to find your *life's task*. There is perhaps a feeling inside you that you want to express your uniqueness. You may feel you have a destiny to fulfil. Expressing your life's task in a mission statement will help you to see what it is that you truly want to accomplish and master.

7.1 Look Back at Life

Remember when you were young and you wanted to solve a maze? How did you go about solving it? It was always difficult to know which path to take first. They all seemed the same, and it just wasn't obvious which route would take you to the end of the maze.

Over time, you probably learned a simple trick—that if you started from the end and worked your way backwards to the beginning, you could easily find the correct route. In fact, once you knew how to solve these kinds of puzzles using the end-to-beginning method, the puzzles became much less challenging, and you probably stopped doing them altogether.

Life is like a maze, and once you know what you want in life, you can work backwards to find out what you should do to get closer to your goal.

The purpose of this step is to put you at the end. How do you want to be seen towards the end of your life? What do you want to tell your grandchildren when they ask, "What did you do for a living? What did you achieve?" By knowing the end, you have a much better chance of getting there, or at least moving towards it, as you can measure yourself against a goalpost.

Exercise 7-1

Towards the End

In this exercise, use a mind map, such as the following, and think of the end goal.

- What would you like to have achieved?
- What legacy would you like to leave?
- How would you like to describe yourself to others towards the end of your life?

Add more branches and BOI as you see fit, or make a new mind map using what is shown as an inspiration.

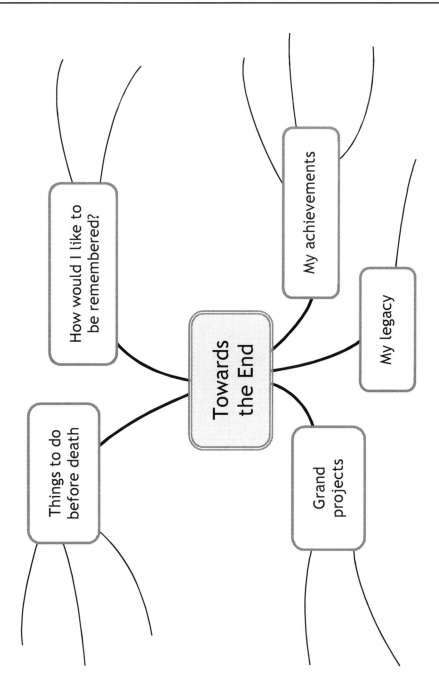

7.2 Mission Statement

Having explored your desires and what you want in the end, it is time to formulate a draft *mission statement*. A mission statement is your ultimate purpose in life. You want to capture the essence of your activities in this statement. It is a highly moral statement. It is what your life is all about. A mission statement is not something you write overnight. It requires thorough examination and a lot of thinking. Drawing up a mission statement is not a light-hearted task, but it isn't as difficult as it sounds either. In fact, you may already have an unconscious mission statement which you have never documented or stated in clear sentences. This step focuses on getting you to draft a statement that closely resembles what you want in life.

Remember, the process of finding this mission statement is just as important as the final product, and it is iterative. You can always come back to review it as you understand what you truly want.

Exercise 7-2

Draft Mission Statement

In this exercise, you need to formulate your mission statement. Having gone through previous exercises, you now have a good idea of your *desires*, *interests*, *needs*, *imaginary heaven* and *roles*. Use the material you have gathered so far for the creation of your mission statement.

To get started, think of the following:

- What is your life's passion?
- What is your grand vision?
- Think of values and desires that you have identified earlier and integrate them into your mission.
- Use the "Towards the End" mind map you created in *Exercise 7-1* while formulating your mission statement.
- Be specific. Use numbers and deadlines.

Some examples of mission statements are shown below. Use your own style, but consider including the following:

- What is your mission?
- What are you willing to give to achieve it?
- When are you going to achieve it?

Don't worry if you don't know exactly how to put it. Read the examples, consider the guidelines here and write something. This is only an initial draft, and you will get to review it several times.

Stephen Covey on Mission Statements

My mission statement is to live with integrity and to make a difference in the lives of others.

To fulfil my mission,

I have charity: I seek out and love the one, each one, regardless of his situation.

I sacrifice: I devote my time, my talent and my resources to my mission.

I am impactful: What I do makes a difference in the lives of others.

Napoleon Hill's Guide to Creating a Mission Statement to Get Rich

Follow these steps to draw up your mission statement:

1. Think of the exact amount of money you desire. Don't say, "I want plenty of money." Be precise.
2. Identify exactly what you intend to give in return for this money. There is no such thing as something for nothing.
3. Think of a plan to put in place at once to get to this end. It doesn't matter whether you are ready or not; you just need to know what your actions are. This step might feed back to your other steps so that you can rationalise your mission. Don't go overboard with this; the real planning takes place later. This is just a warm-up step.
4. Establish a deadline for when you intend to get the money.
5. Write a clear and concise mission statement which includes the amount of money you intend to acquire, your time limit, what you are willing to sacrifice for it and what you are going to do next to start getting there.

My Mission Statement

7.3 Poor Mission Statements

To know what works in a mission statement, it is useful to study examples that don't really work. Consider the following:

Statement	Analysis
"I will do my best to help my community, become successful and have a happy life."	Although this touches on some important values, it does not actually define anything practical. What is doing your "best"? What is "my community"? What does it mean to be "successful"? What would make you "happy" in life?
"I want to live an honest life completely and compassionately and with a healthy dose of realism thrown in. I believe anything is possible if one sets his mind to finding an answer."	Poetic words and highly charged emotional statements can be nice to read, but they do not really help you decide what to do when confronted with important decisions in life. What is an "honest" life? What is a "complete life"? The phrase "healthy dose of realism" is very poetic but absolutely meaningless. Yes, if you put your mind to it, you can get it, but do you actually know what it is that you want to get? This is what you really need to have in your mission statement. A mission statement is not a motivational piece; it is a goalpost.

7.4 Review Roles Based on Your Mission Statement

Having identified your roles and having understood what the ultimate aims of your roles are, you should now be much more confident about where you are going. However, you might have noticed that some roles are more demanding than others and will take up a considerable amount of your time. Hence, you need to balance these roles against your mission. This is a two-way process since your mission is not cast in stone. You need to evaluate your roles and draft the mission you identified earlier to make sure they are all consistent and achievable.

Exercise 7-3

Update Your Roles Based on Your Mission

Go through the final list of roles identified in *Exercise 6-5*. Reconsider the list in line with your draft mission statement in *Exercise 7-2*. Add or eliminate roles accordingly, and update the list.

Exercise 7-4

Roles, Vision and Story

For each role,

1. **Identify your vision.** How do you visualise yourself in this role when you have reached the ultimate goal, as captured in the "Towards the End" mind map in *Exercise 7-1*? In other words, what is it that you ultimately want to achieve in this role?
2. **Identify the story.** Imagine that you have achieved the ultimate goal in this role (as set in your vision) and you want to tell the story of how you did it. What would you say?

Use the example that follows to see how to approach this exercise. Use the blank in the page after to analyse each role. Make as many copies of the form as necessary so you have enough space for all the roles.

Role	Author

Vision	Story
To write a bestselling book on the art of productivity, selling a minimum of 1 million copies internationally and becoming an acclaimed author.	My bestselling book was my fourth attempt at book writing. My name was already out there with my previous books on similar topics. Publishers liked my previous books, but they were not willing to risk too much on the new one. It wasn't until I found a superb agent that my luck turned. I went on a six-month tour visiting at least fourteen countries with my current books and gave hundreds of speeches and interviews. In fact, the idea of my bestselling book came to me when I was on this tour. I came back, and I wrote non-stop for six months . . .

Role	
Vision	**Story**

Role	
Vision	**Story**

8 Design Your Mission Statement: Finalised

"Remembering that I'll be dead soon is the most important tool I've ever encountered to help me make the big choices in life. Because almost everything—all external expectations, all pride, all fear of embarrassment or failure—these things just fall away in the face of death, leaving only what is truly important. Remembering that you are going to die is the best way I know to avoid the trap of thinking you have something to lose. You are already naked. There is no reason not to follow your heart."

Steve Jobs

You have dreamed of a great future. You have set yourself a goal. You have positioned yourself to be lucky, and you think it is going to pay off. With determination and passion, you pursue your chosen line of work and produce results. Gradually, you gain some attention and get very excited. You think this is it. You are through. You can do what you love to do, create value and earn a good living from it. You bask in the success and expect word of mouth to do wonders for you.

Except that it does not.

Your initial mini-success got a bit of attention, and then it slowly died down. It was too isolated a success. You had a well-defined goal and a passion that you were obsessively pursuing. So what went wrong? Why can't you repeat the success you already had? Why do you feel you have to start from scratch again?

Let's look at an example to illustrate. You set out to become an artist and eventually paint something that is admired by people who see it. You may even sell a few more copies than you originally expected. Does this mean that the art community now takes you seriously and starts writing articles about you or collectors queue up to buy your next work? Hardly. You produced a piece of artwork and that's that. There are plenty of good artists who do that every single day. Unfortunately, most of them don't make much out of selling their art. The art community (or the art market at large) doesn't know how to *find* these artists. What should you do to be found then? History, as always, can inspire us.

Consider Pablo Picasso. He was born in Malaga, Spain. His father was a painter and curator for a local museum and mainly painted landscapes. Picasso was interested in art from an early age, and by the time he was nineteen years old, he had already done hundreds of paintings. In 1900, he decided to move to Paris, which was considered the capital of the art world at the time. Picasso befriended Max Jacob, who was a poet and a journalist. They shared an apartment, but both were very poor. Picasso slept during the day and worked at night, while Max did the reverse—worked during the day and slept at night. Picasso focused on his paintings while learning French and getting acquainted with the French culture.

Despite all his efforts and his new paintings, Picasso was not taken seriously. He was clearly talented and was following the styles of the likes of Van Gogh and Degas while shaping his own style of painting. Nevertheless, it wasn't getting him anywhere.

Following a journey through Spain in the second half of 1901 and the suicide of a friend, Picasso radically changed his approach. Between 1901 and 1904 was the time now known as Picasso's Blue Period. He produced a number of gloomy paintings, mainly in the shades of blue and blue-green. The subjects of his paintings included beggars, prostitutes and drunks. Although there was now a kind of pattern in his work, the paintings did not have a style that could make them stand out from what other artists were producing at the time. Picasso struggled to sell them. He was not taken seriously, and his financial situation deteriorated. He became more depressed.

From 1904 to 1906, the period known as Picasso's Rose Period, he started to use more uplifting and warm colours, such as pink and orange, in his paintings. He was now being exposed to more French paintings, and there was a mood of optimism in his new works. His subjects now often included acrobats, harlequins and comedians. They were usually portrayed in chequered clothing.

These started to become Picasso's symbols. He was beginning to understand the importance of a style and the brand associated with it. He was also positioning himself to be lucky.

In 1902, Gertrude Stein and her brother, Leo, moved from America to London and shortly thereafter to Paris, where Leo wanted to pursue art. They would become highly instrumental in the world of art and literature. Gertrude, a writer, and Leo shared living quarters at 27 rue de Fleurus in Montparnasse in Paris. They soon became avid art collectors and set up a salon in which to exhibit the artwork they collected. In the process, they started to collect the artwork of Cezanne, Gauguin, Renoir and Matisse. They also liked Picasso's work. By 1905, the Steins had accumulated so many paintings that they had to continuously rearrange the art on the walls of the salon to make room for the new art.

Due to her character and personality, Gertrude turned out to be a great catalyst in gathering artists and writers in one place and getting them to exchange ideas. Number 27, the Stein Salon, became a hub for the new modernist talents. In 1905, Picasso met Henri Matisse for the first time. The likes of Hemingway and Fitzgerald, as well as artists such as Picasso, Matisse and Braque, became dedicated attendees. Saturday evening became the fixed day for formal congregations. It was like a family-and-friends gathering.

Picasso was beginning to understand how the art world worked and was positioning himself systematically and physically right at the centre of it. At that time, many artists were living in Montmartre, a hilly area in the north of Paris with low rent and a friendly atmosphere. Picasso and several artists lived and worked in a specific building between 1904 and 1909. This maximised his interactions with his peers.

By 1906, after six years of pursuing an art career, Picasso was beginning to understand what was required to completely stand out from the crowd and to get noticed. He was now firmly after attention. He started painting in his signature style, now known as his African Period. Picasso was strongly influenced by African art and perhaps for a good reason. With the extensive expansion of the French Empire into Africa, the press was full of exotic tales, exaggerated stories of cannibalism, discoveries of various artefacts and even mistreatment of Africans by various colonial empires.

In May 1907, Picasso viewed a number of African works of art at the ethnographic museum in Paris. Following this, he experienced a "revelation." He had an idea—not just for a new painting but for a whole new style of painting that would come to define him. The revelation, along with the modernist ideas of impressionist art that he was exposed to at the Stein Salon, came to guide Picasso forward. What he had in mind was expressive, unique and utterly new. He could brand it as his own. With the excitement of starting on a new direction, he set out to work. A couple of months later, he had created his masterpiece—*Les Demoiselles d'Avignon*.

What do you think was the reaction of the art community to Picasso's latest work? Let's just say that even his friends didn't like it. Henri Matisse, Georges Braque, Andre Derain and Guillaume Apollinaire rejected Picasso's painting. In fact, they wrote it off as "some kind of a joke." So you can imagine the views of the rest. The painting was simply way ahead of its time.

Did this bother Picasso? Not in the least. Why should he be bothered? He wasn't there to please the art community, his peers or the collectors. That was not his objective. This wasn't about creating a painting that people liked, which was an activity that many of his peers seemed to be engaged in. His mission was to become one of the greatest artists of his generation. Producing something that people didn't like wasn't going to stop Picasso from achieving his objective.

At this time in his life, Picasso felt that he understood the art world. It was not about producing something that people liked. It was not about showing off skills. It was not about adhering to some academic principles. These could certainly help here or there but would not help him to stand out. What he needed was a specific, well-defined style that he could use almost like a language. He wanted to have a formula that enabled him to produce painting after painting so that people, upon viewing each, could tell that they were part of the same set—that they looked like they were made by Picasso. That's how you create a brand.

This was only the beginning for Picasso, and what he had painted was just example number one of his new style. There were many more to come. He continued to work on this style—to define it further and formulate it. Working with Georges Braque, their efforts led to *analytic cubism*. The idea was to deconstruct images to their building blocks and then understand how an eye or a camera would capture them. They broke down structures "intellectually" to analyse and then construct a scene out of them. The paintings often consisted of multiple complex views of objects. Natural forms were reduced to geometric shapes. Objects were reduced to overlapping and transparent planes laid over opaque planes.

The art world had never seen anything like it. It created a sensation. Gertrude and Leo Stein's influence in both France and America certainly helped to spread the importance of this new modern art movement. Having left Spain for Paris and having worked hard to position himself to be lucky while being in Paris, it was time for Picasso to cash in. The new style came to inspire many artists, who, in turn, started to adopt a similar approach and took these ideas in new directions. It was the beginning of an art movement that would become the most important one of the 20th century. With his approach, Picasso not only created a style, but he also created a strong brand which turned him into one of the most famous artists of all time. More than 100 years later, people can look at a painting and say, "That looks like a Picasso." For an artist, that is perhaps the greatest achievement.

To be recognised, you need to have a style. The easier it is to define, express and brand this style, the more likely it is that you will be found, mentioned, wanted, followed or even copied. Your community will not take you seriously until you have a series of works with a clear *pattern* that defines your specific style. You need something that can be defined by a single brand. This is a universal principle; it is not unique to the art world. No matter which field or industry you are in, your mission statement should lead you to a pattern of success and not just a single, isolated win.

Let's look at another analogy to illustrate, as this principle is rather significant. Consider playing the board game of Risk—the world conquest game. It is usually played between four to six people, and the objective is to eliminate all other players and remain as the sole conqueror. Normally, if you are experienced in a particular game—say chess—you are more likely to win. Risk is rather unusual, which is precisely what makes it realistic and fun to play. Even if you are new to the game and are playing against experienced players, you still have a chance to win the game. You may get lucky, end up with a good starting position or stay out of the way of other experienced players as they compete for power over the territories. They may ignore you, and you can slowly gain strength until it is too late for them to eliminate you.

Now, it is a completely different thing to win a succession of Risk games. This is an entirely different challenge, and only the very best players in the world can win continually no matter the circumstances or their luck. If you win a single game, people will notice you but will soon forget you. If you win several games, they will certainly pay attention to you and will keep an eye on you in every single game, which would make it much more difficult to win another game. In short, it is only when you have a *pattern of success* that you will be taken seriously by your peers, your competitors and the market.

How can you apply this to your world? It means, for example, that if you are an author, you must aim to release a series of books that come to associate your name with the work you have created, and you must strive to ensure that a reader can recognise your work because it has a clearly identifiable style.

If you are a salesman, what you shouldn't do is demonstrate your selling skills by closing a single deal and making tons of money out of people. J. Paul Getty, the American industrialist who in 1957 was the richest living American, put it rather nicely:

> "My father said: You must never try to make all the money that's in a deal. Let the other fellow make some money too, because if you have a reputation for always making all the money, you won't have many deals."

In short, aiming to become successful in one thing is just a gambling mentality; it is as if you are putting all your efforts into a finite, one-off big win. Focused determination is about a series of wins—not just one. It requires forward planning and sustained hard work over a long period to understand the pattern and the style required for a series of successes. The reward is that it leads to much more profound and long-lasting satisfaction and happiness in life.

In the previous chapter, you worked on your mission and vision statements. The exercises would have given you an opportunity to formulate your mission based on your own personal approach. In this chapter, you get a second chance to define your mission statement, and this time you will go through it more systematically. While reviewing your mission statement, consider what you have learned above, and think of a mission that can lead you to a series of successes and not just a single win. Look for a pattern and a style. You may not even know what that style is at this point, but that's fine. You don't have to know it now; you just have to know that you need it. This will help you to think big and at a much higher level when planning your life. This is crucial when defining your mission statement. You can use what you have already identified in the previous chapter as your first draft and update it as you go through the guidelines and exercises in this chapter.

8.1 Create Your Mission Statement

With the exercises you have gone through so far, you have now created a draft mission statement. Let's use it to create a new statement using the following approach:

Mission Statement = Vision + Mission

8.1.1   Vision

Concept:

This captures your ultimate success in life.

Guidelines:

- It is usually an emotional statement.
- It captures your needs and wants.
- It is simple and grand.
- It is only a starting point to help you craft your mission statement.
- It is not set in stone, and you need to update it as you move forward.
- It does not reference how you want to achieve it, but it is anchored in reality.

Example:

"I want to live a happy life and experience as much of what this planet has to offer through adventures, sports, travelling, meeting people and making friends. I want to be seen as a successful professional who continuously helps people whether I am around or not. I want to create and share entertaining and thrilling stories using visual media. I want to feel that I have lived a full and multidimensional life. I want to be well known in my industry, but I also want to protect my privacy."

8.1.2   Mission

Concept:

This should capture your long-term purpose in life. It is how you manifest your vision in your daily life.

Guidelines:

- A mission is a purposeful promise that helps you to move towards your goals.
- It is defined as having goals and deadlines.
- It is specific rather than generic or flowery, such as, "I want to be the best at what I do."
- It is not a to-do list. Instead, it describes who you are and what you want to become.
- It is upbeat and energetic.

Formula:

Step	Example
Describe what you are going to do.	"I am going to get this . . ."
Describe what effort you are willing to put into it.	"In return, I will . . ."

In both steps, describe the specifics and set a deadline so you would know when you have achieved it.

Example:

"I want to become the greatest contemporary comic illustrator by 2020. By then, I want to be able to walk into bookshops in any random country and see my comics on the bookshelves. I want to see shelves completely dedicated to the style I pioneered. In return for this, I am willing to spend countless hours learning everything about the production of comics. I will learn about the history of comics and about other major artists, all production tools, storytelling and marketing. I will aim to improve my drawing skills systematically by training myself every week without exception. As a result of my work in this area, I want to make a million pounds a year by 2020. In return for this achievement, I am willing to sacrifice some of the luxuries in my life. I am willing to work long hours and travel often for my job. I will use all my existing skills and acquire new ones as necessary to achieve my goal. I know that with my determination and enthusiasm for this work, I will succeed despite the challenges. I can already see my comics printed by established publishers. I can see my work winning awards and being printed on the cover of magazines. I can see my bank account with six-digit numbers. My earnings will then allow me to have access to the best tools in my trade. Get out of my way; there is no stopping me."

Exercise 8-1

Create Your New Mission Statement

Use the *"vision + mission formula"* to create a new mission statement. Refer to your roles, draft mission and all the ideas you have captured so far regarding what you want to do in life, and create your new mission statement.

Tips

- Write your mission statement according to the formula as well as you can.
- Leave it for a day.
- Come back and review it again. Read it once, and put it out of sight. Use a blank sheet of paper and write a new version of your mission statement. You are rewriting it to make it sound better, more natural and more of what you really want.

Vision

Capture your ultimate success and grand vision.

Mission
Include specific purposes and goals with set deadlines, and state what effort you are willing to put into achieving them.

9 Set Your Goals

"Much of the stress that people feel doesn't come from having too much to do. It comes from not finishing what they've started."

David Allen

"If you want to live a happy life, tie it to a goal, not to people or things."

Albert Einstein

When dealing with everyday activities, think of yourself as a rider on a horse. As you ride, your horse has a mind of its own. The horse wants to take the path of least resistance. If it finds a path that feels difficult, it immediately wants to move away. On the other hand, if it finds a path that leads to something pleasurable, it takes that path instead.

If you leave your horse in charge, you will end up taking a path to avoid pain or going for pleasure all the time. This powerful metaphor was suggested by Sigmund Freud to showcase the endless conflict between *emotional impulse* and *reason*.

The rider represents reason, and the horse represents emotional impulses. The way you handle the conflict between the two will ultimately affect how you control your life.

The horse has a tendency to go for short-term gains. The horse doesn't have any long-term goals and doesn't really know where it is going. All of this is the responsibility of the rider.

The rider understands that in order to get to the top of the hill and see the beautiful scenery, he may need to go through rocky terrain. He knows that he has to be disciplined and rein in the horse to make sure it doesn't suddenly go off course to avoid potential pain.

Remember this metaphor, and remind yourself every time you get an urge to pursue something that is not in line with your goals. Don't shy away because something is difficult or boring. Don't just pursue something because it gives you immediate pleasure. The horse represents the urge to do something else; the horse resists your command, and you must force it to comply simply because you want to remain in control. The horse has its own short-term whims. Move it back in line to where you want to go. Focus on your goal, and use your horse to get there.

Charlotte reads about the horse and the rider. "Right", she thinks, "I need goals then, and I need to remain in control. Fair enough. I want to be rich beyond my dreams. I want to have expensive jewellery, designer handbags and an extensive shoe collection. I want to be successful, powerful and in charge. I want to become a celebrity who is recognised and asked for her autograph. I want to have my personal chauffeur to drive me around."

Fast-forward five years. Charlotte is still working at the same company, daydreaming the same old dream and slowly realising that none of it will ever come true for her. She is working harder than ever but doesn't seem to get any richer. Her salary has been raised several times. She has got a bigger mortgage and a bigger house. She now has luxury furniture and a cool 4x4 car. She eats out regularly in upmarket restaurants in town. Yet, she doesn't have what she dreamed of and wonders why.

Why hasn't Charlotte succeeded? She certainly appeared to have some goals. Were they not good enough?

If you look at Charlotte's goals, you will see that they are very vague. What does it mean to be rich? What does it mean to have the best jewellery and so on? When and how did she want to achieve these goals? Was she getting closer to any of them as time passed? Did she even think about what she had to do to achieve these results? Was it not more a matter of wishful thinking than goal setting?

It turns out that many people suffer from mixing up goal setting with daydreaming and having desires. Daydreaming and desires have their place and can indeed be influential in driving a person forward. After all, any achievement starts with a desire—a vision that slowly forms and becomes more and more vivid over time until you achieve it. Effective goal setting takes this vision and defines it precisely in reality while keeping it rational and consistent with any other goals you may have set for yourself.

Goal setting should not be mixed up with your life's task or mission. Your focus on fulfilling your mission and mastery of a certain skill is what leads to wealth, success and happiness. Focusing on a random number of short-term goals will not get you anywhere specific. If you want to get somewhere, as desired by your daydreaming, you will need to have a well-defined goalpost.

9.1 Why Should You Bother With Planning?

What is good about planning? Here are a number of benefits:

- It helps you to stay focused on your objectives.
- It gives you a sense of purpose and fulfilment.
- It helps you to monitor your progress and balance your tasks based on your priorities.
- It is easier to change your plans once you know what they are without worrying about not doing something else that you should be doing.
- It reduces your stress level since you are in control.
- By establishing relations between tasks and clustering them, you can take advantage of synergy, which lets you accomplish more by multitasking.

Knowing the importance of setting goals is one thing, but knowing how to set and formulate them is another. Research shows that goal formulation can have a significant effect on whether you achieve it or not. It is important to use established and proven goal-setting guidelines and practise them as much as possible until it becomes second nature to you. Goals are useful when

- They are not generalised and vague.
- There are plenty of details so you know what the goals really mean.
- You know their importance in relation to your other goals.
- They are considered within the context of your life.
- They are not too ambitious to be unreachable but are high enough to get you excited.
- They are prioritised.

These guidelines are only useful if you follow them. To define your goals in line with your mission, you need to follow a structured approach. You can achieve this using what is known as SMART goals. This will help you satisfy most of these guidelines with little effort. Let's look at SMART goals.

9.2 SMART Goals

One of the most famous methodologies to set good goals is known as SMART, which stands for five critical areas that you need to consider when setting goals. Over the years, experts have come up with a variety of parameters that these five letters stand for. They mostly aim to capture the essence of good goal setting, and there is no right or wrong interpretation. All you need to do is focus on the most important qualities.[11] These are presented below:

Specific   Measurable   Achievable   Relevant   Timely

Action-
Oriented

9.2.1   Specific

Examples:

- "I want to get rich."
- "I want to lose some weight."

Analysis:

It is not obvious what it means to be rich or to lose weight. You need to define it so that you know what to aim for. Define your goal as specifically as possible. The clearer you are about it, the more likely it is that you will achieve it.

To Improve:

Use numbers and time scales.

---

[11] Two interpretations are given for "A" in SMART in this session, as they are both critical and should not be ignored just because they don't fit into a beautiful acronym.

Good Examples:

- "I want to be making £200,000 a year within three years."
- "I want to weigh 70 kg by the end of the summer."

9.2.2 Measurable

Examples:

- "I want to improve my relationship with my teenage children."

Analysis:

It is difficult to know how you are progressing. You must define your goals in such a way that allows you to measure your progress and know precisely when you have succeeded in achieving it.

To Improve:

- Use a scale from 1 (poor) to 10 (excellent). Give yourself a score for where you are now in respect to your goal.
- Next, set yourself a target to get to a specific score at a specific time so that you can measure your progress.

Good Examples:

- You think your relationship is about 4 out of 10 at the moment. Hence your goals will be "to have a score of 8 or more for my relationship by the end of the year."

9.2.3 Achievable

Examples:

- "I want to become the CEO by Christmas."
- "I want to run a marathon this year and win."

Analysis:

Setting your aim high is one thing, but setting unrealistic goals is another. If you are currently a part-time assistant manager, aiming to become the CEO of the organisation by the end of the year may be far-fetched. Smaller steps and more realistic goals will help you see what you need to do and how to get there. An overtly idealistic dream might be inspiring but not necessarily helpful in getting you closer to your goal.

Set yourself achievable goals. Big goals are good, but you will need to define sub-goals to manage your progress.

For example, if you are out of shape, have not exercised for a year and want to set a target to exercise, don't suddenly set a goal to exercise for one hour every single day no matter what. Going from nothing to one hour a day is a huge jump, especially if you haven't done it for a while and it is not in your lifestyle. You need to form a habit so that your body habitually feels the need for exercise and you enjoy doing so. This makes it easier than using your willpower every time. The risk is that you may start to exercise one hour a week and then feel that you cannot keep up with the new routine or think of some other excuse and then quit for good. Set a smaller, more achievable goal; reach it; and then push yourself with the next demanding goal until you are where you want to be.

To Improve:

Divide the main goal into smaller specific and measurable objectives.

Good Examples:

- "I want to become the departmental manager by the end of the summer and the division manager in two years."
- "I want to participate in three half-marathon competitions by the end of the year, to win a half-marathon in two competitions within two years and to rank in the top ten in a full marathon within five years."

9.2.4 Action Oriented

Examples:

- "I want to learn a new language."
- "I want to manage my anger better."

Analysis:

A goal may sound like a desire rather than something to do. Desires may become wishful thinking, and you are less likely to achieve them if you don't know what you need to do to reach them.

A goal must be formulated based on an action. Avoid setting passive goals that don't require you to do anything.

Instead of "achievable," "action oriented" is another interpretation for the "A" in the SMART acronym. It is also just as important, so you should consider it in your goal formulation.

To Improve:

Write your goal. Now ask yourself, "Is this actionable?" If so, state the action and formulate it into a goal. If it is not actionable, think of the action required to achieve it.

Good Examples

- "I want to enrol in the evening introductory Spanish course at the local college that runs for ten weeks and spend at least three hours every week, in addition to the course, practising the language."

9.2.5 Relevant

Examples:

- "I want to redecorate the office with new furniture" [when it has already been redecorated six months ago].
- "I want to have several meetings with the receptionist to show her how to use a spreadsheet" [instead of spending more time on running the company and getting new customers].

Analysis:

You may carefully define a specific and measurable goal and identify what needs to be done to achieve it. However, if this goal is not a priority or something that can help you get closer to your main objectives, then you need to replace it, delegate it or prioritise it in line with other tasks.

To Improve:

Ask yourself the following:

- Is the goal you are setting worthwhile?
- Is the goal a priority that is in line with your overall mission statement?

Good Examples:

- "Once we have reached a turnover of £300,000, we can redecorate the office by spending a maximum of £10,000. This should be in line with rebranding the company to reflect our success. The change will also help to improve the office environment for staff and further boost their productivity and enthusiasm."

9.2.6 Timely

Examples:

- "We need to have a meeting next month."
- "I need to do some planning when I get time."
- "I need to get fit."

Analysis:

These goals are vague, and as daily pressures increase, they can easily get pushed down the list of activities or be neglected altogether.

To Improve:

Include specific timing in the formulation of your goals, and give yourself tight deadlines. You must also be aware of the Parkinson Law:

Parkinson Law:
Time expands to fill the gap available to it.

Give yourself tight deadlines and push yourself to achieve more in less time. You can even use the saved time for leisure. The aim is not to get busier in life or to work longer hours but to get more done in a given time by being more focused and on target.

Good Examples:

- "We need to have a meeting at 2 p.m. next Thursday."
- "I need to spend two hours planning every Sunday morning from 9 to 11 a.m."
- "I need to spend a total of at least three hours per week exercising, be it cycling, going to the gym or swimming."

9.3 Goal-Setting Guidelines

- *Set both long- and short-term goals.* Long-term goals help you see which direction you are heading in. Daily goals help you focus and easily measure your progress.
- *Set yourself challenging goals.* Get out of your comfort zone. Try new techniques, tools, methods and new ways of interacting with others. If you don't try them, you will never know the benefits or how well they can work for you.

- *Identify goal attainment strategies*. You need to know how you can go about reaching your goals. This requires precise identification of methods, strategies and techniques that can help you achieve them.
- *Set priorities*. You will always have multiple goals, and some of these can turn out to be partially contradictory. Make sure your goals are consistent, and know which ones to focus on first. The best way to do this is to set your goals within the context of your roles. Since you know the ranking of your roles and how important each one is, you can decide how important each goal is.
- *Understand the difference between outcome, performance and process goals*. *Outcome goals* are usually the most common types of goals, but as they can depend on elements outside your control, they are more likely to cause anxiety. For example, an outcome goal could be to win a weightlifting competition. Instead of setting an outcome goal, you can set a *performance goal*, such as to lift a particular weight. Now, the objective is much clearer and is independent of outside events or contestants. *Process goals* focus on techniques and can be set to direct your attention during a particular activity. For example, your process goal can be to lift any object of a certain weight no matter what its shape until you are comfortable with lifting that weight. As another example, you can set yourself a process goal to draw a still life as accurately as possible using only pastels.
- *Set goals to satisfy different roles at once*. To increase your productivity, consider setting goals in such a way that satisfies several needs in various roles. For example, let's say you have decided to join a volleyball club. You have weekly practice with your team. You get to exercise and get fit. You also get to work in a team. The sport provides an opportunity to compete. It helps you become more agile and improves your hand-eye coordination and reaction times. In addition, the sport also helps you socialise. As you get better, you may even join a league. This, in turn, leads to travelling to other cities to compete with other teams. You then get to meet even more people, sharpen your skills and boost your self-esteem. You can talk about it in social settings to kick-start conversations and potentially make even more friends.
- *Set positive rather than negative goals*.

Consider this goal:

> "I don't want to be the quietest person in a meeting."

It doesn't actually tell you what to do. If anything, it will subconsciously emphasise quietness rather than the opposite. Instead, formulate your goal positively and include an action:

"I want to explain my ideas and talk for at least ten minutes during the next meeting."

9.4 Carry Out Extensive Planning

Now that you have identified your mission and your roles, you need to work out a plan to achieve them. This can take a fair amount of time. Allocate a suitable uninterrupted time, and then go through the following steps to plan your life.

1. *Identify your ten-year plan*. Remember, you should start at the end. Most advisors will tell you to think of your plan for next year and so on. This is similar to solving the maze from the beginning; it is very difficult. Start from the future to figure out what to do now. You have already identified you mission statement. So start from the end, formulate your long-term goals and then work backwards. You should end up with a separate ten-year plan for each distinct role.
2. *Identify your five-year plan*. Similar to the above, focus on a shorter time span.
3. *Identify your yearly plan*. Plan for year 1, year 2 and so on until you reach year 5. You may need to go through several iterations, working backwards and forwards to get it right.

Some people may view such extensive planning as fruitless. They think that we cannot predict the future. We cannot even be certain what will happen tomorrow let alone in ten years, so what is the point of trying? This is a simple mix-up. Such people may indeed have a valid point about our inability to "predict" the future, but that is not what we are trying to do. All we want to do is design our future based on our current understanding of the world and its trends simply because that is all we've got. Naturally, the usability of such plans depends on how much a person knows about the world and its current trends.

While planning for the future, utilise the SMART formula. It is critical to make your goals specific and measurable in order to measure your progress. Vague goals can be misleading, and it is difficult to know when you have achieved them.

The range of planning is limited to ten years. By all means, if you really feel up to it, plan for a longer span. However, there are two points you need to be aware of. As you go further into the future, it becomes very difficult to predict what will happen. It is almost unthinkable to imagine what you could be doing fifty years from now. The world will change significantly. Who knows how humans will respond to this.

The second point is that, as humans, we tend to overestimate what we can do in a year and underestimate what we can do in a decade. The initial excitement may make you think you can achieve a lot in a short time. On the other hand, we really struggle to understand the full meaning of ten years and what a person can accomplish in that time. Hence, planning beyond ten years has the risk that you may set yourself a bar that is too low or overcompensate and aim for something too grand and vague. Just define a series of achievable steps that move you forward.

9.5 The Focused Determination Test

You wake up in the morning. You think of your breakfast and what to wear. You quickly check your daily tasks to make sure you take everything you need before leaving the house. At work, you go through your emails, answer phone calls, attend meetings and work on a number of ongoing projects. Before you know it, it's the end of the day, and you're already thinking about a series of other errands you have lined up for the evening. Today is your gym day, on Wednesdays you go to a French class and on Friday nights you go out with your friends.

The cycle then continues, and suddenly six months pass and you notice how quickly the time went. Now, here is an honest question you must ask yourself: As you go through your daily and weekly routine, how conscious are you of your long-term goals? How conscious are you of your life? How mindful are you of your existence? If someone asks you what your top three goals are at any given time, are you able to answer from memory and directly from the heart? Or do you have to think about it? Are you constantly conscious of your long-term goals?

We call this the *Focused Determination Test*. You will pass the test if you know precisely what you are determined to get at any given moment, night or day, asleep or awake. Precision is critical; so is your immediate response. You must know by heart what it is you are aiming to achieve day after day. What is the point of your life? In which direction are you heading? You must know it while eating your dinner, while engaged in your cross-country mountain biking or while stuck in traffic.

Unfortunately, most people fail the Focused Determination Test. They do not set long-term goals. They don't live consciously. Even if they plan something, they do it as a ritual, like a New Year's resolution, and then forget about it within a few weeks.

If you are not constantly conscious of all your goals specifically, you will *not* achieve them. You cannot afford to forget a goal. A forgotten goal is no longer a goal; it is only a desire . . . just a wish. The chances are very high that you will not reach this so-called goal if you don't know it by heart. As Napoleon Hill beautifully puts it, you must always know your "burning desire" if you ever want to succeed. Be conscious of the fire within, and use it as fuel to power your life.

Persistence

To get to your goals, you need to be persistent. Use the following time-tested approach, which was originally suggested by Napoleon Hill. If you follow this to the letter, you will almost certainly achieve your goal (no, we are not kidding!).

1. *Define your mission statement.*
    a. What do you want?
    b. What are you willing to give to get it?
    c. What is your plan to get it?
2. *Write this up.*
3. *Read it back to yourself twice a day.* Ideally, read it once in the morning and once in the evening before going to bed. DO NOT SKIP THIS STEP!
    a. Print it up, put it on a wall and read it a*loud* twice a day.
    b. Soon, you will memorise your mission. Keep repeating it until it becomes a part of you.
4. *Do a self-test.* If someone asks you what you want in life, can you quote your mission in seconds?

Does this really work?

It definitely does! Just try it. There is no limit to the power of repetition. Countless seriously successful people have tried this and succeeded. You can even extend it to companies. Every successful blue chip company has a simple, yet elegant mission statement that captures the essence of their vision. People in these companies keep repeating their mission statement to themselves and to everyone else quite often.

9.6 Case Study: A Photographer

Let's go through an example. Anushka's main interest is photography. In particular, she likes landscape photography and wants to become very good at it. She has defined several roles, such as "landscape photography", "traveller", "daughter" and "climber" for herself. Having defined her mission and vision as part of her mission statement, she now wants to set her goals. Using the systematic method, she writes the following:

Roles & Goals	
Role	Landscape photographer
Where do I want to be in ten years?	"I will have a TV interview on a mainstream channel where my work is shown to the public. I would be interviewed on my adventures and how I got to take my award-winning shots."
Where do I want to be in five years?	"I would have a set of my photos printed in *National Geographic* magazine, as well as several other mainstream photography websites (such as X and Y). I also want to win the highest photography award—the Z Prize."
Where do I want to be in a year?	"I would have a collection of landscape photos to showcase in a local gallery and sell to the public."

Roles & Goals	
Role	Traveller
Where do I want to be in ten years?	"I would have travelled to several remote places and would have taken at least ten famous landscape photographs of locations that no one else has ever photographed."
Where do I want to be in five years?	"I would have been to at least twenty new countries in all five continents."
Where do I want to be in a year?	"I would have been to African Savannah and shot the landscape and the wildlife."

Exercise 9-1

Prioritise Roles

This exercise will help you to focus on your most import roles in preparation for the next step on setting goals.

PART 1: Recall Mission Statement

One or more days might have passed since you defined your mission statement in the previous chapter. (This will be the case if you followed our advice on not reading the book cover to cover.) It's time to go through a simple test. From memory, write your complete mission statement below. Can you remember it? If not, spend time memorising it. Learn it by heart. You will be using it as a reference in later parts of this exercise.

Vision	
Mission	

PART 2: Identify Important Roles

Consider the final list of roles created in *Exercise 6-5.* Based on your mission statement, review and list your most important roles below—for example, author, manager, kite surfer, real estate investor, photographer and volunteer worker. Include both your automatic and non-automatic roles, though it is more likely that your non-automatic list is changed as a result of this review. Just remember that any role that is left out will not be considered for further analysis.

Role 1		Role 11	
Role 2		Role 12	
Role 3		Role 13	
Role 4		Role 14	
Role 5		Role 15	
Role 6		Role 16	
Role 7		Role 17	
Role 8		Role 18	
Role 9		Role 19	
Role 10		Role 20	

PART 3: Identify Workload

So far, you have identified your roles, chose them based on your contributions, filtered them based on your needs and finally reviewed them based on your mission statement. This process is designed to focus your efforts on what matters most to you. There is, however, one element that you have not considered so far—your time. In this powerful exercise, you will get to see if you have enough time to do it all.

This exercise is rather simple but can provide a profound insight into why you may feel restless because you feel you need to do so much and yet never get a chance to do it all. It can simply be because your excitement leading you to extend your to-do list without realising that you have overwhelmed yourself. You would be juggling too many things as opposed to being focused on a few important areas.

To check your workload, here is what you need to do; Imagine that you have 100% *available time*. This covers all your waking hours minus the time for essentials such as eating or showering.

Now, consider each of the roles listed in *Part 2*. Place a percentage next to each that represents how much of your available time you are willing to allocate to it. This is just a rough estimate. It is not about how much time you spend now. Think about how much time you would *like* to spend in each area. Write the roles and the percentages in the table below.

To make understanding the percentages easer calculate how many *available hours* you have per week and then use the percentage for each role to find the equivalent in hours. Write this in the table in the corresponding column.

While going through this part of the exercise, you will quickly realise that you have very little time available and therefore you should focus your efforts on things that are most important. Feel free to go back and forth between this and previous exercises to prune your roles once more. Your aim is to end up with a set of roles that are important to you and that you have enough time to attend to.

Role ID	Roles	Percentage of Time (%)	Time in hours per week
Role 1			
Role 2			
Role 3			
Role 4			
Role 5			
Role 6			
Role 7			
Role 8			
Role 9			
Role 10			
Role 11			
Role 12			
Role 13			
Role 14			
Role 15			
Role 16			
Role 17			
Role 18			
Role 19			
	Total	100%	

PART 4: Identify Leftover Roles

It is likely that you have listed more roles than you can attend to. In *Part 3*, you examined your roles based on how much time you want to spend on each. It is very likely that you had to remove some roles to make room for others. However, you should still keep track of these leftover roles. Although, you cannot attend to them now; it is possible to explore them in the future. You don't have to do everything at once; you can go through your interests serially.

In the table below, write a list of roles you want to leave for later. You cannot have automatic roles in your leftover list because you always have them. The next time you are going through *Exercise 9-1* as part of your periodic review, remember to examine your previous list of leftover roles to make sure you are aware of them and include any as necessary.

Leftover Roles	

PART 5: Focused Roles

Write a final list of roles you want to focus on now based on all the exercises you have gone through so far. This is a placeholder for all your roles so you can refer back to them in subsequent exercises.

Automatic Roles	Non-Automatic Roles

Exercise 9-2

Short-Term & Long-Term Goals

This 2-part exercise will help you define your SMART goals for all your important roles.

PART 1: Identify Your SMART Goals

Now that you have a final list of roles, let's examine each one in detail to set specific goals. Based on your mission statement, go through your roles one at a time and identify your short-term and long-term goals. Formulate your goals using the SMART method. Include process goals and performance goals. Make duplicate blank forms (as provided on the next page) for each role to review all the roles you identified in *Exercise 9-1, Part 5*.

Role	
Your most important goal for this role	

	10 years	
	5 years	
What do you need to do to accomplish this goal? Formulate these as SMART objectives for each period from now.	4 years	
	3 years	
	2 years	
	1 year	

PART 2: Check Goal Consistency

You have now defined a series of goals for your roles. You must have a series of filled-in forms—one form for each role. In this part, you will be analysing your goals for consistency. You want to make sure that your goals don't contradict each other. If there are any conflicts, you want to highlight them now rather than wasting your effort in years to come.

Note that this is not about evaluating your ability to achieve a goal. It is about logical consistency. For example, you may realise that you have set yourself two goals, such as the following: One is a goal that says you should live in the centre of a major metropolis to do your ideal job, and another goal says you want to live in a tranquil house in a village with an ocean view. You will need to choose or at least be aware of the conflict so you can think more about it. Which one is more important to you? Can you think from a higher level to satisfy the underlying needs for these two conflicting goals? This is the moment to think about them— not years later.

While going through the analysis, go back to your previous forms to update your goals, roles or whatever you need to change as necessary.

Consider the goals for each period shown below on your forms. Go through the goals and check the following:

- Are they logically consistent?
- Can you achieve all your goals in all your roles for this period simultaneously?
- What compromises should you consider?

Use the space below to record your findings and analysis.

Your Analysis for 1 Year	

Your Analysis for 2 Years	
Your Analysis for 3 Years	
Your Analysis for 4 Years	

Your Analysis for 5 Years	
Your Analysis for 10 Years	
Other Notes and Analyses	

10 Maintain a Solid Focus

"A man is but the product of his thoughts; what he thinks he becomes."

Mahatma Gandhi

Barnacles are tiny marine creatures which live in shallow tidal waters. They don't look especially exciting or significant. Not much was known about barnacles until the 1830s. Before that, these creatures were not adequately classified. Not even one species was properly defined. The field needed attention. Earlier in his career as a biologist, Charles Darwin had travelled the world on board the *Beagle* between 1831 and 1836. During this period, Darwin spent a lot of time on land collecting and observing while the *Beagle* charted and surveyed the coasts. In particular, Darwin made a lot of notes about marine invertebrates as he dissected and studied them under a microscope. His voyages provided him ample opportunities to collect a vast amount of information about a variety of species from around the world, and this would later help him to put together his theory of evolution. When Darwin started his journey on the *Beagle*, he was only twenty-two years old, and although he had some experience in collecting beetles and dissecting marine invertebrates, he was otherwise a novice biologist.

By the time he returned home, Darwin had already made himself known to the scientific community. However, upon his return, he wanted to establish himself as a serious biologist and was looking for an area to focus on. A friend suggested that if Darwin ever wanted to work on a theory of evolution, he would need to know at least one species really well. Right at this time, there was also a call to arms to sort out the field by studying barnacles systematically. Darwin recalled his fascination with barnacles in his youth and the various specimens he had collected during his voyages. He decided to take up the challenge. Originally, he thought it should not take him more than a year to do this. As it turned out, it took him eight difficult years to collect every species and then dissect, analyse and describe them in minute detail. The aim was to find variations, similarities, affinities and anomalies. Darwin wrote to museums to send him their collections. He wrote to people whom he had met on his travels and asked them to send him samples. He approached the contacts of his contacts. He wanted to know everything about these little creatures. Soon, Darwin was receiving cargos of samples from all over the world.

The work, however, required tremendous focus. It was a meticulous and delicate task, and Darwin was determined to finish it. Sometimes, he had to dissect a sample and then put it back together just so he could return it to the owner. Just imagine what it means to work on some tiny creatures for eight years day after day with the aim of learning everything about every variation known *in the world*. Darwin had to spend hours bent over a microscope in a room that was filled with the foul vapour of preserving spirits. His health deteriorated, and he was ordered by his doctor to spend less time in the lab. Nevertheless, he persevered. Darwin's fascination with barnacles consumed his family life too. His obsession was seen by his family as a normal part of life. His son, Francis, casually asked another child, "So, where does your father do his barnacles?"

After eight years, the tedious work paid off. The result was a four-volume definitive guide to barnacles, which raised Darwin's profile as a professional scientist. The study helped him to formulate his theory of evolution by natural selection as he classified barnacles based on the principle of *common descent,* the first of its kind in history. Eventually, Darwin went on to publish his theory of evolution by natural selection in *On the Origin of Species*, which made him immortally famous and forever changed the way in which we look at life and God. His theory influenced countless fields, such as zoology, biology, medicine, genetics and philosophy. Before Darwin, we did not understand life. Abrahamic religions dictated that we all came from Adam and Eve only a few thousand years ago. Darwin's evidence gave us a much grander and more realistic view of life—that man was not at the centre of the universe (much like how Earth had been believed to be at the centre just a few hundred years before) or superior to all other life forms. We have simply descended from a long succession of ancestors based on the survival of the fittest, which goes on to connect anything alive today with a giant tree of life. After more than

150 years of research confirming Darwin's theory, we now have a much better grasp of the animal kingdom and know more about our own evolution and why we are the way we are. We no longer need God or intelligent design to explain where we come from or how life is as it is. Things exist because they had the ability to survive. Darwin's breakthrough was immense and brave.

Such is the power of *focus*, *dedication* and *determination*.

Let's look at another example of persistence and determination.

He had won. He was voted the chief executive of the state . . . and not just any state—a very large state with a Gross Domestic Product (GDP) of about 2 trillion dollars. If it were a country, it would be the eighth-highest GDP in the world. With 35 million people to manage, the role was indeed significant.

There was, however, one anomaly. He was not known as a politician, even though he was already world-famous for many other roles he had played in his life. This new role was a new chapter in a life that was as extraordinary as it gets. He was an immigrant who had worked his way up over thirty-five years, from having no money, power or established connections, to become the governor.

Arnold. Do you recognise the name? Who does it remind you of? The chances are high that no matter where you live, you know who Arnold refers to base on this brief introduction. This is the power of a brand and its associated success. You probably have not met him in person, yet he is likely to be very familiar to you.

Whatever your opinion of Arnold Schwarzenegger, there is one thing everyone can agree on; he has been successful. He is a classic case of rags to riches, American style. So, what is the secret to his success? Was he just lucky, or was his success the result of his attitude, actions and decisions?

Let's look more closely at what he has achieved in his life. As a boy of fourteen, he played several sports, including football, and was strongly influenced by his father to pursue it. His father was a strict man. As the local police chief, he was a strong believer in firmness and strength. His mum, as he put it later, was "an ordinary housewife." Arnold lived in Thal, a village near Graz in Austria. He believed that his father tended to favour Arnold's brother, Meinhard. This made Arnold very competitive, and he felt he had to work hard to gain his father's approval, at least at that age. At fourteen, with the encouragement of his football coach, he went to a gym and picked up a barbell for the first time.

Shortly thereafter, he started weightlifting and seriously considered bodybuilding as a career. Arnold studied psychology to understand the power of the mind over the body. He was fascinated with idols in the bodybuilding world, such as Reg Park and Steve Reeves, who were the bodybuilding champions of the time. What he saw in them was the determination to achieve a single goal, along with the huge amount of hard work that went into achieving it. This appealed strongly to Arnold because he could see clearly that the more effort he put into his exercises, the more results he could get and could, in turn, easily show off.

Fascinated by his idols, Arnold covered his bedroom walls with posters of his bodybuilding heroes. Unlike other boys his age, who had pictures of fast cars or beautiful girls in bikinis, Arnold had oily muscle men pinned up on his walls, and his mum soon became concerned about his obsession with these muscle men. Surely, this was not normal behaviour. Behind Arnold's back, she called a doctor to visit the house and see for himself so that she and the doctor could discuss "Arnold's case." The conclusion was simple enough; there was nothing wrong with Arnold, and he was not gay. He was just obsessed, as boys of his age could easily become. Many boys focused on toys, cars or girls. For Arnold, it was bodybuilding.

By the time he was seventeen years old, Arnold attended his first weightlifting competition. By then, he had moved to Graz, a large city nearby, where there was a gym. Once in Graz, he started to go to local movie theatres to watch his idols perform in various competitions.

His father, however, could not see what Arnold was doing with his life. To him, picking up weights in a gym all day long was not a productive use of time. He used to challenge Arnold by saying:

> "If you want to get strong, why don't you get an axe and chop down some wood and deliver it to people's homes? That way, you do some good. This way, you're doing it for yourself. I don't get it. Are you so in love with yourself?"

His father had a point, but the contrast in his mentality and Arnold's signifies exactly how and why Arnold has achieved so much in his life. In fact, as you will see in this book, it is as if Arnold has followed the secret to success to the letter and ticked all the boxes along the way.

Back in Graz, he continued with his training at the gym for five or six hours a day. He was so focused on training that he and his friends used to break into the gym over the weekends while it was closed so that they could continue training. If he missed a session, he would feel sick with guilt.

Most people at such a young age are more interested in hanging around with friends, clubbing or engaging in various "fun" activities—anything but excruciating physical training day after day. Going through the training taught Arnold important lessons which paved the way for his future success. As he put it, "I didn't mind basic training. It taught me that something that seemed impossible at the start can be achieved." This is the mentality of a go-getter. Bear this in mind as you go through the story of his life.

At eighteen, he was recruited for a year of mandatory military service in Austria. This suited him well, as he continued with his strong training regime. His eyes were then set on the Mr. Universe competition that would be held in London. He believed that winning Mr. Universe was his ticket to America, the land of opportunity which he had been dreaming about ever since his teenage years. In 1966, Arnold claimed second place in the Mr. Universe competition. At the time, he was very pleased with himself and his achievement. However, upon reflection, Arnold decided that he had missed a great opportunity. He had overestimated the competition. He could have been standing on that pedestal holding the trophy, but he had lost it, and the only reason for this loss was that he had gone there to *compete* and not to *win*. As he recalled later:

> "After that, I never went to a competition to compete. I went to *win*. Even though I didn't win every time, that was my mindset. I became a total animal. If you tuned into my thoughts before a competition, you would hear something like, 'I deserve that pedestal. I own it, and the sea ought to part for me. Just get out of the fucking way. I'm on a mission. So just step aside and gimme the trophy.'"

He was *determined*.

Eventually, at the age of twenty-one and being able to speak very little English, Arnold moved to the US. His move was sponsored by an American who owned a series of gyms along with bodybuilding magazines and a supply chain to provide supplements. Arnold would advertise for him in his magazines and, in return, would get to be in America. He would then train for his important goal of winning *Mr. Olympia*, the most prestigious competition of them all.

Arnold was a natural at showing off his body on stage. He loved the sport so much that he felt completely at ease when on stage. He thoroughly enjoyed showing off, and the audience could clearly see this. This gave Arnold a great advantage over his rivals, who mostly felt stressed and experienced stage fright. The pressure of performing in front of a scrutinising audience was immense. Arnold was also very competitive—a trait he acquired during his childhood. He fully understood that there was a psychological game to play and that, to win it, he had to use his brain as well as his muscles. The next year, he won Mr. Olympia and went on to win the title seven times, thereby becoming one of the greatest bodybuilding champions of all time!

Meanwhile, Arnold had a simple ambition—to become financially self-sufficient. As he won the titles, people started asking him for guidance on bodybuilding. He took advantage of this attention by setting up a mail-order company to sell how-to guides and supplements. He even wrote a book on the topic, *The New Encyclopedia of Modern Bodybuilding,* which is still selling well today. Next, Arnold started a brick-laying company with a friend. He would get to exercise those muscles while getting paid! Life was good.

Arnold was always interested in acting, and with his fame and impressive physique, he gained some attention in Hollywood. He started with small roles, and it was a struggle in the beginning. He was told by his agents and casting people that he had a funny accent, his body looked "too weird" and his name was too long. In fact, in his first role in *Hercules,* his voice was dubbed in post-production because his accent was considered too thick. He was also credited as Arnold Strong to fix that long name.

Nevertheless, for Arnold, this was just the training ground. He would have to learn the ropes as he progressed. When he went to audition for another small role, he was asked if acting in front of others or a large audience would bother him. He replied that he was very much used to it. He would just block out the audience whenever necessary as he had done in countless competitions before. For his new acting career, he could now tap into what he had already acquired in a different domain and take advantage of his skills.

After a series of small roles, Arnold's major break came in the form of a documentary about the life of a bodybuilder. Pumping Iron, which was released in 1977, boosted Arnold's profile enormously. His first high-budget movie, Conan the Barbarian, was released in 1982 and got the Hollywood machinery behind him. He was now unstoppable. A series of action movies followed—The Terminator, Commando, Predator and The Running Man. These transformed Arnold from a struggling actor into an internationally famous star.

With the money made from his first movies, Arnold moved into real estate with a simple moto: "What can I do to turn one dollar to two?" His aim was to have a source of money that would fund his lifestyle *independent* of the money he was earning from his movie career.

At the height of his movie career, Arnold was constantly reminded of the presence of one other actor—Sylvester Stallone. At first, it was a simple competition between rivals, but as time went by, Arnold turned Stallone into an arch nemesis in his own mind. He started to focus on simple stats—who killed more brutally in a movie, who fired more shots, who had the bigger gun, who had bigger muscles and even who had more oil on his muscles! As he said later, this rivalry simply helped him to push through, as he sometimes felt he was just one step behind Stallone while one action movie was made after another.

As his wage increased, he channelled his money into more businesses, such as Planet Hollywood, a restaurant chain he established with Sylvester Stallone, Bruce Willis and Demi Moore. The investments were also part of his branding as he continued shaping his image. He was an action hero—a macho guy who had to have the biggest of everything—the biggest car (the Hummer manufactured for civilians), the largest private jet (say a Boeing 747!), the most expensive cigars and the largest pay cheque yet for a movie. In the eyes of his audience, he had to look big, because right from the beginning, his aim was very simple and well-defined—to be a successful and supremely famous superstar. This was why Arnold was always extremely reluctant to play the roles of bad characters. He thought that a big, muscly guy with an Austrian accent playing a bad guy would soon lead him to play minor supporting roles and that he would then have no chance to become a leading actor. When James Cameron proposed the idea of *Terminator 2*, Arnold immediately wanted to reject it. He had already played the bad guy in *The Terminator* and did not want to carry on with this kind of role. Cameron then had to correct him by explaining the complicated plot. This time, the Terminator would be a good guy against a much worse enemy—a shapeshifting robot made of liquid metal! Only then was Arnold happy to continue with the role, which, of course, went on to make him very famous. He was offered the role of a Nazi officer, a wrestler and a football player, but Arnold never accepted such roles simply because they would not enable him to convince anyone that he was going to be a star.

While his acting career was moving forward fast, his social life was well in swing too. He fell in love and married Maria Shriver. Maria was the niece of John F. Kennedy (JFK), who was a former Democratic president of the United States. Arnold, in contrast, was firmly Republican. Marrying into a well-established American political family soon helped him to make more connections and to learn what the world of politics was all about. Subsequently, he was strongly influenced and mentored by his mother-in-law, the sister of the late JFK. Now, he had someone who was well versed in the art of politics and whom he could trust completely. Even though Arnold believed in a party that was very much the opposite of the Democrats, it was still in his family's best interest for him to succeed no matter what he wanted to pursue.

Eventually, owing to the heritage of his family and the mentorship he had received, he decided to enter into politics and run for governor of California. His declaration made international news.

Hollywood was traditionally full of Democrats, so he had a lot of contacts and friends on one side while he preached the causes of the other. This placed him in a unique position. Rather than showcasing this as an inconsistency, he thought he could take advantage of it by appealing to both sides, thereby gaining crucial swing votes. This is indeed what contributed to his win in 2003 and made him the governor of California. He was dubbed "The Governator" due to his most famous role as "The Terminator."

Giving interviews and being on stage is something that many people dislike, and new politicians are no exception. Political newcomers seldom get enough experience on the international stage to practise public speaking. Here, Arnold had yet another advantage. Even though he had never held public office before, he was well versed in a crucial skill that most of his rivals did not have. Through his bodybuilding competitions, he was already experienced when it came to performing in front of large audiences. He had already been an international star who had visited countless countries and had given innumerable interviews. He had been on TV an endless number of times and knew well what it meant to be behind the camera. With all this experience of dealing with the press, Arnold felt right at home when he found himself talking about policies. Instead of talking about how he'd built his muscles and what his latest movie was all about, he just had to change the subject and talk about policies instead. Over the years his thick accent had improved as well and even though he still had an accent, it didn't seem to cause problems. His audience was already used to it and in fact it was part of his branding; it differentiated him from his rivals.

The media was already criticising Arnold before he went into politic—"He doesn't know how to act", "he is too money-oriented" and "he is too competitive." When people go into politics, they divide opinions even more. Now, a whole lot more people would comment on Arnold's so-called "inabilities"—"What does he know about politics?" and "What does he know about running a government?" Upon his return to acting after his term was finished, a journalist commented, "He was never in acting to begin with!"

Whatever the opinions—and people are, of course, entitled to their opinions—there is one thing that is clear to an observer; Arnold has been successful and has had an extraordinary life. It is one that many people aspire to, and the secret behind it is rather simple.

Arnold was *determined* to become *successful*.

This is not to say that he is an ideal role model or that you should follow his path. In fact, this is how he puts it himself:

> "I always wanted to be an inspiration for people, but I never set out to be a role model in everything. How could I be when I have so many contradictions and crosscurrents in my life? I'm a European who became an American leader; a Republican who loves Democrats; a businessman who makes his living as an action hero; a tremendously disciplined super-achiever who hasn't always been disciplined enough; a fitness expert who loves cigars; an environmentalist who loves Hummers; a fun-loving guy with kid-like enthusiasm who is most famous for terminating people. How would anybody know what to imitate?" (Schwarzenegger 2013)

10.1 What Makes People Different?

Imagine sitting in a hotel lobby with about ten other people. You are all part of a tour to visit cultural places in Rome. You are waiting for your tour guide to arrive to start the tour. You don't know the others in the group, as you have all subscribed to this tour independently. You look around and wonder about the background of the people before you. What differentiates them? You see a tall, middle-aged man in a suit who looks fairly prominent. You see a woman in her thirties who is dressed casually, much like a tourist. You see an old couple who seem to have come from a different continent. You see a young, talkative man who is full of energy. You see a young girl whom you suspect is a university student. You wonder what she studies. You wonder what these people do as work. You wonder what they do when they don't work.

What is the greatest differentiator between these people? Is it the way they look, the places they come from, their wealth or their manners? If you wanted to describe them to others, what would be the most important quality that you would mention?

The greatest differentiator between people is their skills. Whatever a person is good at comes to define that person. The more skills and experiences people have, the more impressed we are by them. We are also impressed when we begin to appreciate the extent of a person's skills. Going back to the lobby scene, what if each person has written their best skill on a label and stuck it on their chests like a name tag. Now, you see surgeon, competitive snowboarder, network anchor, fashion designer, novelist, robot maker, hair stylist, Boeing 747 pilot and sculptor. Knowing their skills suddenly makes them a lot more interesting. You want to have a chat with every single one of them. They each have a unique world to share, and the more skilled they are in their respective domains, the more eager you would be to learn about them and their world.

What you are good at is all that matters, and every day that passes is an opportunity to get better at something. If a day passes and you haven't improved your skills, you are one day behind others who have.

10.2 Focus on Acquiring Skills

Now, ask yourself a simple question. What are you best at? If you had to define yourself by a single skill, what would that be? Write this below:

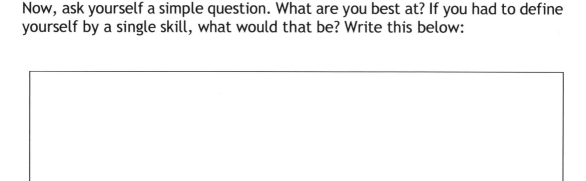

How quickly did you write it? Did you have to think carefully and choose? Were you wondering what to consider as a skill and what to leave out? What does this suggest? If there was *any* delay, does this not suggest that you are unsure of what you are best at? Perhaps you consider yourself good at many skills. Is that how you like to be? Do you consider yourself good at each of those skills, or just merely knowledgeable?

Now, here is another question. Given your skill, how many people out there in the world today are at the same level as you are or even better? If your answer is that there are many people, then don't expect to be treated uniquely. This goes back to your choice of career and interests. Suppose you choose to be a web developer. You can be good at this job. It can pay well indeed. Countless companies need websites and someone to manage them. How many web developers are there in the world? Millions. How many are better than *you*? There can still be many thousands. Unless you choose a specific niche and master it like no other, you will not stand out from the competition.

This is what skill acquisition is all about. Within the scope of your mission statement, roles and goals, you must focus on those skills that can make you stand out from the competition. This requires extensive self-analysis. As you go through this chapter, you will be guided with several exercises that can help you find out what skills to focus on.

10.3 Focus on What Matters the Most

Let's go through a couple of examples to illustrate an important point about what it means to *focus*. Consider a black and white illustration of a person or a scene. This could be similar to those you would find in the comic section of a newspaper or in abstract logos. Imagine those illustrations that use black ink against a white background with no grey-scale tones. In this case, to capture a scene, the artist can use only a single tone but would still need to describe a complex image that would normally have many colours as seen by human eyes. To depict a three-dimensional world on a two-dimensional surface, artists know that the most important element defining a scene is how light interacts with objects. Once this interaction is analysed, understood and captured, they can use it to describe the essential components of a scene on a two-dimensional paper that would illustrate it. If done well, when you look at the abstract illustration, you can understand straight away what it represents. You can see exactly what the shape is and if it is a man or a woman. You can see where the light is coming from and how the form of a person cuts out light and casts shadows on the surrounding environment, further defining a given space.

To get this right, an artist would not aim to capture everything he sees in that image. Instead, he has to carefully *carve out* what is not essential and can be safely ignored. He would analyse the scene, decompose it to its building parts and then reconstruct it in this abstract form so as to capture it in this specific style. In short, he would have to focus on what to leave out in order to define the scene efficiently.

Let's look at another example. Consider Google, which is known for a large number of really successful products. Examples are Internet search, a world-class browser such as Chrome and an insanely successful advertisement platform such as AdWords. In the last decade, they have introduced a cutting-edge mobile OS, such as Android; mapping and navigation; language translation and the YouTube video-distribution system. They are hard at work on some futurist projects, such as automatic cars or automated delivery systems which are yet to be released. The list is long, with countless products and services offered to the professional world too.

Now, suppose you are the head of this large technology corporation. The company has billions in revenue every quarter, and the share price keeps reaching peak after peak. The world is giving you all the money you need. You feel you can do anything you want. If you see any area in which you think there is a market for your products, you can immediately allocate resources, produce outstanding products and services and dominate it. What stops you from conquering every single area you see? Although Google is one of the most successful corporations, the available resources are not necessarily limitless. As the head of the company, there is only so much you can do, and that means *focus*. In short, *it is not what you do, it is what you don't*.

By focusing on what you should not be doing, you can better see what areas are more attractive in the long run. By focusing on what not to do, you can stop investing in risky, fruitless projects. It helps you not to get carried away with your excitement and not to copycat everybody else in the market who comes up with a new idea. Focusing on what you should not be doing helps you carve out a way forward without distracting projects of one kind or another.

This principle can be applied to all aspects of life, especially in today's world in which possibilities are endless because we have access to more products and services than ever before. There are more job types nowadays, and each job has its own niches and complex specialisations. There are simply so many decisions to make. In such a world, focusing on what you *shouldn't* be doing can quickly focus your attention on areas that are more fruitful to you in the long run.

10.4 Close the Loop

It takes effort to learn something new and acquire a new skill. The fastest way to learn is to *close the loop,* and here is how it works. First, acquire some basic understanding about the skill and what it would entail. You can do this by reading about the topic, watching videos about it, attending relevant courses and meeting people who know more about the said skill.

The next step involves producing a tangible result—a product or a service. Continue learning and practising your skill until it leads you to two types of rewards—*money* and *attention*. The money allows you to learn more about the skill. It also covers your basic needs so that you don't have to rely on an auxiliary job. As you gradually become self-sufficient, you can spend *all* your time on mastering the new skill. You can use the money to buy tools, get more training and engage in bigger projects, and this, in turn, leads to acquiring more skills.

Money, however, is not enough. You will also need to gain attention and fans for your work. The fans can inspire and add meaning to what you do, boosting your intrinsic motivators. They will also give you valuable feedback, which will help to improve your skills further. With enough attention and money, you can finally *close the loop* and end up in a *virtuous cycle* whereby producing each product leads to more success. This, in turn, helps you move forward to do the next big thing. Only then will you find your life's task and gain the respect of others as well as yourself, thereby satisfying your high-level esteem needs.

It is difficult not to succeed when you have closed the loop, so bear this in mind as you consider gaining a new skill.

10.5 Use a Timesheet for Self-Monitoring

The total time available to you is limited. Treat time as a scarce resource. You have to manage this resource intelligently. Like any resource, you must find inefficiencies and eliminate them. With ever-increasing content competing for your attention, you must constantly look for ways to increase this resource. Buying time comes by spending less time on something else. Find out which tasks are taking up your valuable time and eliminate them. This will free up your time to do what matters most.

A tool that can help you to identify and eliminate inefficiencies in time management is a timesheet. Most successful companies require their staff to fill in a company timesheet. When collected across the company, timesheets help management to see where resources are being spent. This, in turn, helps project managers to plan and budget current and future projects.

Unfortunately, most people leave it at that. Most employees don't even like filling in the forms and always feel forced by the company to do so. Once filled in, they don't even look at the data themselves. They think the primary use of such data is for someone else. Outside of work, very few people tend to keep a timesheet, but those who do know how powerful it can be. Once you start filling in a timesheet for yourself, you will never stop. It is so addictive. It provides discipline, and you will feel immensely proud when you can see from your timesheet how productive and efficient you have been. The timesheet also allows you to recognise the areas of inefficiency and remove them.

Timesheets have two fundamental benefits. Once you have collected data for a sizable period, such as six months or a year, you will start to see specific patterns of behaviour. You will see that there aren't many productive hours per day and that you need to make the best of every single hour. You will also see where your focus is concentrated, and you can then ask yourself if this is what you want to spend time on.

Before starting to fill in a timesheet, you need to design and customise it for your specific lifestyle. A personal timesheet, as the name suggests, is highly personal. This is why it is different and more powerful than the one you might be required to fill in at work. The work timesheet is designed by someone else for the benefit of someone else. It is for the company to measure your work performance and maximise their profits while you work for them. It is not necessarily for you to measure yourself on becoming successful in all aspects of your life.

Your personal timesheet should be designed to give you insights and answers. For example, you may be spending fifteen hours a week in meetings. Is this acceptable? You may be spending only one hour on physical exercise? You may be spending only one and a half hours on learning a new language when you originally planned to spend at least three hours each week? You may wonder if you are spending enough time with your family. You can add an item to track the time you spend with your family and, after a while, see the answer for yourself. If you only saw your family for five hours a week, would you be content, happy or sad?

In short, you should design your timesheet so that it can give you an insight into your own life—the kind of insight that you would need to have to achieve your goals.

It is up to you what system you want to use, but your time-keeping system must have the following qualities to remain useful:

- It must be very easy to use.
- It must be available wherever you are. This is why you cannot just rely on a system provided by your workplace that you can only use when you are at work.
- It should take very little time to use on daily basis.
- It should make you feel good when you are filling it with data, rather than making you feel it is a waste of time. Complicated software and tons of questions or details don't help.
- It must be forgiving when you forget for a day or two so you can go back and fill it in quickly.
- It should let you calculate weekly and monthly stats easily so that you can get an insight into your average behaviour.

Here is what you can do to create your own time-keeping system that follows the above principles. You can, of course, modify it as you see fit.

To create a timesheet, use a spreadsheet or a table. Use rows as dates and columns as activities/roles. Consider the following when creating one. These guidelines are very effective in maintaining a timesheet over a long period:

1. ***Choose a series of activities or roles.*** Choose these based on what you have already identified as part of your mission, roles and goals. These will end up forming your columns in the table.

a. ***Each column must be specific.*** You need to know exactly what area of your life it covers. To start with, focus on roles, as they provide a good list of areas of your life—for example, project management, website development, mountain climbing and learning Italian. You may also add activities so you can track them. Examples are email processing and marketing.

b. ***Minimise the number of your columns.*** While being specific, as above, you must aim to keep the total number of activities/roles to a minimum. The simpler the system, the more likely you are to use it and stay with it. This means you don't have to account for every minute of every day. Focus on areas that provide insight.

c. ***Ignore anything that is not a role or a useful activity to track.*** For example, you don't need to track the time you spend showering, eating, commuting, drinking coffee or socialising. When you track everything else, the rest of the time in a given day would be for such activities. These activities are necessary for a healthy life, and some are unavoidable (such as shaving). They don't deserve to be tracked, as the overhead of tracking is costly. Unless you have a good reason to track them (because you want to learn something about yourself), you can safely ignore such activities.

d. ***Include sports, as this is a critical area to track.*** Your energy and your health affect everything you do, so you cannot ignore them. You can consider combining all your sports activities into a single column. Only include a sport activity in a separate column when you are mastering a specific skill and want to track how much time you spent learning that particular sport.

e. ***Include your major hobbies.*** These are areas that you specifically spend time on for your pleasure or to enhance skills other than those related to work. For example, if you like to play music, define this as an item that captures any time you spend practising music.

2. ***For each item, record all time entries in hours.*** For example, record one hour and forty-five minutes as 1.75, as this will make calculations much easier. It is not essential to capture when during a day you do something. All you need to know is how much time you spend doing it. This makes timesheet keeping simpler.

3. ***Round all entries to the nearest fifteen minutes (0.25 hours).*** Smaller fractions are simply not worth the hassle to record and can discourage you from using the system.

4. ***Fill in your timesheet every day.*** This is crucial. Do not neglect this. Here is a test. Can you recall what you did this time last week? Probably not, and this is normal. As soon as you realise you are late in making a timesheet entry, make a note of it somewhere until you get a chance to fill in your main timesheet. It is amazing how easy it is to forget what you were doing yesterday, let alone a week before. This is, in fact, why you are keeping a timesheet in the first place. We are bad at it; that's why we need a tool.

The following is an example of a timesheet. It is useful to write a few words for each entry so that you know what the number of hours spent on refers to. This is also useful for not mixing it up by counting something twice. As for totals, it is up to you what you want to include in your calculations. You may want to consider adding up only the important roles and leaving out areas such as sports and hobbies so that you can have a meaningful weekly total that represents how much you have actually worked. Remember, the aim is *not* to maximise the working hours—only to maximise *achieving*. Don't fall for work for work's sake; just aim for results.

Exercise 10-1

Fill in a Timesheet

Create a timesheet as a spreadsheet since it makes calculations easier and automatic so you don't have to spend your precious time constantly adding things up. You can also consider using mobile apps or other software, as long as you can follow the above principles easily.

Example Timesheet

Date	Project Management	Time Spent on Project Management	Website Design	Time Spent on Website Design	Sport/ Exercise	Time Spent on Sport/ Exercise	Total Daily
1/1/2015	Resource management	2	Page designs	2	Gym	1	5
2/1/2015	Spreadsheet calculations	1	Google Analytics Implementation	4			5
3/1/2015	Gantt chart	4	Outsourcing visual design	1	Bouldering centre	2	7
4/1/2015	Dependency Graph	7					7
5/1/2015	New tech project	6			Gym	1	7
6/1/2015	Meeting	2	Analysis	2			4
7/1/2015	Dependency Graph	5	Writing articles	1	Mountain biking	3	9
Total Weekly							44

Timesheet

Date	Role/Activity 1	Time Spent on Role/Activity 1	Role/Activity 2	Time Spent on Role/Activity 2	Role/Activity 3	Time Spent on Role/Activity 3	Total Daily
						Total Weekly	

Exercise 10-2

Analyse your Timesheet

Once you have filled in your timesheet for about a month, go through the following analysis. Carry out this analysis on a quarterly basis, as regular monthly analysis can be overkill. Answer the questions, identify any actions you need to take and record them below.

Questions

Examine the total daily hours spent on all roles/activities. Are you happy with this total considering the rest of the time was spent mainly on unproductive and routine tasks?

Examine the proportion of time spent for each role in comparison with other roles. Are you happy with this time distribution?

Are you spending too much time in one area at the expense of another?

Are you spending too little time in an area that you'd like to spend more time on? Where can you find the time?

Is there an area that you consider significant and that you should be tracking which is not currently being tracked? If so, you will need to update your form for the next period.

Exercise 10-3

What Skills Do You Need?

You have already defined your roles and goals. To maintain a solid focus, you need to concentrate on the required skills for each role. This powerful exercise helps you recognise what you need to learn and which skills you need to focus on systematically. As this is an extensive exercise, ensure you allow enough time for completion and reflection.

PART1: Identify Skills

Your aim is to compile a complete list of skills that will help you perform better in your roles, achieve your goals and ultimately satisfy your mission statement.

Go through the following table while considering the final list of your automatic and non-automatic roles (*Exercise 9-1*). List your roles below. Place the most important roles at the top.

For each role, consider the goals you defined earlier in *Exercise 9-2*. Identify the skills required to help you achieve your immediate and mid-term goals. For example, for a role of "painter" and a mid-term goal of "learning to paint like an old master," you may consider the following skills:

- Colour mixing
- Drawing with pencil
- Glazing
- Composition
- Chiaroscuro

Equally, you may also have another role, such as "photographer" with a mid-term goal of "learning studio photography." Your skills might be listed as follows:

- Mastering the SLR camera
- Learning studio photography
- Directing the model
- Setting up studio lighting

Some skills might be common between two roles. This is fine; just include any skills as necessary.

Role (Ranked)	Skills (Include a comma-separated list)

PART 2: Rank Skills

Consider all skills in *Part 1*. Cross out any duplicate skills. Rank all skills based on their importance to you and the importance of the role in line with your mission statement. Simply go through the above table and place a number from 1 (most important) to N next to each skill shown in the right column in *Part 1*.

PART 3: Focus on the Most Important Skills

Having ranked the skills, the chances are that you are already thinking deeply about what you need to do. Have you ended up with a long list of skills? Do you feel overwhelmed by the challenge you have set for yourself? Does the list of skills excite you enough for you to put energy into mastering them? Do you understand the time requirement for each skill? This depends highly on how you have defined a given skill. If it is too generic, it will take years to master and is difficult to plan for at this level. For example, for a role such as "writer," it is better to put "learning to write a Sci-Fi," which is more specific, as opposed to "learning to write."

Review your skills, and use the table below to write a final ranked list. Your adjustments may also feed back to your role ranking, so you may need to review that list too (*Exercise 9-1, Part 5*).

ID	Skills (Ranked)	ID	Skills (Ranked)
1		11	
2		12	
3		13	
4		14	
5		15	
6		16	
7		17	
8		18	
9		19	
10		20	

Exercise 10-4

Choose Your Top Three Skills

If you remain aware of acquiring a given skill day and night, you will look for every opportunity to do something about it. This mindset will help you discover resources in the most unexpected places. To remain conscious of your skills, consider reminding yourself about the top three skills to focus on every week.

Here is what you need to do:

- On a weekly basis, have a look at your ranked skills list in *Exercise 10-3, Part 2*, and choose the top three skills to focus on during the following week.
- Think of actions you can take to improve yourself in those areas. What can you do? Where can you go? Who can you meet? What do you need to buy? What do you need to read?

Use the following form to record your thoughts and schedule any tasks.

Skill	Actions

Exercise 10-5

Find Your Ideal Role Models

First, transfer your revised ranked list of skills to the form below to prepare for this exercise. Next, for each skill, name a person who best represents that skill. This person will be your role model. For example, for oil painting, you may choose Peter Paul Rubens because you really like his style. You can name more than one person for each skill. They can be historical or contemporary figures, as long as plenty is known about them so you can learn something from your research.

Examine each role model one by one. To become the person who best represents that skill, what would you have to do? Write details on what it would take to learn that skill the same way your role model has done.

Here, you will focus only on the top ten skills. You don't want to get carried away with too much work that can come to undermine all skills. You need to maintain your focus, and this is your chance to make a decision on what you need to spend your time on. As you will periodically review your roles, goals and skills, you will get to update this list.

ID	Skills (Ranked)	Best represented by	What can be learned from the role model?
1			
2			
3			

ID	Skills (Ranked)	Best represented by	What can be learned from the role model?
4			
5			
6			
7			
8			
9			
10			

Exercise 10-6

What Can You Learn From the Masters?

Pick three skills that best represent you *right at this moment*. These capture what you are good at now.

Skill 1	Skill 2	Skill 3

Are you the most representative person for that skill? Answer yes or no.

If you answered no, identify the person who is the most representative for that skill.

This doesn't have to be the world's best in the area. Choose a person who is good at the skill and knows more about it than you do. You can also choose people from history as long as you know about them. For example, you may think that Henry Ford was a great example of a successful and inspiring manager.

Most Representative Person for Skill 1	Most Representative Person for Skill 2	Most Representative Person for Skill 3

Now identify what you can learn from each person in regard to each specific skill. Ultimately, you want to analyse and compare yourself with your ideal role model. The comparison can be quite inspiring and educational, guiding you forward.

What can you learn from the most representative person for skill 1?	
What can you learn from the most representative person for skill 2?	
What can you learn from the most representative person for skill 3?	

Identify a series of actions that will help you to become better than your role model in respect to your chosen skill. What would it take for you to become the most representative person for that skill? There is no reason that you cannot beat the master. It requires determination and persistence, but first you need to know what you are up against. This is your chance to identify the scale of the challenge. This will then help you identify the actions you need to take to outdo the master.

Actions to help you become most representative for skill 1	
Actions to help you become most representative for skill 2	
Actions to help you become most representative for skill 3	

Exercise 10-7

Identify What You Need to Do to Master Each Skill

Now that you have identified your most important skills, it is time to look at each one systematically and see what you need to consider to achieve it. Copy several blank forms using the following template. Use one form to examine each skill.

STEP 1	
Consider a skill from your Ranked Skills List as identified in *Part 3* of *Exercise 10-3*. Write it here.	

STEP 2		
Answer the following questions about this skill.		
What should you do to become excellent at this skill? Name three actions.	1	
	2	
	3	

When can you start each of the three activities identified above?	1	
	2	
	3	
What resources do you need for each of activity?	1	
	2	
	3	

11 Beware of the Skill Plateau

"I fear not the man who has practiced 10,000 kicks once, but I fear the man who has practiced one kick 10,000 times."

Bruce Lee

Let's imagine that you are learning to play badminton for the first time. You find a local club, buy a badminton racquet and join the club. Initially, you want to learn as much as you can. At the club, you are encouraged to play doubles with other players, and you are eager to copy them and learn. You focus on your serve, on where you stand in relation with your partner and on where you need to move to as the shuttle travels to various parts of the court. You probably get coached by some long-term club members who, as part of their efforts to welcome you to the club, feel the need to provide advice. You appreciate their coaching and learn quite a bit at this early stage.

You continue attending the club once or twice a week. Now that you have learned the basics, you start to enjoy the sport more and look forward to each session. You are eager to win the matches and feel you are becoming more competitive. You watch some videos online and get the latest issue of a popular badminton magazine.

As is the case with many badminton clubs, the members in your club are divided into groups based on their skill levels. Having played in the beginners group, you are now eager to move on to the intermediate level. When you watch an intermediate game, you think it is more fun than playing in your beginners group against other newbies.

So far, you have been focusing on learning extensively. You have assessed yourself and put effort into improving your game. You have worked on specific moves, such as serving, sometimes even on your own, so you can play a better game next time around. Long-term members have proved to be very helpful in guiding you, which is why you really feel you have a chance of getting to the intermediate level. You have progressed significantly since your first game only a few months ago.

So far so good.

Eventually, you manage to move up to the intermediate level and get to play against more experienced players. Initially, you feel pushed to your limit. Your aim is to prove that you do deserve to be part of this more advanced group of players. You don't want to be demoted to the beginners group. Since badminton club games are played in doubles, if you are not at a similar level to your partner, no one will be interested in playing with you because they are more likely to lose.

The pressure leads to more focused practice, and you eventually learn enough to play at a similar level to others. At this point, when beginners join the club, you start to feel like an old-timer who is already at a higher level and who has better skills.

You are now enjoying your game. You look forward to the club sessions because they are fun, and there is a social element to them as well. By now, you know many regulars and have become friends with some. You even take pleasure in giving tips to new players, taking on the role of a teacher.

Your focus is now gradually shifting to enjoying every game you play. When you play a game where both sides are equally skilled, you think you had one of the best games ever. The long rallies, strategies and counter-strategies are all very thrilling.

In short, in each game, you think less about the game itself and more about enjoyment. Occasionally, you may concentrate on your serve or a particular shot, but it is no longer a focus. In fact, you are more likely to get frustrated when you cannot do what you have done before.

From this point onwards, any additional time you spend on the court will not substantially improve your performance. You may remain at the same level for decades!

Does this sound familiar? Why would this happen?

When you have become established at an intermediate level, you are just playing a game. You are not practising hitting the shuttle from the same awkward location over and over again to get it absolutely right. No one stands to watch your whole game to give you advice on your posture or how you hold your racquet when hitting the shuttle. In fact, you might have alienated some members and discouraged them from advising you because you no longer want to be treated as a beginner. Your mannerism tells other players that you don't need to be told how to do something; your ego gets in the way. Others naturally stop giving tips. You have now stopped learning and are just there to enjoy what you already know.

You may still desire to get better at badminton, but you may not realise that you have stopped progressing at the skill. You may not see that you are slowing down. Here are a number of common questions people ask themselves when they are frustrated with their progress:

- "Others tend to learn faster, memorise faster and remember longer than me. Why?"
- "How come others have learned so much in a short time and I am still not very good after all these years?"
- "Why don't I learn?"
- "Why do I find learning difficult?"
- "Why do I tend to get excited, start something and then quit halfway?"
- "I don't get much out of training courses, and I wonder if I am the only one?"
- "Do I need to attend some training courses to learn something because I cannot learn anything on my own?"

If this is you, you have reached a *plateau* that you may have difficulty leaving. Reaching such skill plateaus is extremely common. Think about the skills you have already acquired, especially those that you are not spending much time on these days. On the other hand, some people seem to cruise along and reach much higher skill levels more quickly than you do. This is quite frustrating, as it can make you feel inferior. The solution is actually quite simple in principle, but before exploring the solution, it is useful to carry out some self-analysis.

Exercise 11-1

Do You Have Any Skill Plateaus?

Based on the example about learning badminton, think of your various skills to see in which areas you are progressing well and in which areas you have reached a plateau. Focus on those skills that are important in line with your mission and goals. Use the form below for analysis.

Current Skill	How proficient are you in this skill? 1: Beginner 2: Intermediate 3: Advanced 4: Professional 5: Renowned expert	How long have you been at this skill level? A few weeks A few months About a year A few years	Have you reached a skill plateau? (Yes/No)	Do you want to leave this skill plateau to achieve a higher level given your goals? (Yes/No)

11.1 The Gap of Disappointment

You may have situations in which you feel that no matter how much effort you put into learning a new skill, you don't get good results. This can be frustrating, and you may wrongly conclude that you are not good enough to learn that specific skill.

It is actually quite natural to feel frustrated at some point during the learning process. Let's illustrate how this pattern works using the following graph.

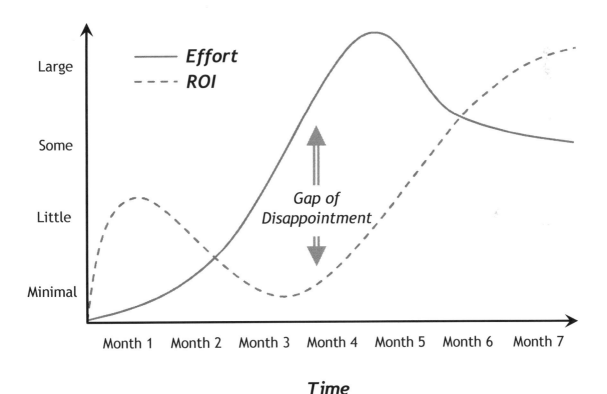

Two curves are shown on this graph over time. One is *effort* and the other is *Return on Investment* (ROI). ROI is a common term used in business, and it often refers to the amount of money that can be made from an investment. You can also use ROI for any other resource, such as your time. For learning, ROI can represent the results you achieve per unit of time spent on learning a new skill.

Let's walk through the graph. You start by putting effort into a new skill, such as drawing or painting. As you are focused on learning this new skill, you immediately start to get results. Hence, your ROI increases rapidly. You paint a face that is fairly convincing. A few weeks ago, you couldn't draw any better than a five-year-old. You are happy. You can feel that you are progressing quickly, and so you put more effort into learning more.

So far so good.

As you put in more effort, you become more skilled. After a couple of months, you are no longer a beginner; perhaps you have reached the intermediate level. At this point, you start to see the extent of the skill. You now realise that it is actually much more difficult to become a master than you originally thought. You now appreciate what it takes to be good at painting. You start to understand what other artists have created with their high-level skills throughout history and how difficult it is to produce something similar. In fact, it starts to feel a little bit overwhelming. You decide to achieve a certain effect in your painting, but you fail. You try various methods to get it right, but you still struggle. You are putting more effort, but you are not necessarily getting immediate results. Your ROI starts to drop.

At this point, you may start to feel that the more effort you put in, the less results you are getting. This is the so-called *gap of disappointment*, and it is in this particular phase that many people feel very frustrated. The disappointment can eventually lead to getting stuck at this skill plateau and never achieving high-level expertise. Some even quit at this point.

Several factors lead to the gap of disappointment:

- *Impatience about learning and wanting immediate results.* This can be because of that initial high ROI, which can make you think that you will always get the same level of return as you put more effort in.
- *Delay in getting results.* With some skills, effort doesn't necessarily lead to immediate results. You have to be patient until you can see measurable results. A prime example for this is bodybuilding or losing weight. Due to the nature of the human body, you may not see observable results, such as a toned body or a smaller stomach, even though your sustained efforts to diet and exercise would have already helped to burn a lot of fat somewhere. You cannot see the results, yet you need to put more effort into it. It means you need to remain patient and focused and simply persevere.
- *Treating learning a skill as a "tickable" task.* Another wrong belief is that some people think that once they have learned about a particular area for a given skill, they can completely leave it and move on to something else. Hence, they only focus on learning about new areas within that skill. What they forget is that they still need to spend effort *maintaining* what they have already learned. This leads to

disappointment as they think that they are not getting enough return for their increasing efforts.

Continuing with the graph, as you stay focused and put more effort into mastering a given skill, there eventually comes a time when your efforts peak. After this, you start to see higher and higher ROI until both your efforts and ROI stabilise at a certain level. By this point, you are well established with the new skill. You don't have to put tons of effort into it all the time. It comes naturally to you, as it has become routine.

Managing what happens during the gap of disappointment is the key to overcoming your frustration and reaching a higher level of productivity and satisfaction. What happens during the gap of disappointment can also be related to your expectations. Consider the popular wisdom that "the secret to happiness is to have low expectations." The logic is that since you don't expect too much, then you won't be disappointed when things don't work out well. People are expected to lower their expectations to increase their happiness. Unfortunately, this logic is flawed; research consistently shows that people with higher expectations are generally happier irrespective of their success.

Here is an example study. Psychologists Margaret Marshall and Jonathon Brown asked students to guess their grade in a midterm exam (Marshall & Brown 2006). This is what they observed; those students who expected an A but got a C were naturally surprised. However, in comparison with those who expected a C and got a C, they did not feel any worse. This is because the two groups arrived at different conclusions. The group of students who expected an A but got a C concluded that they would need to put make effort next time to get the A they want. Regarding the group members who expected a C and got a C, it just reinforced their belief about their lower abilities in the subject; they were just not good enough at this, and here was their confirmation. Interestingly, this reaction was similar to another group. Those who expected an A and got an A also reinforced their belief about themselves; they were clever, and this is why they got an A. Some students who expected lower grades but got an A attributed the result to luck.

In principle, people with higher expectations are generally happier no matter what they achieve.

11.2 Self-Fulfilling Prophecies

Psychologist Sara Bengtsson carried out some amazing research (Bengtsson *et al.* 2011). Each one of the twenty-one healthy participants in the research was given a series of scrambled sentences one at a time. Each sentence consisted of six words, and participants had to judge whether the words could be arranged into a grammatically correct sentence. There was, however, a twist as participants analysed the set of words one after another. Each set of words was chosen based on a specific condition and directly related to it. The conditions were "clever", "stupid", "happy", "sad" and "neutral". For example, the six words chosen for "clever" were: "the brightest nothing idea everything promoted." The six words chosen for "stupid" were: "welcome not morons one are here."

Therefore the subjects were primed as "clever", "stupid", etc. and some were left as neutral to act as a control group. Interestingly, the researchers also used an MRI to scan the participants' brain activity while they went through the task.

What the researchers found was quite fascinating. The results showed that those who were primed as "clever" were more successful than those who were primed as "stupid." Those who were primed as "clever" spent more time checking for errors while analysing a given sentence, while those who were primed as "stupid" spent less time. In other words, being primed as "clever" evokes a number of self-concept associations, such as competent, bright and skilled. Once self-concept was affected, people reacted differently to their own behaviour. Those who were primed as "stupid" triggered associations, such as inefficient and forgetful, which, in turn, reduced their performance on the task.

This, as well as other research in this area, has led to profound insight. People who are made to think that they are doing well are more likely to learn from their mistakes and subsequently do better. Those who are convinced that they are likely to fail are less interested in learning from their mistakes and are, hence, more likely to fail. People's beliefs in their own abilities lead to self-fulfilling prophecies that confirm their original beliefs.

If you relate this principle to expectations, you can see why you gain tremendously by having positive beliefs about yourself and your capability to achieve more.

In short, higher expectations suggest that you have what it takes to achieve the expectation. This, in turn, creates a positive self-fulfilling prophecy that makes you more capable until you achieve your higher expectations.

The key to our well-being and happiness is not to have low expectations or take anything negative and unexpected as simple bad luck. Instead, it is about our ability to take an unexpected negative outcome and learn from it so that we can do better next time.

11.3 What Is the Right Kind of Practice?

Let's go back to the example of playing badminton. To move on from a given skill plateau, you will need to focus on practising more; but what kind of practice do you need to engage in?

What is missing, and what is stopping you from progressing, is a lack of effort. You are attending the club to have a good time; you are no longer eager to get out of your comfort zone and to put effort into learning new skills. Effortful practice would allow you to get feedback about specific areas of your game in order to improve them. This is the essence of *deliberate practice* that is required for the mastery of any skill. Deliberate practice involves two kinds of learning:

- Improving skills that you already have
- Extending your skill set

By constantly focusing on both, you can maximise your chances of success. Deliberate practice is an incredibly important topic when it comes to learning how to succeed. This topic is explored further in the next chapter.

Before moving on, let's review the list of skills you have identified earlier, and based on what you have learned in this chapter, let's examine what you can do to improve each specific skill.

234 ◆ Chapter 11: Beware of the Skill Plateau

Exercise 11-2

Define Actions to Leave a Given Skill Plateau

From the list of skills identified in *Exercise 10-3*, select those that you think you are stagnating in but wish to move up from the skill plateau. Write the skills below, and then based on what you have learned in this chapter, specify what you need to do to move on.

Current skill that you want to improve on	What should you consider doing to leave the skill plateau?

12 Practise Deliberately

"It is only human nature to want to practice what you can already do well, since it's a hell of a lot less work and a hell of a lot more fun."

Golf champion Sam Snead

"I am always doing that which I cannot do, in order that I may learn how to do it."

Pablo Picasso

"Do one thing every day that scares you."

Eleanor Roosevelt

In 1453, after a seven-week siege, Constantinople (present-day Istanbul), the capital of the Eastern Roman Empire, fell to the invading Ottoman Empire. Sultan Mehmed II conquered the city, and thus marked the end of an era for the Roman Empire, which had been in existence for 1,500 years. Historically, the event turned out to be a significant one which affected Europe and the world in many ways. Constantinople was the heart of Christendom, as established by Constantinople in 500 AD. Its capture had an immediate and major effect on the people and political powers in the area. The Ottomans could now expand more freely without expecting much resistance. Sultan Mehmed II decided to declare the city the capital of the Ottoman Empire. This was indeed bad news for many of the intellectuals living in the great capital. Many of them were Greek intellectuals who feared what the new invaders had planned for them. As a result, they fled the city before and after the siege, most of them leaving to settle in Italy. This led to a great cultural movement across Europe—a movement we now recognise as the *Renaissance*, which is a French word meaning "rebirth."

The Renaissance started in Florence, Italy. In contrast with the past, when scholars were more interested in studying Greek and Arab works on mathematics, the natural sciences and philosophy, the new Renaissance scholars were more interested in cultural texts from ancient Greece and ancient Rome.

Interestingly, the new breed of scholars did not reject Christianity. In fact, they embraced and devoted some of their greatest works to it. The church patronised many works during the Renaissance. The church needed to spread its message of Christianity to all corners of the world. Similar to modern-day mass-marketing techniques, the church needed engaging and effective works of art. As European trade expanded into the Eastern world and luxuries were brought back by the crusades, money became more available to merchants and patrons, including the church. In Florence, some merchants, such as the Medici family, became ever more powerful and rich. With their interest in art, the Medici supported many young artists.

In this new world, money and art went hand in hand. The artists depended on patrons to support their living, and the patrons needed money to support the artists as they could then use the art for their political gain or as marketing resources for the church. This led to a major trend, whereby art flourished and many great artists emerged. Among them were the likes of Da Vinci, Michelangelo, Rafael and Botticelli. The new cultural movement spread slowly, and soon, the Netherlands started to go through a vibrant artistic movement which led to major inventions in art techniques and materials. Jan van Eyck had a great influence on the development and spread of oil painting on canvas, which eventually came to dominate painting as the medium of choice for centuries to come.

To become an artist, a student had to go through a particular style of training which is now known as the *atelier method*. Atelier is French for "workshop." Students would become apprentices at an early age—about twelve. They would then learn the skills from a master by copying him and getting guidance on how to approach the "craft" of painting. They would also help the master with day-to-day activities in the studio, such as preparing paint, which was a tedious process. Each morning, the apprentices had to grind pigment powders and then mix them with various oils and mediums, pass the mixture through a sieve and continue the process several times until it was ready for the master to use. In the process, the apprentices would learn the ins and outs of how to create a painting or sculpture. They were fully immersed in that world and had access to a mentor for guidance.

From the 17th century, academies started to flourish in France. These places were primarily founded to distinguish art from manual labour and to define an artist as a "gentleman practicing a liberal art" rather than just a craftsman. In 1803, under Napoleon's rule, academies were classified into four categories to cover all subjects, and one of these was the *académie des beaux-arts.* Beaux-arts is French for "fine arts." This model, which was used to train artists, proved to be very effective, and it soon spread across Europe. Academies organised official exhibitions called *salons,* which became an aspiration for many artists. Their works could be seen by a large number of visitors, and the resulting fame could come to financially support their lives. As a result, by the 18th century, the centre of art activity had moved to France. Many new artistic talents emerged, and some became famous worldwide. The quality of their work was comparable to that of the old masters.

Since the Renaissance, and for the past 500 years, European artists have been busy producing some of the world's most famous paintings, sculptures and artwork. The great masters produced stunning works of art that are universally admired today. Anyone who looks at Rembrandt, Vermeer, Bouguereau or Jean-Léon Gérôme can easily see the significance of their work.

What was the secret to their success? Why did the model used by the French academies prove to be so effective? What did it take to become an expert? Is it that the students were gifted and had some innate talent, or was it something else? Did they just start painting and producing masterpieces, or did they also need to practise their craft and skill? Fortunately, finding the answer is rather easy. We just have to look to see what they went through.

French academic art is very inspiring. It was based on classical approaches to art, much like those used during the Renaissance, and it helps us to understand what it takes to become a master in a given skill. The core idea of the training was based on *systematic progression.* Becoming an artist or a painter was much like becoming a craftsman before focusing on the creative aspects of art. It was critical for a good artist to know how to draw well and develop an eye for details in an incredibly systematic way before focusing on the "liberal art" aspect.

If you wanted to become an academician artist, this is what you had to go through. First, to get into an art academy, you had to develop a portfolio that showed off your skills and initial interest in the subject. You had to be able to convince the academy that you had enough interest in the craft to be worthy of attending the academy.

After being accepted into the academy, you had to learn how to draw. Initially, you would be allowed to draw in black only. You would not be allowed to go anywhere near colour or, for that matter, even paint for a couple of years. Using pencil, you had to draw from still life in studio conditions. You would place an object inside a black box with fixed unchanging light, such as an overcast light coming from a north window or from a candle. You would then spend the next month drawing this object in as much detail as you could. The aim was to be representational. You had to learn what nature looked like and be able to depict it as accurately as possible using methods such as the "sight-size" technique. You would then repeat this process using more complex objects, such as plaster casts which were made specifically for training and were often made out of the works of famous sculptures. You would practise drawing lips, ears, hands, feet and heads. The advantage was that the casts remained still, and the lighting and shadows could be controlled to enable you to focus independently on each aspect of the drawing skill.

Each work had to be signed off on by an academician before you could move on to the next stage. This is, in fact, the essence of systematic progression. Once you mastered drawing using a variety of techniques, such as comparative measurement or sight-size, you would be allowed to start using charcoal. Once mastered, you would then be allowed to paint a cast in black and white only. A few months later, you would be allowed to introduce a third colour, such as brown, so that you could start learning about colour temperature. After being signed off on that, you would move on to use more colours, albeit still using a fairly limited palette.

Up until this point, you would not have been allowed to draw a real model. You had to master drawing and develop an eye for detail before you could draw the complex shapes and tones of the human skin. Having gone through the rigorous training for two or three years with a fair amount of academic criticism, you would have developed an eye for details. By this point, you would not even need to use the initial systematic methods to draw because you would have trained so much that you could draw more quickly and easily. You would be ready to move on to the next level—drawing a live human model.

Here, the approach was systematic too, as you had to start focusing on just pencil drawing, then charcoal, then black and white painting and, eventually, full colour painting. By now, you had drawn so many times that you had developed a pattern of what to expect when drawing a human. You knew the pattern of how the elbow rested next to the hip while standing and knew that hands were much bigger than we expected and that our brains are fooled by what we want to see rather than letting us make accurate observations in nature. Having mastered the craft, you could now express your personal style and creativity in any direction you wanted. Indeed, students of such ateliers, such as Delacroix, Ingres and Jacques-Louis David, expressed a great amount of creativity and led the art world with their work. Even many of the impressionist artists who kick-started the modern art movement went to the very same academies, where they mastered their skills.

This is what it takes to become an expert. It doesn't come out of nothing. No one is born with some innate gift that enables him to draw. You learn to draw, and learning requires persistence, passion and hard work. With training and hard work, you aim to rewire your brain. With passion, you persevere to rewire it. Once you have "programmed" your brain, you become unique and special. You are then seen as "gifted" because you know how to go about a craft much more quickly and easily than the average person could. Along with your passion, accumulated life experiences and unique interests, this "gift" (read "programmed brain") can lead you to produce major work that can be admired for many years to come and can even outlast you.

In previous chapters, you identified your mission, roles and goals. Next, you identified what skills you needed to focus on to achieve your objective within each role. Learning a skill requires practice, but what does it really mean to practise? What does it mean to undergo systematic training? It turns out that not all training styles are effective; in fact, many are useless. How can you make sure that the training you choose will be effective and will utilise the least amount of your time to learn something well? What principle will give the most ROI? It is, in fact, fascinating to see what happens to our brains as we undergo systematic training. In this chapter, you will be introduced to such studies and will see what is required to become the master of any skill.

12.1 How Memory Works

You are a high school student, and you have an important physiology test at the end of the month. You need to learn how the human body works. You are a businessman who needs to give a presentation on the technical aspects of your company's latest product. You need to provide a long list of features, making sure that they are compared positively with the competition. You are a bus driver, and you need to learn a new route and ensure that you never miss a single stop. You are a historian who is interested in learning about the Napoleonic Wars so that you can give a lecture on this topic. In all of these seemingly unrelated examples, the best way to learn quickly is to memorise. A good memory is so impressive and influential that we have learned to consider anyone who demonstrates good memory as someone who is intelligent. The obvious benefit of having a good memory is that your ability to recall something quickly or a sequence of activities accurately will allow you to get things done more quickly. In many cases, a good memory also helps you solve problems creatively by simply enabling you to be more aware of related topics and ideas.

Let's see how the brain handles memorisation at the cellular level. We know that learning takes place when new connections are made between brain cells. But exactly how does this work? It is rather fascinating.

Studies by researchers such as Dr. Joe Tsien show that special communication channels in our brains—nerve cells called NMDA—can facilitate the process of learning (Li & Tsien 2009). When a nerve signal passes from one cell to another, a "receipt" is sent back to acknowledge that the signal has been received. This receipt is picked up by other nearby nerve cells that were firing at the same time.

The mechanism of exactly how this works in practice was presented by Prof. Aryeh Routtenberg. When a nerve signal crosses the gap between two nerve cells, a "receipt" molecule is sent back by NMDA receptors to acknowledge it. The receipt molecule activates certain proteins, known as GAP-43, which, in turn, make it easier for the next signal to pass through (Holahan *et al.* 2007).

So what does all this lead to? It means that the more you repeat and the more you fire specific neurons, the easier it gets for the signal to pass through and create a better connection. This leads to the ultimate magic—*the more you repeat, the easier it is to learn*. Research by other neuroscientists confirms that continuous repetition leads to a fundamental change at the neural level in our brains.

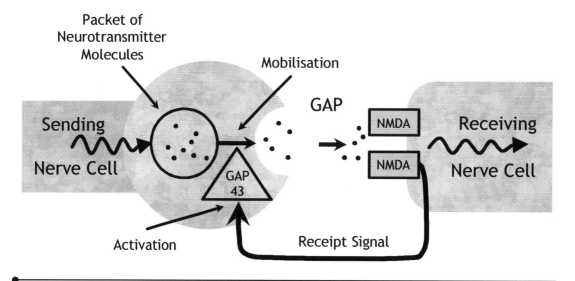

However, not all repetitions work, and there is a particular pattern that is most effective. This is known as *spaced repetition*. Let's see what this is.

12.2 *What is Spaced Repetition?*

In spaced repetition, you have increasing intervals of time in between learning attempts. Each learning attempt fires the appropriate neural connections and makes them stronger. The technique also relies on what is known as the *spacing effect* in psychology; we learn a list much better if we repeatedly study it over a long period as opposed to a short period.

There is an interesting explanation for this; it is known as the *deficient processing view*. It suggests that short-term repetition is not as effective because we get bored while going through the same exact material repeatedly over a short amount of time and hence pay less and less attention to it. There is also minimal variation in the way in which the material is presented to the brain when it is repeatedly visited over a short time. This tends to decrease our learning. In contrast, when repetition learning takes place over a longer period, it is more likely that the materials are presented differently. We have to retrieve the previously learned material from memory and hence reinforce it. All of this leads us to become more interested in the content and, therefore, more receptive to learning it.

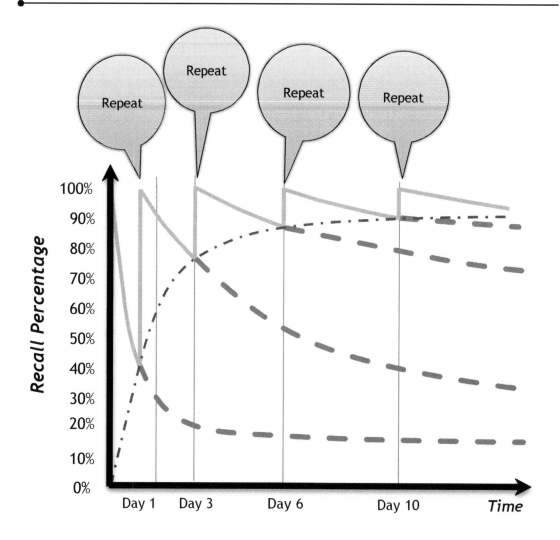

12.3 The Great Brain Transformation

You have seen how powerful spaced repetition is. It gets even more interesting. It has long been believed that people who are exceptionally good at a particular skill are good at it simply because they are gifted in one way or another and their skills cannot be topped by mere ordinary men. This belief is so strong that, even today, many people still think it is true.

However, research conducted in the past thirty years has changed our view of mastery forever. This research has been captured in several popular science books promoting new insights and shedding more light on this fascinating topic. Why do some people go on to become elite while others do not (Greene 2012)?

The research on mastery is, of course, highly related to what we now understand about how our brains work. In cognitive science, two contrasting terminologies are used to describe the processes within the brain (Goleman 2013):

- *Top-down.* This refers to mental activity which is carried out mainly within the neocortex, which is located at the top and front of the brain. It can monitor or impose on subcortical activity. It deals with voluntary, effortful behaviour. It has control over automatic behaviour, can learn new models of the world and makes new plans. It is responsible for willpower and intentional choice. From an evolutionary standpoint, this is a fairly new addition to the brain; it took place about 100,000 years ago.

- *Bottom-up.* The lower part of the neural machinery, which is located right at the top of the spinal cord, deals mainly with routine; involuntary, automatic and emotional behaviour; and as our mental model of the world. It is fast in brain time, operating in milliseconds. This is a much older part of the brain, and it has evolved for our basic survival.

On balance, the brain prefers to go through its cognitive effort using the bottom-up approach, and it does this for a good reason; it costs more energy to use the top-down approach. As you go through a routine several times, some parts of the brain (in particular, the basal ganglia) start to take over the task from other parts. This then helps the brain to spend minimal effort and energy to achieve the same result. As we practise more, the routine requires less and less effort. It becomes more automatic until its takes no effort at all, much like riding a bike or hitting tennis balls with a racquet. Once you have practised it countless times, you may even remain oblivious to the effort that goes into hitting that tennis ball. You will then be able to focus on other aspects of the tennis game you are playing, such as which direction to hit the ball based on your strategy and guessing what your opponent will do as a result.

Learning requires you to practise enough that rather than using your top-down approach, you can utilise the bottom-up approach, which is much faster and takes less effort. To master something, you need to have practised a task so many times that your basal ganglia starts to take over and carry out the task in routine mode. While faster to execute, this will also free up top-down thinking and allow you to carry out additional analysis. This is why there is a fundamental physical difference between the brain of a master who has gone through extensive practice in a specific area and that of an enthusiast who is still learning and must think about every step of the way. This is why it is very

244 ◆ Chapter 12: Practise Deliberately

difficult to compete with a master without having gone through a similar extensive training experience. Another way to look at this is that once you have reached the mastery level, you become irreplaceable.

This is also why you can't cheat your own brain. Utilising the bottom-up approach and freeing up the top-down approach takes a specific amount of sustained deliberate practice over a long period.

Deliberate practice means spending countless hours on a single skill with the aim of improving it. It is this constant improvement that leads to mastery. You may wonder what "countless" and "deliberate practice" mean. Let's look at some examples.

William-Adolphe Bouguereau was a popular artist in the 19th century. His figurative paintings of classical subjects and his emphasis on the female human body proved to be popular. He became the quintessential salon painter of his generation. At the time, the salons attracted a crowd of 300,000 people a year, and Bouguereau soon became well known all over the world. His artwork was sought after by collectors in Europe and America. He was considered one of the greatest painters in the world by the art community too. He was indeed a master of the art.

At a late stage in his life, and after a successful career, Bouguereau described his love of art:

> "Each day I go to my studio full of joy; in the evening when obliged to stop because of darkness I can scarcely wait for the next morning to come . . . If I cannot give myself to my dear painting I am miserable.
>
> I fill every moment with painting, with painting furiously. First of all because that is what I love—and then just look at my white hair. At my age it gives pause for thought, and *an hour lost can never be recovered*. Look at these portfolios filled with sketches and drawings. Perhaps I would need more years than I have left to live. As soon as I finish painting I know which portfolio contains such and such a sketch, and I start on a new canvas."

Bouguereau painted 826 paintings in his lifetime, making him one of the most prolific academic artists. He did this in addition to all the administrative duties of the various offices he held along with being a professor at Ecole des Beaux Arts, the most famous French art academy. Bouguereau was one of the academy's longest-serving members, and in 1885, he served as the president of the institute.

You don't even have to go that far in the past to find such masters. Great contemporary artists have a similar level of passion. Consider Boris Vallejo with his amazing fantasy paintings. In one of his books, he describes his obsession with painting when he was in his twenties. After a full day of work, and just before going to bed, he would place his half-finished painting next to his bed so that when he woke up the next day, the first thing he would see would be his painting. He could then get up and work on it straight away.

The secret to mastery, success and the subsequent happiness that comes as a result is *focused determination*.

12.4 What Does It Take to Become an Expert?

Determination must be guided. Much like how a lens focuses light in a specific direction, your determination must be focused too. It is this intense, focused determination that leads to real expertise. Perhaps one of the best places to look for insight on expertise is the work of K. Anders Ericsson, a Swedish psychologist who is widely recognised as one of the world's leading researchers on this subject.

Ericsson has summarised this research, including contributions from more than 100 scientists, in a 900-page handbook called *The Cambridge Handbook of Expertise and Expert Performance* (Ericsson *et al.* 2006).

The following are a number of critical highlights and conclusions from this volume of amazing research on what makes a person an expert. The highlights can help you improve your learning and help you see why your own style might not work as well as you hope.

12.4.1 There Is No Correlation between IQ and Expertise

The research shows that there is no correlation between IQ and expert performance in fields such as medicine, sports, chess, music and many others.

For sports, the only innate differences that may be significant are body size, height and, to a certain degree, date of birth. For more on this, see *Outliers* by Malcolm Gladwell and his great stories on how date of birth can influence a sportsman's performance (Gladwell 2009).

12.4.2 Experts Are Always Made, Not Born

All related studies indicate conclusively that all the great performers who were investigated for the research practised intensely, were supported and coached by informed teachers and had enthusiastic families for many years while developing their skills.

12.4.3 Learning Must Be Measured

The British scientist Lord Kelvin famously stated that, "If you cannot measure it, you cannot improve it." This is why you need to have SMART goals and, of course, a timesheet.

12.4.4 Practise Deliberately

Not all practice is the same. You need a particular kind of practice, which is known as deliberate practice. Most people practise by focusing on things they already know. This kind of practice won't help you become an expert, because you are not challenged. Deliberate practice, in contrast, is sustained, specific and concentrated practice on something you cannot do well or at all. In short, deliberate practice is high-concentration practice *beyond one's comfort zone*.

12.4.5 There Are No Shortcuts

To become a genuine expert, you need to struggle, sacrifice and engage in honest and sometimes painful self-assessment.

You will need to practise those tasks that are beyond your current level of comfort and competence.

12.4.6 You Don't Need a Different Brush

Many people hope that they can suddenly improve their performance by using better methods or better tools. They think that if they just had a better brush or canvas, they could do a better painting. They think if they had a better racquet, they could ace every game.

Changing tools can actually reduce performance, as you then need to get used to the new tool. Having obtained better tools, if you still fail, you have no other conclusion than to think that you just don't have what it takes.

In reality, the key to improved performance is careful, consistent and deliberate effort. You might be better off investing in training materials and accessing mentors and coaches than worrying about tools. In due course, you will get to update your tools when you know what difference they make after having practised with the ones you already have.

12.4.7 It Takes More than a Decade to Become a True Expert

Research on exceptional performance shows that to become an expert in a domain, you need about ten years of sustained effort. This applies to a wide range of domains and is observed in expert musicians, scientists, chess players, poets, mathematicians, swimmers, tennis players and several other domains (K. Ericsson *et al.* 1993).

Research also shows that, on average, there is about a ten-year gap between when a scientist or author publishes his first work and when he publishes his greatest work.

12.4.8   You Need 10,000 Hours of Practice to Become an Exceptional Expert

Further research, as noted by Ericsson, suggests that to achieve exceptional expertise, you need to spend about 10,000 hours of effortful practice to master a subject.

These 10,000 hours go hand in hand with the observation that it takes a decade to master a topic. The idea of practising for 10,000 hours is widely circulated in blogs and recited almost religiously in training courses, but unfortunately, a critical part of it is left out. Not any 10,000 hours will make you an expert.

First, there is the matter of pace. As you have already seen, there are no shortcuts with the brain. You must practise regularly, over a long period and with high concentration and focus to master a skill. You are aiming to rewire your brain to utilise the bottom-up instead of the top-down approach. Packing in sixteen hours a day every day of the week to quickly get to the 10,000 is not necessarily a wise move. The problem is that this level of work gets tiring, and the quality of the practice and concentration drops over time due to the extensive and potentially boring repetition of various activities. This reduced concentration means that you may no longer be practising at a level which places you out of your comfort zone. It means you may not be exploring new ways of approaching a problem and might simply be following a habit. In other words, you are not rewiring your brain at all.

The 10,000 hours are not the time spent on a topic by just being there to clock in and clock out. You need smart practice, which always includes a *feedback loop.* You must be able to assess your performance, compare it with a well-defined ideal and take actions to improve yourself so you can reach this ideal. Without this feedback loop, hours spent on a given skill cannot be counted towards your 10,000-hour target.

Here are some examples of how a feedback loop is established:

- Just about all world-class sports champions use coaches. For example, a tennis coach can observe a tennis player and provide invaluable feedback on posture, movement and placement on the court.
- A ballet dancer practises in front of mirrors, constantly seeing herself and comparing what she sees to how she ought to be seen.

- A world-class windsurfer gets help from a coach or a friend by getting filmed while performing various moves. By reviewing his posture, position and direction in relation to wind, the board and the sail, he can improve his skills.
- A stand-up comedian measures his performance based on the laughter he receives. If no one is laughing, he has not been funny enough for his audience and should move on to a different topic. Audience laughter provides him with invaluable feedback on what works and what doesn't.

Learning a new skill requires a top-down approach by the brain, as well as focus and concentration. Concentration is critical, as it enables the brain to rewire the bottom-up circuitry to turn a learned skill into a routine one. Hence, if you do several unrelated things at the same time, your time spent cannot be counted towards the 10,000 hours. If you are browsing TV while working out, you will simply not be pushing hard enough, as you will be distracted.

Recall the example of the badminton player who was stuck at the intermediate level. This also explains why the badminton player reached a skill plateau. After about fifty hours of training—whether badminton, skiing or kayaking—many people achieve a satisfactory performance, which is enough for them to be able to go through the motions routinely and without much thinking. From this point onwards, they may no longer feel the need to focus and instead want to "enjoy" the newly acquired hobby that is now easy for them. From this point onwards, it doesn't matter how many more hours they put in, because the time will be mainly spent using the bottom-up approach. Learning will be minimal, because practising is not carried out by the top-down approach to rewire the brain. This is what differentiates amateurs who are stuck at a certain level from experts who constantly improve.

Once you have gone through 10,000 hours of concentrated smart practice, you are likely to have made many related skills into a routine. Rather than the top-down approach, the brain can now use the bottom-up approach for a variety of required skills while freeing up the top-down planner brain to focus on much higher-level tasks. It is then that such a brain becomes an asset because it has become supremely skilled in a given area. It can process information with extraordinary creativity and speed while still having enough capacity to carry out additional higher-level thinking with the top-down brain. Naturally, the society will honour such a brain and will credit the person accordingly with attention, prestige, wealth and immortality.

To succeed, consider the following simple and practical plan. Spend two hours a day engaged in smart practice for a total of 700 hours a year. In a decade, you will have clocked 7,000 hours. If the two hours a day is effortful, taking you out of your comfort zone, a decade will get you very nearly there.

12.4.9 Intuition and Gut Feeling Come After Expertise, Not Before

Some think that performance can be improved by relaxation or by just "trusting your gut feelings." It is certainly true that intuition can be valuable in certain situations. However, intuition can be formed *as a result of* deliberate practice—not the other way around. You cannot improve yourself by intuition without any considerable practice on a given task.

12.4.10 Use Your Head

Focused concentration makes all the difference. If you are not mentally engaged in an activity and are not constantly thinking about ways to improve your performance, you will not achieve much.

The famous violinist Nathan Milstein wrote the following:

> "Practice as much as you feel you can accomplish with concentration. Once when I became concerned because others around me practiced all day long, I asked [my mentor] Professor Auer how many hours I should practice, and he said, 'It really doesn't matter how long. If you practice with your fingers, no amount is enough. If you practice with your head, two hours is plenty.'"

12.4.11 Find the Right Coach and Mentor

Having coaches and mentors can make a huge difference in a number of ways:

- A coach can accelerate your learning process by providing you with direct, customised feedback.
- A coach can introduce you to new directions, tools or methods that you may not be aware of or that will take you longer to come across on your own.
- The best coaches can identify areas of your performance that need to be improved and provide advice to get you to the next level. A bad coach is one who could push you too hard when you are not ready for the next level, thereby putting you off practising altogether. You will need to avoid such coaches and look elsewhere for better ones. To be placed outside of your comfort zone is one thing, but being put off by humiliation due to a lack of skills is another.
- A good coach is not there just to tell you that you are doing well. A good coach should help you rewire your brain by helping you challenge yourself systematically.

12.4.12   Learn to Self-Coach

All exceptional performers learn to self-coach. Here is a great example of self-coaching. Benjamin Franklin wanted to become more persuasive. He used to read from a popular British magazine, *The Spectator*. He used to pick his favourite articles and then reconstruct them from memory in his own words. Franklin would then compare his writing with the original and then correct his writing based on the differences. This is what deliberate practice is all about—sustained effort along with performance evaluation, assessment of results obtained and correction to create a feedback loop. As you can see, they are all there in this simple method used by Franklin.

12.4.13   Spend on Obtaining Quality Training Materials

Roger Bacon, a philosopher in the 13th century, once observed that it takes thirty years to master mathematics. Today, teenagers can master calculus in only a few years. Is this because we are so vastly more intelligent than before?

As much as we may like to believe this to be the case, unfortunately, this is not true. The difference is access to well-designed training materials and guidelines that have been developed over centuries by a variety of educational organisations. Quality training materials can act as an always-accessible coach that helps an individual to engage in effortful practice even when a live coach is not present.

12.4.14   Get Enough Rest

Focused and deliberate practice takes effort, and you will become mentally and physically tired. Once tired, the tendency of the brain is to start relying on routine and bottom-up thinking. After all, it takes less energy. This means you lose your top-down learning and rewiring function. Any further practice will have little benefit. Take a break by switching your attention to something completely different. Get enough rest so that when you go back to practise the skill, you are enthusiastic enough to engage in top-down learning. The test is simple; if you are no longer out of your comfort zone, relying on routine or your mind is drifting, then you need to take a break.

12.4.15   Work Is Different from Deliberate Practice

Let's examine the nature of deliberate practice more carefully. It is very easy to think that an activity constitutes deliberate practice when, in reality, it does not. Activities can be divided into the following three types:

What is Deliberate Practice?		
Type	**Activities**	**How It Compares with Deliberate Practice**
Work	Includes commissions, services for pay, public performance or any activity with an external reward.	When working, you are simply referring to what you already know and using it to offer a service or provide a performance. There is no attempt to improve your skills, and hence, this does not count as deliberate practice. Sometimes, there are opportunities to learn at work, but given hard deadlines and financial limitations, these are usually very minimal.
Play	These are activities that have no explicit goal. You just do them for pleasure.	There are no external rewards. The goal here is the activity itself. When you are engaged in an activity and are enjoying it fully, you can end up in a state of "flow." This state is in total contrast with the concentrated and focused attention that is required for deliberate practice.
Deliberate practice	These are activities that are specifically designed to improve your current level of performance.	As with play, there are no external rewards for deliberate practice. However, in contrast with work or play, the explicit goal here is to improve performance. New tasks are created to target weaknesses. Performance is carefully monitored to provide cues on how to improve it. It requires effort and is not inherently enjoyable. Deliberate practice doesn't generate monetary rewards; instead, it costs you, as you need access to training materials, teachers and suitable training environments.

12.4.16   Repetition, Repetition, Repetition

When Arnold Schwarzenegger was living in Graz and training at the local gym, he and his peers had set up a system. They had a piece of plywood on a wall. Each day, they would write down in each person's dedicated section exactly what they intended to do that day. They did this right at the start of the day while changing into their workout gear.

It looked something like this:

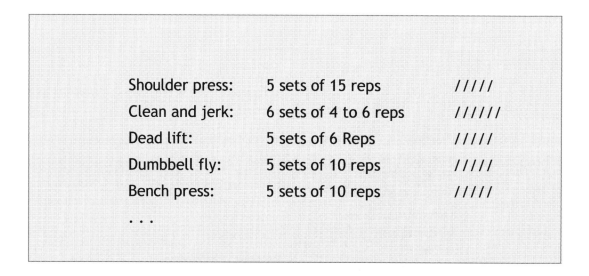

Shoulder press:	5 sets of 15 reps	/////
Clean and jerk:	6 sets of 4 to 6 reps	//////
Dead lift:	5 sets of 6 Reps	/////
Dumbbell fly:	5 sets of 10 reps	/////
Bench press:	5 sets of 10 reps	/////
. . .		

The list continued to cover the entire programme of about sixty sets for the day. The list represented a target even if Arnold didn't know he could achieve it. The lines at the far right of each item presented a visual target—one line for each set. After each set was completed, one line (/) was crossed and turned into an X. Collecting the Xs became the aim of the day. Each time he made an X, Arnold felt he had made an accomplishment. He had done what he had set out to do. He was doing well! Then it was on to the next set.

Arnold learned the power of repetition early on in life. It would take him thousands of repetitions to develop a single muscle. He accepted that everything else would also require the same sort of effort. It was the same when he was learning his lines for his movies, how to reload a shotgun in *The Terminator*, how to dance the tango in *True Lies* and even how to deliver a speech at the United Nations in 2007.

It doesn't matter what skill you are learning in life; in the end, it comes down to *repetition* and *mileage*. If you are learning kite surfing, time on water is critical; you need to get out there, practise and become immersed in the task.

If you are learning how to paint, you need to spend hours every single day for years before you can produce something that showcases mastery. It is the same when learning to play the guitar, dance, cook, negotiate, write a software program or any other skill.

Exercise 12-1

Deliberate Practice

Consider an area that you want to become skilled in. Refer to the ranked list of skills you identified earlier in *Exercise 10-5*.

In this exercise, you get to analyse yourself with respect to a given skill and draw up a number of actions that will help you practise deliberately to master it. The aim at this point is to plan ahead based on what you have learned in this chapter and formulate a number of actions.

1. First, describe the skill under analysis below. Use duplicate forms for each skill so that you can analyse all ten skills one by one, as identified in *Exercise 10-5*.
2. Next, go through a question on the form and provide your analysis.
3. Based on your analysis, formulate a number of immediate actions that can put you in an environment in which you can practise the skill deliberately.

Here are example actions for a given skill, such as painting:

- Pick a painting by a master painter that I admire and aim to replicate it.
- Compare my achievement with the original to correct my mistakes.
- Redraw the piece over and over again until I can produce a satisfactory copy.
- Make a print of mine and the original using the same printer and show it to friends or experts to see if they can tell which is which.

What skill do you want to analyse? Describe the skill you want to learn or are already learning below.

How can you improve your current skill set?

Analysis	
Actions	

	How can you extend your skill set in new directions?
Analysis	
Actions	

	How can you challenge yourself and take yourself out of your comfort zone?
Analysis	
Actions	

	How can you access an informed coach, teacher or mentor?
Analysis	
Actions	

	How can you assess your performance and accurately measure it?
Analysis	
Actions	

	What targets can you set for yourself?
Analysis	
Actions	

	What training materials can you use to improve your skills or add new ones?
Analysis	
Actions	

	What do you need to change so that you don't work or play but practise deliberately?
Analysis	
Actions	

	What schedule can you use, and how many hours a day are you going to spend on this area, to improve your skills?
Analysis	
Actions	

13 Engineer Your Environment

"To be an enlightened master is to be mindful that it is not what you do that brings about a miracle, but that you do it. Doing something, almost anything, in the direction of your dreams, every day, is all that you need to drop a few jaws."

From the Universe

Josie was twenty-two years old, and like many girls her age, she was adventurous and full of energy. She had a degree in history, but she had chosen the subject as a teenager without knowing much about what she liked. She now found history incredibly boring. Adventure, however, was exciting. A friend suggested to Josie that she join her on an active holiday to Dahab, Egypt. Josie's friend was a keen windsurfer, and Dahab, which is on the southeast coast of the Sinai Peninsula, was world-famous for windsurfing. Josie thought she'd give it a try. They booked a holiday and went to Dahab for two weeks of adventure.

The place was lively and was full of young tourists from across Europe who were keen to improve their windsurfing skills. The area thrived on windsurfing tourism. There were various windsurfing clubs catering for each nationality, and the place was popular with Germans, Russians, Britons and North Europeans. Periodically, they all mingled in various parties, enjoying the hot weather and other people's company.

The atmosphere was energetic. There were windsurfers of all levels; people who knew nothing about the sport but wanted to give it a try, as well as some international freestyle competitors who wanted to perfect their stunts to impress their fans.

Josie had a great time on holiday. It was as if she was given fresh blood. She learned the basics of windsurfing. The windsurfing club offered structured tuition at various levels. One of Josie's instructors was Tom. Tom was a classic "surfer dude," except that he was older than others, in charge of running the club and, therefore, more grounded. This appealed to Josie a lot. Before long, they became good friends.

After returning home, Josie kept in touch with Tom. In fact, it did not take long before she felt she was falling in love. As she was still undecided as to what to do with her history degree, she decided to leave for Dahab, go to Tom and change the direction of her life.

Shortly thereafter, Josie joined Tom in Dahab. While there, she was determined to make her own mark. She despised the idea of living off someone else, and she was determined to pull her own weight. She started focusing more on windsurfing. This was, after all, what the place was all about.

The environment was perfect for learning. Most tourists would come for a week or two to practise their windsurfing skills and then leave. Josie had access to all of this environment constantly; there were ideal wind conditions and a flat ocean surface for most days of the year. In addition, she had Tom, who was now her boyfriend, by her side. He could teach her everything she needed to know. Tom was a competitive windsurfer and a good instructor, and Josie knew how fortunate she was.

Life was treating Josie well. She practised every day. She learned to sail in stronger winds and using smaller boards. She learned tacking, speed tacking, beach starting, water starting, jibing, planing, heli tacks and other techniques. As soon as she learned one skill, she was already thinking about learning the next one.

These new skills made Josie feel more comfortable and confident. She now knew that she belonged to the place. With Tom giving her support, she could consider becoming a windsurfing instructor as a career. Having started windsurfing only a year earlier, becoming an instructor felt like a giant leap. Josie, however, was not a normal windsurfer. She was entirely immersed in the world of windsurfing and focused on the sport.

Just about everyone who was involved in the day-to-day running of the club, including the instructors, participated regularly in competitions or even organised them. Tom was a professional windsurfer, and competing for prize money was, in fact, part of his career and a source of income. Josie went to every competition with Tom, and soon she was hooked. Before long, she started competing at her own level. This created a new focus for crafting her skills, and it wasn't long before she began winning prizes. Josie was petite and very light. She took advantage of this for certain stunts that other heavier windsurfers could not even dream of pulling off. She was becoming more and more confident in her own abilities. The alternative world of sitting behind a computer and researching history all day long was not even on her mind.

With Tom's encouragement, Josie started to teach. The first week was difficult, but she was focused and determined. She learned quickly which methods and instructions worked best. She knew that the best way to learn windsurfing was by visualisation and by doing rather than just hearing about techniques. When teaching, she showed plenty of diagrams to learners. She used a simulator and got every student to practise the moves on land several times before heading out to practise them on water. While on water, she was accurate with her instructions, always using visual signals to help her students. In effect, she was using the principles of *accelerated learning* in her teaching.

Two years after first setting foot in Dahab, Josie was living in a dream holiday destination. She was an experienced windsurfing instructor, a participator in international competitions, second in command at a famous windsurfing club and, because of her friendly personality, well-liked and respected by colleagues and guests alike. This was no small feat. Windsurfing is considered one of the few sports that has a very steep learning curve, and it usually takes years of practice to learn to do anything decent. Yet, Josie had done so much in just two years. She had also turned her life around for good.

What was the secret to Josie's rapid success? What made all the difference?

Josie had managed to immerse herself fully in the world of windsurfing. Her boyfriend's work and hobby was windsurfing, and she was exposed to it constantly. She was surrounded by people, staff and guests who either knew windsurfing well or wanted to learn it. The place had all the gear a learner could dream of, and it was available to use any time she desired. She had access to sails of all sizes from a variety of manufacturers, as well as quality surfboards with different capacities. Above all, she had access to an ideal ocean, along with ideal constant winds at her doorstep 24/7. These were the kinds of conditions that people were willing to pay thousands of pounds to fly to. They came all the way from another continent to spend a week or two practising windsurfing. Josie had access to all this all the time.

This immersion meant that Josie lived and breathed windsurfing. It was the only thing on her mind. She had nothing else pulling her away from it. She wanted to have adventure, placed herself in the right environment and practised deliberately in that environment to perfect her skills. It did not take long before she excelled.

What does it mean to be immersed? What does it mean to create an environment that allows you to stay focused on a given skill? In this chapter, you will learn about a series of techniques that will help you do that.

Bill was sitting behind his computer in an open-plan office. He had to finish writing the report by lunchtime. He had written one paragraph before the phone rang. It was a colleague from another branch "just wanting to catch up." Bill had not talked to her for a while and felt it would be rude not to. Besides, he wanted to stay in the loop with company gossip, so he could not miss this chance. Half an hour later, Bill put the phone down and resumed his work. Five minutes later, Emanuel, who was just passing by Bill's desk, said, "Have you seen the email from the boss? Couldn't believe it!" He then disappeared down the corridor. Bill was now curious. He didn't want to check his email, as he had to focus on the report, but he could not resist it. Maybe it really was important. He fired up the email program and checked his emails. He read the boss's email along with various replies from his colleagues. The email was an update on some project that some supplier had pulled out. No big deal really; it just meant finding another supplier in that area, and there were plenty of them. It happens all the time, but obviously Emanuel thought it was shocking news. Bill could have easily read it later. While he was checking his email inbox, he thought he might as well check a dozen new emails too. Other than junk, there were some requests from other colleagues about some data. Bill spent another fifteen minutes digging the data out and sending the information off to his colleagues. By now, he felt he needed a coffee, so he headed for the canteen to make one. He saw Rana there and started chatting with her. He liked Rana . . .

By the time Bill got back to his desk, it was 11:30, and he had only another hour before he had to send off the report. He needed at least a few hours of work. He was beginning to panic . . .

Fast-forward to 6 p.m.

During his drive home, Bill's mind wandered off to his conversation with his boss in the afternoon, and he thought to himself, "How dare he speak to me like that? Who the hell does he think he is? I work my ass off here! It's just a bloody report. So what! I will send it off tomorrow. And that sneaky Emanuel checking on us while we were chatting. I hate that man. I can never trust him. I bet he is broadcasting my conversation with the boss to everyone. Can't believe how intimidating he was to Juan the other day. Rana is right; he is just an a*****e. What a job. What a place. Just about to arrive home now and screaming kids are next. What a life . . . I feel so tired . . ."

What is happening to Bill? Is there any hope to rescue him from this negative spiral downwards to depression and burnout?

As you may have guessed, one area that Bill could improve to get immediate results is handling distractions in his work environment. In fact, he is suffering from two types of distractions:

- *External distractions.* This type includes all interruptions that are mainly in the environment, such as a cluttered or noisy workspace. It also includes distractions in regard to one's body, which is situated in that environment, such as a headache or a broken fingernail.
- *Self-talk.* This includes the mind's chatter. When your mind drifts, the chatter is likely to be negative and unpleasant. A wandering mind is usually the cause of unhappiness and can be quite disruptive.

All distractions can be divided into these two types. Both sources of distraction are problematic, and you must engage in strategies to eliminate both types. Some of the strategies explored in this chapter will indirectly help you eliminate such distractions, but you may also need to consider strategies that can address them directly.

13.1 Design Your Environment

A great way to eliminate external distractions is to engineer your environment. The following are a number of strategies to consider:

- *Remove all sensory distractions.* Remove distracting paintings, posters or notice boards that are in your field of view. These images can distract you without you even noticing. Similarly, eliminate noise, including background chatter. Consider changing your room, asking chatty people to leave if possible or using headphones and listening to music (preferably without lyrics) to block out external distractions. The key is to remove sudden sensory distractions, be it someone suddenly talking loudly or loud music starting to play. The test is simple. If you suddenly become aware of it, it has distracted you. Analyse it and prevent it from happening again.
- *Surround yourself with messages about your goals.* The more you are reminded of your goals, the more likely you are to reach them. Make a custom poster about your targets and hang it on a wall in front of you at home or at your workplace. If you use computers, make a custom desktop background with a motivational message that is relevant to your goal.

- *Avoid having moving images or messages in your field of view*. Our eyes have evolved to be extremely sensitive to movement, helping us to find food and escape predators. As a result, we have evolved to become very sensitive to visual change. This is why advertisers are fond of using moving images to grab our attention. If you have a moving image, such as a screensaver or a TV, in your environment, you will be constantly distracted by it.

- *Disable flash in your browser to block moving ads*. How many times have you gone to a website looking for something and become completely distracted by some flashing advertisement on the side flicking between yellow and blue? Have you seen that rather freakish image which seems to constantly shift by about three pixels? They scream for your attention, and your brain cannot ignore it. Your brain is hijacked by a shrewd, greedy advertiser whose only concern is making money out of you. Use a flash blocker or ad blocker extension in your browser to stop such ads from showing. You won't miss much. If that's their ad, their products can't be worth buying.

- *Remove disruptive pop-up messages*. Remove notifications for your email, messenger or social networking sites from your computer or your mobile phone. They can easily distract you and lead to procrastination.

- *Limit the amount of time you spend browsing*. This is an increasingly common problem. Rather than working on something useful, you get an urge to check a favourite website instead and, in the process, end up procrastinating and wasting valuable time. Fortunately, there is a great way to control this. Use a browser extension such as *StayFocused*, which is available for Chrome browsers, and customise it to limit your access to a select number of sites defined by you. Once you have used your predefined allocated time per day, all these sites will be blocked, and instead, you will see a beautifully worded warning: "Shouldn't you be working?" Stay focused.

- *Close your used browser tabs*. You want to search for something relevant to your task. You open your Internet browser and find twelve tabs already open, with one of them in the front. The open tab can easily distract you, sometimes to the point of making you forget what you wanted to search for! This is particularly damaging if an open tab is from a self-updating page, such as a news site, which means every time you see the page it will show you something different and distracting. This is becoming increasingly problematic, as some major websites, such as popular social networking sites, tend to update their pages regularly. People develop a habit of leaving such pages open and subsequently becoming distracted by them when working.

- **Control *when you want* to receive messages.** Checking your social network status every few minutes is much like checking your email every few minutes. You are advised to check your emails once or twice a day—maximum. Apply the same rule to social media messages. Mobile phone text messages can be incredibly disruptive, as you can be alerted to every single one of them wherever you are. In this day and age, sending text messages has become part of normal life, so the solution is not to avoid them completely. You must, however, take actions to control how you get disrupted by them. When concentrating, a simple text message can throw you off completely. Consider using features such as "Do Not Disturb" on your mobile device to silence it while you are engaged in deliberate learning or in a task that requires concentration.

13.2 Eliminate Self-talk

Recall that there is a top-down planner in your brain. This is responsible for your consciously planned activities while learning something new or while you are engaged in analytical reasoning. In contrast, the bottom-up planner is responsible for routine tasks, emotional signals, reactions such as fight or flight and survival behaviour.

Now, imagine that during the course of a day, you have been working hard and have been using your top-down brain. This part of the brain uses much more energy than the bottom-up part. Just like a muscle, your brain gets tired. Having used a lot of energy, your brain can also become deprived of glucose, which is the main source of brain power. If the brain gets tired, what do you think happens next? It is very much like a computer that is low on power. When a computer tries to save on battery power, it switches off its most processor-hungry functions. Similarly, the brain tends to utilise the bottom-up part more than the top-down part since the former uses much less energy. This leads to a profound shift. Rather than thinking logically while analysing the environment, a tired mind starts to rely on routine behaviour. This, in turn, leads to more emotional thoughts and reactions. It causes an enhanced sense of frustration when things don't go right, or it results in anger towards others, whom you blame for various inadequacies. It also leads to more self-talk. A tired brain starts to daydream, and this is not the good-quality, creative daydreaming. It includes emotional, anxiety-inducing thoughts with negative exaggerated consequences of one kind or another.

To stop such negative self-talk, you must simply take a break. You may think that this is kind of obvious—except that you cannot take just any type of break. To understand what type of break you need to take, let's see what a tired brain needs. The aim is to give the top-down part a rest so it can recover. This means engaging in activities that do not involve the planner and analytical part of the brain, which consumes most of the energy. To put this into everyday context, it means that during your break, you should not engage in activities that involve the top-down functions of the brain.

Below is a list of activities that many people engage in when they are trying to have a break. The problem is that none of them offer a true break; in fact, they only make you more tired!

- *Browsing.* Browsing the Internet is not really a passive activity. It strongly involves the top-down planner. You will end up checking your email, Twitter account and social network among other things.
- *Playing certain computer games.* Games, whether on a console, PC, tablet or your mobile phone, often involve solving some puzzles. You need to navigate a complex environment, use a strategy to conquer or click on a sequence as quickly and accurately as you can. This all requires a lot of learning and concentration. A computer game remains interesting as long as it is challenging. As a result, most games involve the top-down brain and won't provide any rest for a tired brain.
- *Solving Sudoku.* This is a logical game that primarily involves the reasoning part of the brain—the top-down part. If your brain is already tired, Sudoku won't provide much rest.
- *Eating chocolate.* As tempting as it may be to have that bar of chocolate while you keep concentrating on something highly analytical, it is really bad for you. The energy kick from sugar doesn't last long, as it is released too quickly and leads to a lethargic state. It creates a craving for the wrong kind of food, which can lead to all sorts of health issues, including decayed teeth.
- *Learning music.* Even if the activity is completely different from your day job (say accounting), it still doesn't mean you will be giving yourself a rest just because you are switching to something different. When you are actively engaged in learning a new piece or a new instrument, this involves the top-down part of the brain.

The list goes on, but this should give you an idea of the kinds of activities to avoid. You may now wonder what you should engage in instead. The answer is simple. Choose any peaceful activity that uses the bottom-up sequence of your brain. Here are some examples:

- *Play learned music.* You may have had an objection when you were reading about playing music above, thinking that playing can be relaxing. Indeed, you are right to feel this way. When you are playing music that involves learning, you are engaging your top-down brain. However, if you have mastered a piece that is treated as completely routine by the brain, you will only involve the bottom-up part, and this makes it a perfectly acceptable activity while you want to rest your brain and enjoy your hobby.

- *Go for a walk.* Any activity in nature will help you calm your top-down mind while the physical activity will help with your circulation and general health.
- *Go for a swim.* Once you have learned how to swim, this activity can be quite calming and therapeutic. Swimming is considered an ideal exercise for the human body, as it helps you exercise many muscle groups that normally don't get much attention. Swimming is also much gentler on your body than high-impact exercises, such as running.
- *Do yoga.* Much has been said about the benefits of yoga along with concentration and breathing. It can do wonders to calm a raging and tired top-down brain.
- *Play immersive games.* Some games can be relaxing because they involve your bottom-up brain most of the time. Immersive role-playing games that place you in a natural, tranquil environment, such as the world of Skyrim (The Elder Scrolls V: Skyrim), can be incredibly addictive and therapeutic. With modern computer-processing power, recent enhancements in computer graphics, the creation of immersive environments and endless customisation by modding communities, you can immerse yourself in your own customised world. As beautifully put by the game developers, "Live another life, in another world."
- *Feed your brain.* In addition to calming activities, use the break time to feed your brain. The main fuel for the brain is glucose, which is made from the carbohydrates in your diet. Wholegrain is ideal, as it releases energy slowly and steadily. The best kinds of food for the brain are oily fish, which are rich in omega-3 oils, proteins and B vitamins[12] and have plenty of water. Avoid sugary foods.
- *Go to a spa.* The relaxing, almost meditative environment of a spa can do wonders to calm you down and engage only your bottom-up brain. Using a sauna, steam room and hot Jacuzzi engages all your senses. The extensive sweating also helps you get rid of the chemical waste that is present in your body, making you feel physically lighter. Heat up in the sauna and then jump in the freezing plunge pool. You are guaranteed not to have any negative self-talk left. You can get high on this. No need for drugs of any kind. You will also get to sleep better afterwards. In fact, with all such benefits, one wonders why we don't

---

[12] You can find a list of sources for various B vitamins here: www.nhs.uk/Conditions/vitamins-minerals/Pages/Vitamin-B.aspx

have more spas in towns than churches and mosques. The spa business is a booming industry, particularly in mainland Europe, and its continued commercial proliferation is indeed a welcome trend for all societies.

- *Make love.* This is an activity that seems to tick all the boxes. Sex relaxes the brain, utilises the bottom-up brain in routine mode, provides a good physical exercise and satisfies your need for intimacy and sex. It also makes you feel good.

Tiredness, however, is not the only reason for engaging in negative self-talk. Here are some strategies to utilise as soon as you catch yourself engaged in self-talk:

- *Count backwards.* Start from 100. Subtract seven from it, and keep subtracting seven each time until your mind goes quiet.
- *Count the number of words in a paragraph.* Pick any paragraph from any book. Count the words. You can even extend this to count the number of words on a whole page once or twice.
- *Use mindfulness.* Go through the following exercise for the next ten minutes and no less. Consider eating a single raisin. Focus on it with all your senses. Feel the sweetness. Hear the sound as you chew it. Focus on the texture and the feel of it on your tongue. Enjoy the richness of the flavour. Let the sensation of the moment go through your entire body. Now, while immersed in the joy of eating the raisin, focus on your breathing. Concentrate on the air going into and out of your lungs. Continue to focus on your breathing, feeling your entire body until you have spent about ten minutes on the activity. You should feel calm now.
- *Focus on a fruit.* Take a fruit, such as an apple, orange, banana or peach. Hold it in your hands. Focus completely on the fruit, and do not let any other thoughts interrupt you. Focus on its texture, how heavy it is, how it would taste, how colourful it is and how cold it is. Do not think about where it comes from, its supply chain, the global economy or your next investment opportunity! Only focus calmly on the fruit that you are holding in your hands for five minutes.
- *Immerse yourself in a challenging activity.* While absorbed in a challenging task, you cannot get carried away by negative self-talk. You will have to focus to perform, and this will help silence the chatter.
- *Immerse yourself in a challenging physical sport.* By engaging in a challenging physical activity, your mind can focus only on the task at hand, and everything else fades away automatically. Consider sports such as mountain climbing or windsurfing. When you are climbing up a rock that is twenty metres high, your survival instincts will kick in. All that matters is going up, spending less energy and getting on with the

climbing task. It is guaranteed that your self-talk will stop when you are hanging on to a little ledge and your entire body and mind are focused on not falling. Similarly, while windsurfing at thirty knots, maintaining your balance against the waves, the gusts and the sheer thrill of speed will stop your mind drifting to anything else. You cannot worry about your clients suing you while riding waves at thirty knots or hanging from a rope with fifty metres of empty space beneath you.

Why do the above techniques work? When you engage in self-talk, you can become emotionally preoccupied. Emotional distractions are the worst type of distraction, as they lead to a deep level of anxiety. You become preoccupied with everything to do with *yourself* and nothing to do with the present moment or the external world. The medial prefrontal cortex fires away as you engage in self-talk. In contrast, when you concentrate, this medial area is inhibited by a nearby lateral area in the brain. In other words, your sustained attention shuts off the area that is preoccupied with "me," self-talk stops and you get on with more useful stuff in your life.

13.3 Use Total Immersion

Most people are familiar with the power of immersive learning, and yet very few utilise it. The idea is to consider as many methods as you can and surround yourself with the information and the topic at hand so that you are constantly exposed to it both directly and indirectly. Perhaps it can be summarised in the following statement:

> ### Treat learning as an all-out war, not just a battle.

If you focus on just one aspect of learning or use just one set of tools or techniques to learn, you are limiting yourself significantly. You will be aiming to win a single battle when, in reality, you should be focusing on the war. You should consider the big picture and utilise all resources to attack the topic from all fronts. This will then help you to immerse yourself in the topic and live and breathe it, just like how Josie learned windsurfing in Dahab.

13.4 Focus on Immersion Rather Than Flow

A state of flow occurs when you are completely absorbed in a given task and are enjoying it. It happens because you know exactly what you need to do to achieve your target.

Studies show that people are rarely in a state of flow in daily life. For example, sampling people's mood at random shows that during a typical day, people are mostly either stressed or bored and occasionally experience brief periods when they are in a state of flow. Fifteen percent of people never enter a state of flow during a typical day, while only 20% have at least one state of flow a day (Csikszentmihalyi & Larson 1984).

Immersion, in contrast with being in a state of flow, is about surrounding yourself with materials that will help you learn more. In a state of flow, the objective is not learning; it is enjoying. Immersion, in contrast, is about engineering an environment that will maximise the likelihood of deliberate practice.

Here are a number of techniques to help you immerse yourself in a topic:

- Enrol in short courses to boost your knowledge and skills in a given field.
- Ask a tutor to help with your learning in a formal private session.
- Subscribe to online courses.
- Watch videos and tutorials related to the subject matter.
- Visit industry exhibitions.
- Attend workshops.
- Find a learning buddy for the subject matter.
- Enter a competition to compete at a higher standard than you are already at. This will push you to focus and will set you very specific and measurable targets.
- Compile a guide about the subject you are learning, and prepare it to a standard that will be useful to a new learner.
- Find opportunities to teach other enthusiasts about your acquired skills.
- Find a meet-up group of people with the same interest for networking.

13.5 Replace Negative with Positive

Your mood can be easily affected by what you see and hear in your environment. Negativity makes you less productive. Positivity does the reverse. Let's look at some strategies that can help you avoid negativity:

- ***Avoid the news.*** The news is inherently negative, sad and exaggerated. Today's sensationalist media can exaggerate to make the smallest incident sound like a catastrophe. The sensational stories can then trick you into seeing more content and advertisements, thereby making money for big news corporations. Be selective in the type of news you expose yourself to; avoid distractions and negativity. Of course, you still need to be aware of what is going on in your environment, but you can get important and useful news from other people through social interactions.

- *Avoid unrelated news.* Some news is not really news and is not worthy of your time and attention. Do you really need to know how the cat got stuck in the chimney? Reading extensively about yet another sex scandal is not the best way to spend your precious time. Stay in charge of your emotions and expose yourself to such content *only when you want to*. Don't let others hijack your emotions for their own benefit.

- *Avoid drama.* Avoid watching dramatic, depressing or horror movies. Instead, watch a comedy, a thriller or an adventure movie where the hero overcomes adversity despite overwhelming challenges. Watch something that inspires you rather than something that depresses you.

- *Avoid listening to sad music.* It can significantly change your mood without you being consciously aware of it. You end up feeling depressed without having any good reason.

- *Avoid watching soap operas.* These TV programmes are often about relationships that go wrong. The interactions are usually dramatic, negative, aggressive and provocative simply because people don't want to watch normal life. Despite their popularity, soap operas can have devastating effects on people's general emotional intelligence. Repeated exposure to such programmes can make some people think that the behaviours and mannerisms portrayed in these programmes are acceptable and normal. Imitating such behaviours and actions can cause countless problems for families and societies. Banning an entire society from watching soap operas is perhaps too simplistic. However, you can always start with yourself. Impose a ban on yourself and your family for such useless content, and if enough people do it, we can certainly lift society.

- *Avoid a messy environment.* An untidy desk or a messy office is a recipe for failure, procrastination and lack of productivity. Organise and tidy up! Use well-known systems such as Getting Things Done (GTD) to do this (Allen 2001).

13.6 Give Yourself a Fake Constraint

Artificially limit yourself based on a particular parameter. This can help you stay focused and feel challenged. It can sometimes totally change the task from boring to absolutely exciting.

Here are some example strategies:

- **Limit the time available to do a task**.
  - o Make a full comic in twenty-four hours
  - o Record an entire album in twenty-four hours
  - o Fix the garden shed by lunchtime
- **Increase the complexity.** Use Guy Kawasaki's formula to make presentations that have no more than ten slides, use thirty-point fonts and are no longer than twenty minutes. (This is known as the *10/20/30 rule.*)
- **Use unorthodox methods.** If playing a basic racquet game with your ten-year-old is not challenging enough for you, play the game with your other hand and see how well you do.

13.7 Use Status Boards

Set up a screen with your targets, and keep it updated to reflect the current trends in your life. This board can be physical or it can be a computer screen.

Here are examples of what you can include:

- Number of days left to a major deadline for a project
- Amount of sales so far and how many more sales are needed to reach a target this month
- Number of calls left to reach this week's marketing calls quota
- Number of errors made in the production line this week in comparison with the past twelve weeks
- Number of books read this month
- Total number of hours spent exercising this week in comparison with the last four weeks

13.8 Don't Get Carried Away

Suppose you want to learn about a new programming language. You may think you need to read a whole book on the language, read lots of blog posts on the topic and go through the help files to learn about the Application Peripheral Interface (API). This could work, but it will take a significant amount of time.

Besides, you may not even like the language or may not have much use for it after all. All this time would have been wasted.

As an alternative approach, focus on a small achievement. For example, write your first "hello world" program and run it. Once you have gone through the exercise, you can decide how to proceed.

Sometimes, getting carried away is a way to procrastinate and avoid doing more important tasks. You justify this by convincing yourself that you need to spend more time on a new topic, while in reality, you only need to spend a small amount of time considering your initial goal.

13.9 Use a Reminder System

To develop new habits, or to catch yourself when you are procrastinating, use an automated reminder system. For example, use your mobile phone to periodically remind you to stick to your task. It can also remind you to log what you are doing at a given moment so that you feel guilty if you are not doing what you have planned to do.

13.10   Involve a Friend

To overcome indecision, share your thoughts and what you need to do with a friend. Commit to your friend that you are going to do it. An external commitment is a great motivator since quitting will be more difficult and embarrassing.

13.11   Block Escape Routes

Imagine that you are on a battlefield and are confronted by a fierce enemy. Sun Tzu, a classic Chinese strategist, noted long ago that soldiers fought most ferociously when they thought they were fighting to the death. You don't want to fight an army in such a state. To avoid fighting such an army, he suggested that a general must always create an illusion that escape routes are available to the enemy. Knowing that they can escape prevents the opposing army from fighting as hard as they can.

When it comes to procrastination, you can turn this strategy on its head. You can block all escape routes so that you are forced to "fight to the death" to get through the task. You are committed and unable to quit. There is no *procrastination escape*; you are trapped until the task is completed.

Here is an example of how you can block escape routes. Put up a large poster with your image and the following statement in the main lobby of your company: "If you catch me smoking, anytime, anywhere, I will give you £5,000." You may end up quitting smoking much sooner than you think!

13.12   Maximise Your Creativity

It is unfortunate that the media often portrays creativity in a sensational and dramatic way, as if breakthroughs are created in one go and by people who haven't had much experience with the subject. This is an exaggerated portrayal of what actually happens.

In reality, creativity is achieved in a series of small wins. These are minor innovations and solutions to specific and well-defined problems. Each solution and each step gets a creator or innovator closer to a larger goal. As we have seen in history, solutions do indeed come at unusual times. There is, however, a pattern. A creator knows the problem very well and has usually been working on different aspects of it for a long time. After an intense thinking session, the creator leaves the task and focuses on something else. For example, he may go for a walk, take a bath or lie in the sun with his eyes closed. It is often in such unusual moments that a connection is suddenly made and the pieces of the puzzle fit together to create a breakthrough.

To achieve creativity, you must have *all* the following:

- *Clear goals*. To know your goals, you need to understand the problem you are trying to solve. Innovation and creativity do not manifest spontaneously. You need a direction, a bounded problem and a good understanding of what you are trying to achieve.
- *Total freedom in reaching these goals*. If your resources are too limited or you are worried about your direction—for example, in terms of ethical issues—this can dampen your creativity. Similarly, external threats, such as political instability, imposed policies or health-related issues, can also influence creativity negatively.
- *Protected time with no interruptions*. You need uninterrupted time to think freely. Any interruption can easily disrupt your thought process and make you miss the chance to chase non-obvious but promising associations, which are the building blocks of creativity.

13.13   Adopt a Tool's View of Life

> *You are only as good as your tools and your knowledge of using them.*

Use this slogan to approach your time management system. Your time management system works if it passes three simple tests. You should be able to do the following:

- *Quickly process anything.* If something new comes into your world (physical or digital), you should know exactly where to put it within ten seconds and should be able to find it easily at any time in the future. In other words, you need to have a system in place and know how to use it by heart.
- *Know your next actions.* At any given time, you should know exactly what you need to do next according to your goals and priorities.
- *Keep your mind free.* If you cannot keep track of an important task in your time management system, then it becomes an "open loop" in your brain, constantly nagging you not to forget. Open loops will slow your brain down as you lose focus and concentration. Your time management system and your 100% trust in it should allow you to completely eliminate these open loops.

Time management systems, such as GTD, can help you satisfy these requirements (Allen 2001).

Whether we like it or not, there is going to be even more information to process and deal with as we move into the future. There is no escaping this. The only way to stay on top is to adopt and use new technological tools against the demands of a connected and fast-paced world.

New technologies come to market all the time, and some can be quite powerful for certain applications of productivity. Consider the following as an example. *Pocket Informant* is an excellent calendar app that is available for iOS and Android devices. The latest version supports *Informant Beacon*. This is a little electronic device which can be placed indoors to mark positions. When your phone is in the proximity of the device, or basically in a specific zone nearby, it will let the calendar know its position. The calendar can now remind you of various tasks and appointments that you have preprogramed to be reminded of when you are in that specific location. This takes GPS geolocation one step further by making location-based reminders available even when you don't have a good GPS signal. Even though, technologically, this is not that complicated, the result is that it can give you tremendous power over your environment and free your mind. Rather than constantly thinking about what to do and where, you focus on higher-level tasks. Less on your mind means less information overload.

In short, to stay competitive, you need to be able to filter through useless information manually and automatically so as not to be overwhelmed by information. Those who fail to get through the clutter of information or don't see the importance of spending time to set up a system that deals with it will be at the mercy of being bombarded by junk and getting buried underneath it. You will not have a satisfied life if all you do is react to whatever your environment throws at you without you making a conscious effort to move towards an identified goal.

13.14   Take Action Now

Don't think about consequences. Clear all that junk and throw it out. Make a decision and follow through. As soon as you start to take charge, especially of those areas that you have neglected for a while, you start to feel more energised and happy. Use this energy to follow through with other critical and more demanding tasks and projects.

Be persistent, constantly think of your burning desires and continuously revise your plans until you achieve every goal you set for yourself. It is just a matter of time. Engineering your environment may sometimes feel like such an indirect activity that you may wonder if it will have any effect. It does, and you will be amazed by how much you will gain through simple changes. Stay with it; make the plan, and follow the plan.

Exercise 13-1

Identify Actions to Engineer Your Environment

Go through the techniques and guidelines provided in this chapter, and see which ones you can take advantage of to engineer an immersive environment. Design an environment that is suitable for your goals, roles and mission statement.

- Draw a number of actions to set up your environment. Be as specific as possible.
- Rank these actions based on their importance.
- Start by focusing on the top five and see when and how you can implement them. Schedule each action for a particular time, knowing that you are committed to doing it.

Use the form below and extra blank sheets as necessary.

Actions	Rank	Scheduled Time

14 Motivate Yourself Automatically

"It's not that I'm so smart; it's just that I stay with problems longer."

Albert Einstein

As a struggling entrepreneur living in the US, Bruce Lee decided to write the following letter to himself:

> "By 1980, I will be the best known oriental movie star in the United States and will have secured $10 million . . . and in return, I will give the very best acting I could possibly give every single time I am in front of the camera and I will live in peace and harmony."

Lee went on to act in several movies until 1973, when he was about to release his first major US title—*Enter the Dragon*. Unfortunately, he died before the movie was released due to a rare allergic reaction to certain painkillers. Several months later, *Enter the Dragon* was released in the US and China, and it became an international success, making Bruce Lee an international star and a legend.

As a young comedian struggling to break into Hollywood, Jim Carrey started to have doubts. One day, after performing a stand-up comedy in one of the night clubs in Los Angeles, he was booed off the stage by the audience.

Looking down at the city from the top of Mulholland Drive, he wondered if this was what he wanted. He wondered whether the city held his future success or failure. He then decided to pull out his cheque book and write himself a cheque for $10 million. He also made a note on it, "For acting services rendered." He carried this cheque in his wallet everywhere he went.

The rest is history. Carrey went on to act in a series of blockbuster comedies, such as *Mask* and *Dumb and Dumber*. Eventually, he acted in *The Cable Guy* and earned $20 million for his role in it. This was the highest sum a comedy actor had ever received!

What is common between Jim Carrey's approach and that of Bruce Lee? What did they do by writing such notes to themselves?

The answer is rather intriguing. Lee and Carrey tapped into a great secret. It is actually not a real secret, but so few people use it that it seems mystical or even supernatural.

The secret is known as the *law of attraction*. It can be expressed in a variety of forms:

- Positive thinking brings positive physical results; negative thinking brings negative physical results.
- If you wish for something, you will get it in the end.
- Thoughts become things.
- If you constantly aim for something, you will eventually get it.
- If you are constantly negative, you will miss opportunities, which can, in turn, make you feel unlucky and even more negative.

The law of attraction suggests that your persistence will help you succeed. In other words, if you really want it, you will get it. This is not because if you want something then the universe will align itself to give it to you or some god will answer your prayers. It is the other way around. Your mind, in its quest to reach what it is *determined* to get and *believes* it can have, will find the way. If the mind stays on a given problem long enough, it will *always* find a solution to it. Give up too soon, doubt yourself or wonder if it is really worth the effort, and before long, you will be confronted with failure.

14.1 Be Persistent

To be persistent about a given desire or goal, you need to be constantly conscious of it.

To create this constant awareness, you can engineer your environment in a way that helps to remind you of your goals.

Consider using the following strategies:

- *Use self-advertisement.* We know that advertisements can be incredibly powerful. Ads are used everywhere because they work. It is well known that the real power of advertisement lies in the repetition of a clear, noticeable message. You can take advantage of its marketing power by self-advertising a specific goal. The more you are reminded of your goals, the better.
- *Place statements about your goals in your environment.* Constantly look for inspiring quotes. Choose the best ones, print them in large fonts on posters and place them somewhere you can see them on a daily basis. For example, place them in front of your desk, in your home office, by the door as you leave the house or on the door of your office. Seeing a poster of a goal every day is a great way to be reminded of a principle or purpose. However, it is crucial that the message is created by the people who are subjected to it rather than designed by a third party.
- *Create a dreamboard.* This is basically a visual representation of a collection of desires and goals. Being visual, it can constantly remind you of your aims. It is also inspiring to reach your goals and achieve all that you placed on your dreamboard.

14.2 Use Weekly Slogans

Have you ever come across an inspiring statement in a movie or a book that made a lot of sense to you? Next time this happens, stop and make a note of it in your notebook or on your mobile phone so that you can add a statement to your collection as soon as you see one. Keep collecting slogans that have a personal meaning to you.

Here are some examples of such inspiring statements:

- Life is to be enjoyed, not just endured.
- My best work is my next work.
- No matter what happens tomorrow, I am happy today.
- You cannot build a reputation on what you are going to do.
- What a man can be, he must be.
- Focus on causes that are bigger than yourself.
- Focus more on lost sales than losing money.
- Give and you shall be given; take and you shall not.
- Nothing lasts forever.

- If it is not working, do something else.

Now, here is a powerful technique you can employ that allows you to take advantage of *autosuggestion, repetition* and an *engineered environment*. Go through the following instructions step by step:

1. Print each of these slogans on a separate sheet of paper in a very large font so that it is easily readable from a distance. Keep a collection of these print-outs. As you come across more slogans, keep printing a new batch, and add them to your printed collection.
2. Find a suitable wall or surface in your environment that you see every day. Think like an advertiser. If an advertiser were to grab your attention with a poster, which area would he pay the most to place it? Find this spot in your home, in your office or both. Just like an advertiser, you may need to experiment to see which area works best.
3. On a weekly basis—say, on Monday morning before you start to work— browse through the printed collection of slogans. Choose one that most appeals to you for what you are going through that week. The better it captures what you are going through at that point in your life, the more effective it will be.
4. Attach your weekly slogan to its designated place as you identified in Step 2.
5. Look at it every day, and think of it all day and for the whole week before you change it the following week.

A more comprehensive list can be found in *Appendix B*. As a guide, the best statements are those that condense a really useful idea or concept into an elegant sentence. The context you get them from can have a direct effect on the meaning you get from the statement, which is what makes this personal approach effective. It is not good enough to go through a library of inspiring quotes where you can read statement after statement and enjoy them but will forget them soon afterwards. By being aware of each one for a whole week, you are more likely to be more conscious of what it really means as you go through your daily life and think about how it may apply to what you are going through.

Exercise 14-1

Define a Series of Weekly Slogans

Now that you have seen examples of slogans, pause and use the space below to quickly write down a series of statements that you find most suitable as weekly slogans. This can then be your starting point for this activity.

14.3 Automate Your Exposure

As stated by the law of attraction, you need to constantly expose yourself to your mission and goals so that you remain conscious of them. Fortunately, computers and sophisticated smartphones can do a great job of taking care of this.

To take this concept one step further, consider placing your slogans everywhere in your environment and not just in one or two places on your walls. Think like a shrewd advertiser who aims to bombard you with this message everywhere you go. The best way to think about this is to consider yourself as being in charge of designing an advert that will expose you to the message at all times. You can borrow from the tricks advertisers use.

For example, advertisers always search for spots that are frequently looked at. They always place their ads on the most visible parts of a web page. They show their logo five times during a one-hour TV programme. They find the busiest locations in town and erect enormous billboards. No wonder we buy so much stuff that we don't need. Advertisements work, and now you can use the same technique to help yourself.

You have already placed your weekly slogan on a wall in your office. Now, set up a reminder on your mobile phone which pops up periodically to remind you of the slogan. When you turn on your laptop, see the message on the desktop background. When you get into your car, see the slogan placed on the dashboard. Hang it on a wall right on top of your TV in the living room. Every time they start to show advertisements on TV (and there are plenty these days), mute the TV, look at the slogan hanging above it and think about that instead of the ad on TV. You will be much better off looking at your own personally targeted ad than looking at someone else's generic ad, which most of the time doesn't benefit you at all.

You don't have to limit yourself to only your slogans. You can use the same self-advertisement technique to remind yourself of your goals or whatever *you* think is important to be reminded of all the time.

Consider using the following strategies to automatically motivate yourself:

- *Automatic reminders.* Set up automatic reminders on your digital calendar, such as Microsoft Outlook, or on your smartphone calendar to remind yourself to read your mission statement. Include your mission in your reminder so it simply pops up on your computer or mobile screen.
- *Automatic notifications.* Similarly, you can set up goal reminders on your mobile phone. To make life easier, use a synchronised calendar that keeps these reminders in sync between your computer and your

mobile devices. This allows you to program everything once and use it everywhere knowing that no matter where you are (even while travelling), you will be reminded of your goals.

- *Receive positive messages*. Subscribe to services that offer positive and inspiring daily messages. Imagine receiving a personalised positive message everyday by email. You will start your day by reading a nicely crafted message that gives you hope, puts a smile on your face and prepares you to face the day with more energy and determination. A great example of such a service is Mike Dooley's *Notes from the Universe*.[13]

- *Automatic reviews*. Set yourself monthly, quarterly and annual reminders in your digital calendar to review your mission statement and goals. It is all too easy to set goals and forget about them. As discussed before, goals change, and you will need to review your current situation, where you are heading and how your situation and environment might have changed since you last set your goals. A handy reference is provided in *Appendix A* for all periodic reviews and exercises that you can carry out based on what you have learned in this book.

---

[13] Check out his website for further information: http://www.tut.com/theclub

Exercise 14-2

Define Automated Actions

Based on what you learned in this chapter, draw up a number of actions for how you are going to automate your exposure to your goals, mission statement and inspiring slogans. Record them below, and then schedule them.

Actions	Schedule

15 Make Yourself Happy

"No matter what happens tomorrow, I am happy today."

You wake up in the morning and prepare to go to work, and you have a routine every day. Once at work, the first thing you do is make yourself a cup of coffee with the new Nespresso machine, which makes really good coffee. You look forward to this coffee every day, as it is a good kick start to your day. You simply *expect* to get your coffee every day.

One day when you come to the office, you realise that the machine is broken. The other coffee machine on the ground floor was sent out to be serviced yesterday and won't be back until next week. It means no coffee this morning! You are upset. You wanted a coffee, and your *expectation* is not met. Your energy level goes down.

Your colleague, Marla, doesn't drink coffee. On the day the coffee machine broke, she had no particular feelings. She had no expectations and so was not influenced by the lack of coffee.

A week later, both coffee machines are back in operation, and you have been drinking your coffee for several days. One day when you arrive, you see a large triple-chocolate cake in the coffee room. It was somebody's birthday and they brought in a cake. This is a pleasant surprise. You prepare your coffee and get a slice of the chocolate cake. The chocolate cake has *exceeded your expectation* and has made you happier.

Let's put this into a graph.

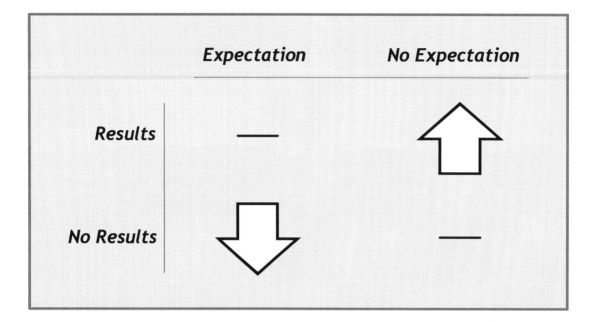

The graph captures the four possibilities. When you have an expectation and it is met, your energy is neutral. The same applies when you don't have an expectation and nothing happens. When you have an expectation and it is exceeded, you become happier. On the other hand, when you have an expectation and it is not met, you become unhappy. You may think this is rather simple and straightforward; however, the graph leads to an interesting point: You only become happier *when your expectation is exceeded*.

Unfortunately, people are not good at managing their own expectations or those of others. If you have an unhappy client, the chances are very high that some expectation was not met and that this is the source of your client's unhappiness.

To manage an expectation, you can approach it in two ways—work to meet that expectation, or express it in a way that leads to satisfaction. To illustrate, as an example, you can set a lower expectation for selling a product by not promising a world of features. Instead, you can focus on advertising a few core features and leave the rest of the more minor features to be discovered as an unexpected surprise.

If you are confronted with an angry customer, you will need to address his unmet expectation. You will need to see what it is that the customer wanted and take steps to address this or at least provide something that compensates for this failure in communication.

15.1 Managing Your Expectations

Now, let's apply this to managing self-expectations. Managing expectations is about eliminating the gap between your expectation and the results you get from reality.

Let's pause at this point and go through the following self-analysis exercise.

Exercise 15-1
What Are You Unhappy About?

Are you happy with your life? Do you feel angry about something? Are you disappointed with your life in any particular way? Do you engage in self-talk, often feeling bad about what has become of your life? Consider your routine, commitments, endless chores, workplace inefficiencies and people's interactions with you. Use the space below to list everything you can think of that makes you generally unhappy and dissatisfied. You will shortly address them one by one. The aim here is to analyse yourself. Be honest, but don't be hard on yourself.

ID	Your Dissatisfactions
1	
2	
3	
4	
5	

15.2 How to Address Your Dissatisfactions

As you saw, eliminating your dissatisfactions mainly comes down to how you manage your expectations. To get positive energy, you need to create an environment in which you are positively *surprised*. Fine, you may say, "I will just lower my overall expectations and I will be constantly surprised." As you saw earlier in *Section 11.1*, you cannot just aim to lower your expectations as a whole. In the long run, this doesn't lead to a happier and more successful life. Instead, you should aim for high expectations while managing them in a way that lets you exceed these expectations. This is actually not that difficult to do. The following are a number of approaches and techniques that you can utilise.

15.2.1 Set Specific Goals and Be Aware of Them

Managing self-expectations starts with knowing what these expectations are. The more precisely you know them, the less likely you are to get confused by some vague expectation, thinking that you have failed rather than succeeded.

Example:

> You have accumulated savings over the years and were thinking about investing it. After considering several options, you decide that investing it in a house is perhaps the best option, as you expect the house prices in your area to rise quickly in the coming years. Besides that, you can take advantage of tax benefits for buying a house as an asset.
>
> A month after you purchase the house, you start to feel unhappy about various features of the house. It is a classic case of buyer's remorse. It is not the ideal home you wanted. Before purchasing it, you thought you could knock down a wall that separates the living room from the dining room to create an open space. Now you realise that you cannot remove the wall. You hate the giant black cast iron radiators that are scattered around the house. The style of the house is old-fashioned and doesn't appeal to you. You just cannot get comfortable in it.

How to Address:

> Here, your dissatisfaction is a result of you expecting an ideal, modern house. The root of your dissatisfaction is your vague goals. Your specific goal was to invest and increase your asset value. That goal is still valid, and you are likely to achieve it. Along the way, however, you wished that the house appealed to you more. As it turns out, it doesn't, but that was not the original goal. You invested in a big house in a good area of the town, and it is going to make you a lot of money when you

sell it. Once you remind yourself of your original goal and realise that it is on its way to becoming a reality, you will immediately start to feel better about the current situation and your expectations.

15.2.2 Aim for High Expectations—But Not Foolishly

As you saw in *Section 11.1*, reducing your expectations is self-defeating. Similarly, if you aim for a foolish and outlandish target, you can make yourself unhappy for a long time.

Examples and How to Address Them

Suppose you are a short person. Your chances of becoming a great basketball player are very slim. You can enjoy the sport by setting moderate targets, but don't frustrate yourself by setting an unreasonable and unachievable goal.

Here is another example. You may set yourself a goal to become the first person on Mars. If you are in your forties now, this is simply not going to happen. By the time humanity gets its act together and sets up a human mission to Mars, you will be in your sixties or older. Considering the cost of such a mission, it will then be too much of a risk to choose you to send to Mars as opposed to someone much younger and physically fitter.

15.2.3 Don't Lower Your Expectations; Just Reframe Them

Since you cannot lower your expectations, you can instead aim to formulate them in a different way so that they will benefit you but will not lead to strong dissatisfaction if they are not achieved.

Example:

Suppose you are an artist and want to submit your painting to a competition. If you set your expectation as winning the competition, any result you get other than winning can make you feel bad. To address this, you certainly cannot reduce your aim to just participating. With this lower aim and no will to compete, you won't produce anything that is worthy of winning. It then becomes a self-fulfilling prophecy.

How to Address:

Instead of lowering your expectations, you can *reframe* them. For example, you can aim to create your best work yet while adhering to the expected style and requirements of the competition. You can aim to provide your best within certain criteria. This aim will push you to create something better than what you have ever done. The process itself will be immensely satisfactory if you think that you did well. If people recognise your effort, you will get more satisfaction too. Winning is then just a bonus on top of it all. Your expectation is rephrased.

15.2.4　Beware of Low Expectations

If you set the bar too low, you cannot expect a lot when you get it. You might be upset that you have gained little, but that might just be because you aimed too low.

Example:

> Your social life is not as extensive as you would like it to be. You like to make new friends and spend more time with your friends. This is a natural expectation as you aim to satisfy your specific social needs. Now, ask yourself how much time you spend every week meeting new people. If your answer is pretty much none, then you don't really have a goal. Your expectation is very low. All you have is a *wish,* and you are not doing anything specific to address this need. With no goal or expectation, you are unlikely to improve in this area.

How to Address:

> You should consider setting a higher and more defined expectation. For example, you can set a target to get to know at least two new people every month. Now, you can take actions to satisfy this precise expectation. You will also need to define what "knowing" means. For example, you can define it by having exchanged contacts and arranged at least one specific meeting during which you can spend time learning more about each other.

Exercise 15-2

Rephrase Your Expectations

Go over the list of dissatisfactions you made earlier in *Exercise 15-1*, and examine each one using the following form. Use a single form for each dissatisfaction, and answer the questions listed below if they apply.

Use the responses to prepare to answer the final question about defining your new expectations. Use the space to remind yourself of your revised expectations in relation to your dissatisfaction so that you no longer feel unhappy.

Your dissatisfaction under consideration: **(or just the ID from Exercise 15-1)**	
What were my original expectations that led me to be dissatisfied?	
What are my specific goals?	
Have I set my goals foolishly high?	

Have I set the bar too low?	
Can I reframe my expectations?	
What are my new expectations?	

15.3 How to Make Yourself Happier—Now

Consider the fascinating experiment conducted by George Loewenstein, a professor of economics and psychology. A group of undergraduates were asked to indicate the most they would pay now to obtain or avoid certain outcomes (Loewenstein 1987). One outcome was gaining $4. The participants then stated the most they would pay to get the $4 or to get it at some point in the future: Three hours, one day, three days, a year or even ten years later. As you can imagine, the results showed that people preferred immediate results. What they were willing to pay gradually declined as the reward (the $4) was delayed. The same was true for avoiding the loss of $1,000. Again people would pay more not to lose now and were less concerned about losing it in the future—say, in ten years.

So far so good. The researchers then introduced a couple of clever outcomes in the mix to further test participants' behaviour. The results were intriguing indeed. This time, they asked the participants how much they were willing to pay now to obtain a kiss from a movie star of their choice in three hours, one day, three days, one year or ten years. This time, the results were different.

It turned out that the participants were willing to pay the most for a kiss that was delayed by three days. Similarly, they would rather get the kiss in one day than in three hours. In other words, they were willing to pay extra for an *opportunity to wait*. Unlike gaining $4, an immediate kiss was no longer more valuable than a delayed one.

To test this further, researchers also asked to see how much the participants would pay to avoid receiving a non-lethal 110V shock. The results showed that participants were willing to pay much more to avoid a shock in one or ten years than they would to avoid it now or in three hours. Even studies on rats show similar results. For example, in one experiment, when rats were faced between choosing an immediate shock and a moderately delayed shock, they preferred the immediate shock (Knapp *et al.* 1959).

The results of these and similar studies suggest that expecting something good to happen leads to an *anticipatory pleasure*; hence, we like to wait to enjoy it. Similarly, when it comes to unpleasant experiences, we would rather have it now than go through the pain of waiting and dreading it until it happens.

The body of research in this area suggests that such results can be interpreted using a concept known as *vividness*. This is the imaginary picture of what we create for the future state of our behaviour or work. The more vivid the imagination, the stronger our response as we anticipate it.

This can be used very effectively to motivate people, including yourself, to influence behaviour. For example, consider road safety videos targeting young drivers. The accidents shown are usually created to be very shocking, but research shows that they have a limited impact. To take advantage of the vividness concept, some schools have used the following device to address this. Students were put on a specially designed wheeled chair that was sped up to five miles an hour and then abruptly stopped. The effect was total sensory stimulus to create maximum vividness. Naturally, this proved to be more effective than just showing passive videos.

You may wonder how this relates to self-motivation. Vividly imagining your positive future can give you pleasure *now* as you anticipate it. It means that optimism and positive expectation of the future along with your vivid imagination of this future lead to a more pleasurable life right now. Optimists expect a better and more rewarding future, and such positive expectations boost their well-being and happiness today. Be an optimist all your life; see the glass as half-full—never ever half-empty.

15.4 Keep and Update a Personal Journal

Anthony Robbins, the world-famous guru of personal growth, once said, "If your life is worth living, it's worth writing about." Much has been said about the power of keeping a personal journal, and believe it or not, everything they say is true.

On a fundamental level, the journal acts like a companion you can talk to. Writing is very different from thinking about something. When you want to write, you have to formulate your thoughts into sentences. The process also slows you down, which allows you to focus more on ideas, feelings, thoughts and insights.

Writing about your feelings in your journal will make you feel lighter. You have got it out and expressed it *and* you have recorded it so it will not be lost. You can always go back to it for reference or just leave it.

To keep a journal, you can use a digital solution or a traditional notebook. Whatever system you use, it must have the following qualities:

- *Must be easily accessible*. When you have a thought or just find time to write something down, your journal must be within reach. This is why a digital solution, which is easily accessible on your mobile phone, is ideal because you will have it with you almost everywhere.
- *Must be secure*. If you are going to be writing your most intimate thoughts, you cannot be worried about your journal being discovered by other people. If you are even slightly worried, you will automatically sensor yourself. Remember, you cannot fool your own brain. Censoring

will, of course, reduce the quality of your journal and prevent you from fully expressing yourself with all the benefits that you get from it.

- *Must last.* As months and years go by, you will end up with a rather large journal or volumes of it. After spending so much time writing your journal, you certainly don't want to lose it. Your journal will become like your best friend who knows everything about you. You cannot, therefore, risk accidental damage, loss or theft—especially theft. Again, digital solutions are superior, as you can easily add more content, and they allow you to back up the data securely and even automatically.

There are plenty of good digital solutions. A good solution consists of a system that works across various devices, such as computers, mobile phones and tablets, so that you can access your journal wherever you happen to be.

You can start by using a simple MS Word document and add content under headings of dates. You can consider syncing it across devices and backing it up as you would normally do with your other files. For synchronisation, plenty of cloud solutions exist that can facilitate this for you; these include Microsoft OneDrive, Google Drive and Apple iCloud. You can password-protect your file to make it more secure.

You can also use apps that are made specifically for journaling and note taking. Examples are DayOne and Evernote.

Some people dislike putting personal content online. In that case, you can use a local synchronisation system between your device and your computer. You can write your journal in a Word document and sync it across various devices with a tool such as Microsoft SyncToy without using any third-party synchronisation services.

15.5 Measure Your Happiness

Being happy is the ultimate goal in life. A happy life is a high-quality life—one in which you are satisfied with everything that you have achieved. Throughout the book so far, you have seen many methods on how to maximise your happiness. However, while it is important to take steps towards becoming happy, it is equally important to take steps to *maintain* that happiness. A great way to do this is to monitor yourself regularly, analyse what bothers you and address it.

To do this, go through the following exercise once a month. Answer the following questions:

- "How happy are you?" Rate yourself from 1 to 10 (from not happy to happiest).

- "What three things would make you happier?"

These questions are simple yet direct. The key to happiness is knowing exactly what you need most and then going after it. It is about getting rid of wishes and half-thought desires and instead asking yourself what it is you really want the most. You might be surprised that you will always know the answer. It is just that while going through day-to-day errands or work, we tend to forget what they are, and we end up responding to life as opposed to being in charge of it.

Consider the following guidelines to get the most from this monthly activity:

- Make a reminder task in your digital calendar so that the message pops up on your computer or smartphone every month.
- Include the questions in the task, and use your digital device to answer the questions.
- Do not look at your previous answers before you rate your happiness for this month or identify the three actions that would make you happier.
- Once you have written your answer, transfer it to an archive document or note-taking application next to all other monthly ratings you have recorded in the past. You can even archive these ratings in your journal.
- Now, you can compare your happiness rating and the three actions you have identified with what you recorded in previous months. Are you getting any happier? Have you addressed the previous three areas that were the source of your unhappiness last month, or are they still in your list and troubling you? Are you making any progress? What can you do to become happier next month?
- Since it is critical that you fill in the form without looking at what you have entered in previous months, you cannot just open up an archive document that contains previous entries to add your new rating. You would inevitably glance at the previous entries, which would influence your new answers. Instead, you want an independent analysis. You want to ask yourself to see how happy you are first and *only then* compare yourself with how you have been in the past.

Exercise 15-3

Rate Your Happiness

Use the form below to rate your happiness as of this moment.

Date:	
Happiness: **1 = Not happy at all** **10 = Extremely happy**	

What are the top three areas that can make you happier?

Include the source of your unhappiness for each area, and identify actions that can make you happier.

1	
2	
3	

15.6 How to Raise Your Overall Happiness by 25%

Consider the fascinating study conducted by Emmons and McCullough (2003). The researchers divided college students randomly into three groups. Each group was assigned a specific "condition." One condition was "gratitude," another was "hassles" and the third was "events." On a weekly basis for nine weeks, the students were given a pocket notebook in which to write a series of statements based on their "condition." In the gratitude condition group, the students were asked to write about some of the experiences that they were grateful for. In the "hassles" group, the students were asked to write about the annoyances they experienced during the previous week. The "events" group was used as a control group; these students were asked to write about the events of the previous week. No specific instructions were given to indicate what type of events to include. This neutral group was then used to compare the other two groups with. In addition, the students were asked to answer a series of questions that required them to rate their health, mood and physical symptoms.

Here are some examples of what the participants recorded:

Research Results on Gratitude	
Group	**What Each Group Recorded**
Gratitude Group	• The generosity of friends • Sunset through the clouds • The chance to be alive • Having wonderful parents
Hassles Group	• Finances depleting quickly • Hard to find parking • Messy kitchen no one will clean • Doing a favour for a friend who didn't appreciate it
Events Group	• Cleaned out my shoe closet • Learned CPR • Attended Whole Earth Festival • Talked to a doctor about medical school

The results showed that the students in the "grateful" condition reported greater optimism, significantly more life satisfaction and fewer physical symptoms. They were 25% happier. Surprisingly, these students also reported that they exercised one and a half hours more than the students in either the "events" group or the "hassles" group.

The results are profoundly interesting. Just by focusing on things that made people feel grateful, their optimism, life satisfaction and even their health improved. By focusing on benefits received from others, people feel loved and cared for. It helps to strengthen their friendships and their social bonds. It has also been shown that gratitude leads to more optimism not just for now but also for the future. It facilitates coping with stress and adversity and even helps creative thinking.

Here is a question. Would this positive effect remain the same if you compared yourself with others to look for signs that proved you were better off than they were? In fact, the same researchers conducted a very similar study by changing a simple control condition. This time, they asked the participants to list ways in which they were better off than others. The idea was to make positive comparisons but without necessarily thinking gratefully. Again, the results showed that those in the gratitude condition were significantly happier.

Within the field of positive psychology, gratitude is perhaps the most studied subject. Studies show that there is a causal link between gratitude and well-being. Research indicates that gratitude is most effective in increasing happiness for people who are not already happy. It is as if there is a "happiness ceiling" beyond which it is difficult to become happier (Wood *et al.* 2009). For those who are depressed, are less happy or are stressed, gratitude can be quite effective. They are the ones who would get the most from gratitude exercises.

The next question that comes to mind is how often you should exercise being grateful. Again, studies shed light on this. In an experiment that took place over six weeks, the participants were asked to list things that they were grateful for. One group had to do this exercise three times a week, while another group did it only once a week. The results showed that those who listed what they were grateful for about once a week had higher levels of well-being than those who listed them three times a week. The study suggests that people who counted what they were grateful for several times a week developed a routine or simply got bored by the intervention. As a result, the task no longer had a positive impact on them. This is also similar to expressing gratitude to some god in prayers several times a day; the meaning and importance of it is no longer registered. The prayers then become a waste of time and do not contribute to well-being or happiness.

15.7 How to Exercise Gratitude

The following exercise can help you get the most from gratitude:

- *Keep a gratitude journal.* Use a paper-based or digital solution to keep your thoughts on what you are grateful about in one place.
- *Record what you are grateful for every week.* It is important that you think about what you appreciate in life regularly, but not too regularly to make it a boring routine. Make a note or set a recurring weekly task in your digital calendar to remind you to go through the weekly gratitude exercise.
- *Be original every time.* Every week, add a series of statements to your journal on what you are grateful about. Don't look at your previous entries before you write about different aspects of your life. Remember, you cannot fool your own brain. Fresh thinking will help you to truly appreciate what you have.
- *Remember the bad.* One way to see how fortunate you are now is to recall a time when you were not as fortunate. This helps put things in perspective. The contrast will help you feel grateful. Think about the time when you thought having a certain amount of money would make you feel very happy. Now that you earn ten times more than that, how can you not feel grateful?
- *Mentally subtract something valuable from your life.* Use counterfactual thinking to create meaning. This is thinking about the past that did not happen. Thinking of what might not have been can be extremely helpful in appreciating what you have.
- *Analyse your relationships.* Pick a person to analyse. Think of what you have received from this person. Next, think about what you have given to this person. Third, think of what trouble you might have caused this person. Considering these three, you may discover that you owe the person more than you thought.
- *Use the power of self-talk for gratitude.* Take advantage of the voice in your head and develop the habit of telling yourself that you are grateful. Tell yourself the following:
  - "I exist, therefore I am happy."
  - "Every day brings a positive surprise."
- *Say "thank you."* Don't keep your gratitude to yourself. Tell people that you are grateful for them and for what they have done for you.
- *Spend money on someone.* Buy a present for a friend. By giving, you will feel good about yourself. Spending money on others helps to cement stronger social ties; it shows that you express your gratitude

with actions, not just words. It makes your gratitude feel genuine to you.

To put expressing gratitude into a regular activity, consider going through the following exercise on a weekly basis. Do the exercise now to kick-start the new gratitude habit. Remember, it will come to benefit you the most when you are feeling unhappy or depressed. Including this exercise as part of a weekly routine will help you cover such times automatically and, therefore, increase your well-being systematically.

Exercise 15-4

Gratitude

Choose a particular day of the week to go through the following exercise and reflect on your life during the previous seven days. Repeat the exercise on a weekly basis.

PART 1: Be Grateful for Your Previous Week

There are many things in our lives, both large and small, that we might be grateful for. Think back over the past week, and write down five good things that happened to you. It doesn't matter how your week was as a whole—you can always find something good if you think hard enough.

1	
2	
3	
4	
5	

PART 2: *Be Grateful to a Person*	
Pick a person to analyse. Preferably choose one whom you think you will meet next week.	
What have you received from this person?	
What have you given this person?	
What trouble (if any) have you caused this person?	
Considering the above three questions, do you think you might owe the person more than you think?	

Plan to express your gratitude to this person next week. What will you say? Don't just promise yourself to say, "Thank you for lending me your book." Think about deeper aspects of your relationship and how it is helping you in your life. Next time you meet the person, simply express it with all your heart.

Part 3: Be Grateful to Yourself

Mentally subtract something you value from your life. Write it below.

What if you never had the above? What if you never had that job, or met your partner or got that degree? What would life be without it? Walk through life as if you didn't have it, and visualise what happens so you can appreciate what you have now. Describe your thoughts below.

16 Final Remarks

"Life isn't about finding yourself. Life is about creating yourself."

George Bernard Shaw

"You're in the midst of a war: a battle between the limits of a crowd seeking the surrender of your dreams, and the power of your true vision to create and contribute. It is a fight between those who will tell you what you cannot do, and that part of you that knows—and has always known— that we are more than our environment; and that a dream, backed by an unrelenting will to attain it, is truly a reality with an imminent arrival."

Anthony Robbins

It is our observation that with most books on self-development or popular science, once finished, they are put back on the bookshelf never to be read again. You have learned the message and hope that the new insight will provide a significant change in your life. For a couple of weeks, you think about the book and its message. You share the main points with your partner, family members or close friends. Gradually, as you get on with normal life, the book starts to fade away. You feel you learned something new and your life should automatically improve as a result—except that you fall back into the same old routines, and life goes back to what it was before.

Nothing much changes.

With most self-help books, you don't get to apply the insights directly to your life. This is because they have not been written that way. They often provide valuable insight and inspiration but are not designed to be easily applicable to your everyday life. They can be full of useful information but lack the structure that would allow you to apply the knowledge to life.

This is where this book is different. Having gone through plenty of exercises, you have already had an opportunity to apply what has been covered to your daily life and draw personal insights from this. The book also aims to help you acquire new habits. This is why we have designed the book from the outset to help you do just that by providing you with plenty of exercises for you to be able to systematically set aside time to review your life in a structured way. Only then can you be sure that you are adapting to change.

If you are not doing anything about something, you won't get the change you desire no matter how much you want it. If you are not conscious of what you want to achieve at any given moment, you are more likely to be controlled by life than to be in control of it. If you are trying to get somewhere very fast using all the tricks in the book to be productive, you can be greatly disappointed if where you end up is not where you wanted to be because you didn't think it through.

A summary of exercises is provided in *Appendix A* along with a recommended schedule. Make a plan right now to go through the exercises on a periodic basis so that you know where you want to go and remain in control of your life knowing that you are benefiting from all the principles presented in this book.

Maslow tells us that the highest human need is self-actualisation—achieving something profound that has a personal meaning to you and comes to define you. Only a few ever reach it, but everyone aspires to get there. There is a key point here that should not be missed. Happiness is not about getting results and recognition. That places the focus on the external world—on how others think of you instead of what you think of yourself. Happiness comes from the *process* that you go through to achieve results. It comes from the *act of* creating, solving, discovering, loving and living. This way, it doesn't matter what others think, because you find your happiness in the act that can never be taken from you. People, the society or your rivals can ridicule, ignore or vehemently oppose your results, but they can never take away your pleasure if your pleasure is in the act of creating.

You are here to live the life of your dreams. You are not here to be tested and challenged. You don't have to endure life. You are not here to beat others. You are here to rule and conquer, motivated by your desire to achieve. You are a heroic being on a quest to achieve happiness as your sole purpose in life. Keep gaining, and never settle for less.

Never ever compromise your dream; pursue it with *focused determination*.

*"If you always do what you've always done,
you'll always get what you've always got."*

Anonymous

Wish You the Best in Life

Skills Converged

Appendix A: Summary of Periodic Actions

The following is a handy summary of actions you need to take on a periodic basis. Actions are referenced to the exercises presented in the book to show you what you need to do for each period.

There are actions for daily, weekly and monthly basis. These actions are accumulative. For each period pick a day as a reference. For example, for weekly, you may choose Sundays. For monthly, you may choose the first of the month. For quarterly, you may choose the first of the month starting from January. As an example, on 1st of July, you will need to go through your daily, monthly, quarterly and six-monthly actions. If it was a Sunday you also have to do your weekly actions.

Period	Tasks	Exercise References
Daily	Fill in your timesheet.	Exercise 10-1
Weekly	Read your mission statement. Aim to memorise it.	Exercise 8-1
	Remind yourself of your top three skills and formulate actions.	Exercise 10-4
	Express gratitude.	Exercise 15-4
	Update weekly slogans on your wall.	Exercise 14-1
Monthly	Analyse your timesheet for the month.	Exercise 10-2
	Rate your happiness.	Exercise 15-3
Quarterly	Review your needs using Maslow's Hierarchy of Needs.	Exercise 4-1
	Review your timesheet.	Exercise 10-2
	Review your skills.	Exercise 10-3 Exercise 10-5 Exercise 12-1
Six Monthly	Analyse your skill plateau.	Exercise 11-1 Exercise 11-2
	Prioritise your roles. Review your workload and leftover roles. Consider refocusing your time on your most important roles. In addition, also consider including some of your leftover roles if you now have time to address them.	Exercise 9-1

Period	Tasks	Exercise References
Annually	Review your roles.	*Exercise 6-5*
	Review your mission statement.	*Exercise 8-1*
	Review your goals.	*Exercise 9-2*
Every Two Years	Review your ideal heaven.	*Exercise 5-2*
	Comprehensively review your skills.	*Exercise 10-3* *Exercise 10-5* *Exercise 12-1*
Every Five Years	Comprehensively review your roles.	*Exercise 6-5*
	Comprehensively review your mission statement.	*Exercise 8-1*
	Comprehensively prioritise your roles.	*Exercise 9-1*
	Comprehensively review your goals.	*Exercise 9-2*

Appendix B:
Weekly Slogans

Here is a list of weekly slogans that you can use, or more importantly, get inspired by so you can come up with your own.

- Life is to be enjoyed, not just endured
- My best work is my next work
- No matter what happens tomorrow, I am happy today
- You cannot build a reputation on what you are going to do
- How much is the fish?
- What a man can be, he must be
- It will be what it will be
- Focus on causes that are bigger than yourself
- Everybody is looking for something
- Nothing lasts forever
- Focus more on lost sales than losing money
- The chase is better than the catch
- Stay hungry, stay foolish
- Hindsight is always 20/20
- Practice deliberately
- Give and you shall be given. Take and you shall not.
- If it is not working, do something else
- There is no spoon
- Your name is a brand. Your brand is a community.

- What did you do, what result did you get?
- You worry about yourself
- You are defined by the communities you belong to and the ones you don't. I am definitely this, this and this but not that, that or that.
- You never know what worst luck your bad luck had saved you from
- I can't believe I was so lucky that I didn't win. It was way too close.
- Fortune comes to the prepared mind
- Self-education is the only education I know
- Respond to every call that excites your spirit
- How can I be unhappy, if I exist?
- Don't paint to sell

More slogans can be found online at:

www.SkillsConverged.com/Books/FocusedDetermination.aspx

The online list also includes suggestions from other readers for inspiration. Please also consider submitting your own favourite weekly slogans.

Appendix C: Recommended Reading

If you only had to read ten books on success, productivity and happiness, what would be the most useful books that could have the most profound effect on you? This is our recommended list. Full details are provided in references.

1. *7 Habits of Highly Effective People.* How to be in control of your interpersonal interactions, mission in life and most important of all, how to be proactive. If something is not working, it is your fault.

2. *Think and Grow Rich.* Have burning desires, a plan and persist. If you really want it, you will get it.

3. *Getting Things Done.* If you want more time, you will need to be organised. Holding things in your brain will slow you down. Dump it down to your reliable time management system to free your mind and get more done.

4. *Atlas Shrugged.* What is the role of man's mind in existence? How reason and selfish individualism can actually be greatly beneficial not just for a person but also society.

5. *Free Agent Nation*. The world of tomorrow belongs to people who work for themselves.

6. *4 Hour Workweek*. You don't have to do everything and you don't have to do it yourself. One way to save time is to know when you shouldn't bother. Success comes with efficiency. Do the least to get the most. Focus on automation to save time. Don't work for work's sake.

7. *A Whole New Mind*. The world of tomorrow belongs to people who are creative and make their living in creative industries.

8. *Outliers*. Success is not about some magical gift or IQ. It has got much more to do with emotional intelligence, luck, hard work and cultural environment.

9. *Mastery*. Discover your life's task. To become a master, as great masters have done in the past, you need to go through a systematic apprenticeship with access to mentors and work hard to transform your brain. You will then need to be good at social intelligence to resist manipulation.

10. *Black Swan*. Life does not have regularity and is practically random. We should use our common sense to think defensively about the unknown unknowns.

References

Allen, D. (2001) *"Getting Things Done, The Art Of Stress Free Productivity"*, Penguin Books.

Bengtsson, S.L., Dolan, R.J., Passingham, R.E, (2011) *"Priming for self-esteem influences the monitoring of one's own performance"*, Soc Cogn Affect Neurosci. Sep 2011; 6(4): 417–425.

Buzan, T., Buzan, B. (2006) *"The Mind Map Book"*, BBC Active, ISBN: 978-1406612790.

Covey S., (1989) *"7 habits of highly effective people"*, WS Bookwell.

Csikszentmihalyi, M. & Larson, R. (1984) *"Being Adolescent: Conflict and Growth in the Teenage Years"*, New York: Basic Books

Emmons, R. A., McCullough, M. E., (2003) *"Counting blessings versus burdens: An experimental investigation of gratitude and subjective well-being in daily life"*, Journal of Personality and Social Psychology, 84(2), 377-389

Ferriss, T. (2011) *"4 Hour Workweek: Escape the 9-5, Live Anywhere and Join the New Rich"*, Ebury Digital.

Gladwell, M. (2009) *"Outliers"*, Penguin, ISBN-13: 978-0141036250

Goleman, D., (2013) *"Focus: The Hidden Driver of Excellence"*, Bloomsbury Publishing.

Greene, R. (2012) *"Mastery"*, Profile Books, ISBN-13: 978-1781250914

Hill, N. (1937) *"Think and Grow Rich"*.

Holahan, M.R., Tabatadze, N. and Routtenberg, A. (2007) *"GAP-43 gene expression regulates information storage"*, Learn. Mem. 14: 407-15.

Jackson, T., Soderlind, A., Weiss, K.E., (2000) *"Personality traits and quality of relationships as predictors of future loneliness among American college students."*, Social Behavior and Personality, Vol 28(5), 2000, 463-470.

Knapp, R. K., Kause, R. H., Perkins, C. C., JR., (1959) *"Immediate vs. delayed shock in T-maze performance"*, Journal of Experimental Psychology, 1959, 55, 357-362.

Lepper, M.R., Greene, D. & Nisbett, R.E. (1973) *"Undermining children's intrinsic interest with extrinsic reward: A test of the 'overjustification' hypothesis"*, Journal of personality and social psychology, 28(1), pp. 129-137.

Li, F., Tsien, J.Z. (2009) *"Memory and the NMDA receptors "*, N Engl J Med. 2009 Jul 16;361(3):302-3

Loewenstein, G. (1987) *"Anticipation and the Valuation of Delayed Consumption"*, The Economic Journal, Vol. 97, No. 387 (Sep., 1987), pp. 666-684, Blackwell Publishing for the Royal Economic Society

Marshall, M. and Brown, J. (2006) *"Emotional reactions to achievement outcomes: Is it really best to expect the worst?"*, Cognition and Emotion, 2006, 20 (1), 43-63, Psychology Press Ltd.

Maslow, A. H., (1954) *"Motivation and personality"*, New York: Harper.

Pink, D. (2008) *"A Whole New Mind"*, Marshall Cavendish.

Pink, D. (2001) *"Free Agent Nation"*, Business Plus.

Rand, A. (1957) *"Atlas Shrugged"*, Random House.

Schwarzenegger, A. (2013) *"Total Recall"*, Simon & Schuster UK, ISBN-13: 978-1849839730

Taleb, N. (2008) *"Black Swan: The Impact of the Highly Improbable"*, Penguin.

Wood A.M., Froh, J.J., Geraghty, A.W.A., (2009) *"Gratitude and well-being: A review and theoretical integration"*, Clinical Psychology Review, doi:10.1016/j.cpr.2010.03.005

Index

About
Skills Converged

Skills Converged is based in the United Kingdom and specialises in the design and development of soft skills training courses. Our training materials are used world-wide by the training community to train some of the world's most prestigious and successful organisations. As course designers of personal and interpersonal skills, we are passionate to learn what it takes to provide effective training with long lasting results. Our books written for the general public are designed as self-study courses based on the same principles of learning that we use to produce our successful training courses. Our self-help books are suitable for anyone interested in improving their personal and people skills.

For more information please check **www.SkillsConverged.com**

About Ehsan Honary

Skills Converged was founded by Dr. Ehsan Honary in 2008. He is a training specialist with years of experience in the training industry. He has an interest in a diverse set of subjects such as psychology, artificial intelligence, social sciences, business management, fine arts, computer graphics and software engineering. Through Skills Converged, Ehsan has enabled thousands of trainers worldwide to deliver outstanding training courses on soft skills and has empowered people to realise their full potential. He is an advocate of using the latest training methodologies that help speed up training while simultaneously make learning last longer.

The Concise Version

This book is also available in a digital format on the Kindle platform. The concise version is the same as the main book here but without the exercises.

We have released the concise version based on our readers' request so that you can read through the text on your favourite devices and go through the exercises at a later time.

The concise version is available on the Kindle platform which can be read on a variety of digital devices such as Kindles, tablets, phones and PCs.

**The Concise Focused Determination:
How to Engineer Your Life to Maximise Your Happiness**

By Skills Converged

Made in the USA
San Bernardino, CA
19 April 2019